HIGH FRIENDS IN LOW PLACES

(An epic romp through the riotous
avant-underground of Eighties
Montreal, New York and Europe)

MIROLAND IMPRINT 37

**Canada Council
for the Arts**   **Conseil des Arts
du Canada**

**ONTARIO ARTS COUNCIL
CONSEIL DES ARTS DE L'ONTARIO**

an Ontario government agency
un organisme du gouvernement de l'Ontario

Canada

Guernica Editions Inc. acknowledges the support of the Canada Council
for the Arts and the Ontario Arts Council. The Ontario Arts Council
is an agency of the Government of Ontario.
We acknowledge the financial support of the Government of Canada.

HIGH FRIENDS IN LOW PLACES

BY ALAN LORD

GUERNICA EDITIONS
TORONTO · CHICAGO · BUFFALO · LANCASTER (U.K.)
2022

Guernica Founder: Antonio D'Alfonso

Connie McParland, series editor
Michael Mirolla, editor
David Moratto, cover and interior design
Cover image: Photo of Alan Lord (left), with Tristan Renaud.
Cover backdrop is a photo of the Foufounes Électriques in the 80's
Guernica Editions Inc.
287 Templemead Drive, Hamilton, ON L8W 2W4
2250 Military Road, Tonawanda, N.Y. 14150-6000 U.S.A.
www.guernicaeditions.com

Distributors:
Independent Publishers Group (IPG)
600 North Pulaski Road, Chicago IL 60624
University of Toronto Press Distribution (UTP)
5201 Dufferin Street, Toronto (ON), Canada M3H 5T8
Gazelle Book Services
White Cross Mills, High Town, Lancaster LA1 4XS U.K.

First edition.
Printed in Canada.

Legal Deposit—Third Quarter
Library of Congress Catalog Card Number: 2022933475
Library and Archives Canada Cataloguing in Publication
Title: High friends in low places / Alan Lord.
Names: Lord, Alan, 1954- author.
Description: "MiroLand imprint; 37"--Page preceding title page.
Identifiers: Canadiana (print) 20220177104 | Canadiana (ebook)
20220177228 | ISBN 9781771837545 (softcover) | ISBN 9781771837552
(EPUB)
Subjects: LCSH: Lord, Alan, 1954- | LCSH: Lord, Alan, 1954-—Friends and
associates. | LCSH: Musicians—Québec (Province)—Montréal—Biography. |
LCSH: Arts—20th century. | LCGFT: Autobiographies.
Classification: LCC PS8573.O68 Z46 2022 | DDC C811/.54—dc23

This book is dedicated to everyone in it.
They were part of a vast conspiracy
to make my life interesting.

CONTENTS

1
PLEASED TO MEET YOU

I smoked a joint with Burroughs at sunset and fucked Kathy Acker's brains out at dawn. At the time I was a hot shit sunglassed guitarist in the coolest band in town, single and miserable, lonely with six girlfriends and a few unspellable venereal diseases. And stoned whenever possible. We were well into the Eighties and I was still not using condoms. Splodging into gummy plastic wasn't in my DNA. Sure, it was high risk, but what's the point if things aren't exciting?

Welcome to my Eighties. I had high friends in low places. Mostly at the *Foufs*—or *Les Foufounes Électriques*[1]—Montreal's première pisshole club that looked like its toilets, and the place where I organized the *Ultimatum* series of cutting-edge literary festivals and generally held court as king of Montreal's avant-underground scene. My reign as louche Minister of Counterculture lasted a handful of years, until I collapsed exhausted from being a glorious failure. I used to fly poets up from New York instead of paying the rent. I blew my paycheques inviting *Between C & D*[2] luminaries from the Lower East Side. *Of course* I was sick in the head. *I wanted Art.* The kind that's alive and could give *me* life. I asked Karen Finley if I could film her stuffing yams up her ass. She said "sure".

Thanks to cheap Laker Airways, I could afford shuttling back and forth to New York on a regular basis. For me the most thrilling thing in the world was the cab ride from La Guardia into Manhattan, passing

---

1. Pronounced "Foo-foon Elect-treek"; Translation: The Electric Buttocks
2. A literary magazine run by Joel Rose and Catherine Texier out of New York's Lower East Side

by the tombstones of St. Michael's cemetery in Queens—a mini teaser
of the Manhattan skyline that was about to swallow me whole as I
exited the Midtown Tunnel.

My fondest memory is of walking up Fifth Avenue with Beat saint
Herbert Huncke telling me the story of his life, under the waking lights
of the Empire State Building towering over us at dusk. I brought him
up to Montreal for readings several times, but it also went the other way
around. I brought Montreal artists down to New York for a group exhibit and graffiti fashion show. Because I was doggedly determined to
promote the countless great local artists, literati, and brilliant misfit
geniuses I knew. Yet despite my efforts, the best minds of *my* generation
still remain unknown, or else self-destructed. I was friend to all losers.
The bright ones. Because they're way more interesting than the most
respectable hedge fund manager I sincerely hope you don't know.

Not all of my bright friends were losers. Chris Kraus and Sylvère
Lotringer—of *I Love Dick* fame, much later[3]—moved into my place for
a month. She was working on her video *How To Shoot A Crime*, and he
needed a space to do work on his countless Semiotext(e) projects. My
fridge was empty and they felt sorry for me, so as a parting gift they
gave me new bedsheets, which was a subtle comment on my cruddy old
sheets flung with the sperm of my various flings with things picked up
in the clubs. Nearing closing time at the Foufs, in 4 AM desperation I
could always count on dragging home some unappetizing groupie.
Because I was the guitar slinger of *Vent du Mont Schärr*[4]—or VDMS
for short—the best agitrock band in the world you never heard of. We
toured Europe, playing in *Concerts Sauvages*—shows set up in abandoned office buildings, spread by word of mouth at the last minute.
They tapped power off nearby electric poles, and the show lasted until
the cops arrived and everybody scattered. We played at a bona fide anarchist commune in the Swiss town of Bern, and in Brussels we got to
destroy a lugubrious goths-with-synths festival at the famed Plan K, by
getting the audience to snap out of its wake and have some dancing

---

3. To say the very least!
4. Pronounced "Vaughn-doo Moh-Sharr"

good fun. That killed any idea of going back to acting like dead vampires. After we left, the cavernous dark space emptied.

乙 Anything else to declare? You bet. I was a veteran of the Punk/New Wave scene as documented in two movies[5], I put out several albums with several bands, had poems published in anthologies, and got mentioned in more books than I've published. I opened for the B-52's and The Ramones, and even gave Dee Dee a joint on the fire escape during soundcheck. I had my picture taken with the Ramones but lost the photos. Story of my chaotic life. I later opened for Nina Hagen but didn't need any pictures, it was satisfying enough to hear her having a diva fit backstage, swearing at her guitar player in German.

In the French town of Bourges, after a VDMS show in a concert featuring the cream of Europe's punk bands on the *Boucherie* label roster, I got to jam at 3 AM with Tony Chao—brother of Manu Chao—Rock's Che Guevara. Back then he was with his sizzling band Mano Negra, before he found solo fame in the late Nineties. We also got to open for the legendary anarchist band Bérurier Noir[6]—in front of 1000 people, twice—once in Fribourg, Switzerland, and a week later in our home town. I crashed at their place in Lausanne and was there when CBS records was on the phone with their manager, once more pleading to sign them. They were being offered a million dollars. He told them to go fuck themselves.

Throughout all this incredible madness I somehow still managed to have a semblance of a career as a civil/structural engineer, designing buildings and bridges and other cool stuff, minus a few gap years as an art/music bum.

The highlight for me was meeting Burroughs and getting to visit his Bowery bunker, still intact after he'd move to Kansas, not knowing that a couple years later I'd be dropping by on his upstairs neighbour—the poet John Giorno—whom I invited to Montreal many times. I also read my poems at a Kerouac conference in Quebec City and got to share

---

5. MTL Punk movie trailer: https://www.youtube.com/watch?v=rHPUKTq0xGw, Montréal New Wave movie trailer: https://www.youtube.com/watch?v=0LG7bo3e6xk

6. Pronounced "Bih-roor-yih N'wah"

the stage with Allen Ginsberg and Lawrence Ferlinghetti. Then a few years later, when living in Paris, I stood up *Mr. Speed*—the urbanist and philosopher Paul Virilio. He still graciously re-invited me to hang out with him at La Coupole in Montparnasse.

Or how about the time in New York, when Pop artist James Rosenquist poured me a glass of champagne, Chris Burden explained to me how to drop steel beams from a helicopter clean through concrete pads, Grace Jones had a fit during her birthday party, and Divine walked in on my brunch? I also once had a hilariously futile phone conversation with Nam June Paik, and J.G. Ballard wrote to me on the back of photos of his cat.

⇒ This is not boasting, it's not name dropping, it's the icing on the cake of the crazy life I had throughout the Eighties—which were my Sixties, except I remember 'em better because blow and champagne don't fog up your brain like weed and acid. I lived my life in fast forward and always kept wondering how I could ever decelerate. Well, one day I got the answer: you smack into a brick wall. Nervous breakdowns were only for people on The Soaps, so I never noticed one sneaking up on me. Fortunately, within weeks of my decisive meltdown I met the blonde mini-skirted angel who saved me from myself. I knew instantly we'd be together for years, and it's been 34 and counting.

Lucky gal, she was with me for my last hurrah in a tumultuous decade: Burroughs was coming to town for a gallery show of his *Shotgun Paintings. Of course* I jumped in to help organize. I became the publicist, and for the occasion I put together a *Hommage to Burroughs* show at the Foufs. I had a few local bands play, and the highlight was Huncke reading from his work. We sat down the two old junkie compères in a private room, with little piles of cocaine, heroin, and joints of hash laid out on a small table between them. And there you go—the highest of friends in the lowest of places. Start at the top of the bottom, whyncha. Burroughs came out onto the mezzanine and placed his elbows on the railing to watch the proceedings. Someone in the audience looked up and saw him, and the whole place started clapping, cheering and whistling. Old Bill lit up and waved back smiling, like the iffy royalty he was. The most precious item in my 75-book Burroughs collection is a monograph signed *"For Alan Lord with memories of a great visit to Montreal."*

≥ For all the big names I got to meet and even know, there were dozens of totally unknown, unsung heroes in my local cherished pantheon, and you'll get to meet them all, one after the other. The parade of fascinating characters is endless, unforgettable, and enough videos survived to prove it.

We were punks, poets, mischievous artists, anti-artists, post punk anarcho-nihilists, Situationists, Neoists, mad subversives of every stripe and shadiness. You can slap any label you want, it doesn't matter, because each generation has a different word for the same thing: fearless young angels of whirlwind apocalypse art mayhem, who will always turn up out of nowhere to make trouble, try to shake the collective mind out of its everyday coma, then disappear ignominiously into sad, monk-like obscurity and poverty, burned out from the sheer naïve superhuman effort. Most of my friends ended up glorious doomed heartbreaking souls, that for a minute froze time in a wild spontaneous jewel-tipped fireworks spectacle for the crowd to stop and gawk for a minute, shake their heads in disbelief, shrug and get back to work. Most of the time we were high on drugs and booze. Because it made life livable. But more importantly, we were high on our music, poetry, art, and gratuitous fuckyou provocations.

No, we weren't "high on life". We were high on killing normality before it killed us, and living overwhelmingly creative lives lived wide-eyed *in the moment*. We were at war with artlessness and the dull forces of workaday accommodation that conspired to pound us flat. We wanted things to happen. And if you want things to happen, you have to *make* them happen.

This is the story of my wild decade, which in retrospect now seems like a golden age in music, poetry, writing, and general artistic exploration, when boundaries were smashed to smithereens—an age of exhilarating freedom of expression which now seems near impossible. So much stuff happened—that I often *made* happen—and was involved with so many amazing people—why, even decades later my head's still spinning.

And now *you* get to sit in the front row of my life that was so exciting it nearly killed me. But things take time. You don't make it to the gutter with an all-star cast overnight.

2

MY LIFE BEFORE I GOT ONE

My parents kicked me out of the house when I was 20. Rather, they sold the house we had in the Rosemount neighbourhood, and moved into a new one on The Plateau, announcing matter of fact they didn't have a room for me. My father had intercepted a letter from McGill University, and even if he didn't know English, he sussed out I'd been kicked out of the civil engineering program. Ok, fair enough. Message received loud and clear. No room for losers.

So I had to start playing house with my girlfriend Joss for real now, and get to pay the bills. Joss had only a high school education. She looked like a young pre-Jackie-Kennedy-Onassis Jacqueline Bouvier—and was equally allergic to employment. Except I was no Onassis. After a few weeks spent together in a rooming house on St. Denis street, I got a job with Armand Sicotte, as a surveyor for the construction of Highway 30. For which I had to live near the work site, so we moved to the bumpkinfuck village of Saint-Roch-de-Richelieu. Saint Rock indeed. The house across the street was a stoner pad blasting Pink Floyd's *Dark Side of The Moon*, 24/7: *"Money... get away..."*—well *we* certainly couldn't get away. It played every 45 minutes ... all ... day ... every ... day.

We were broke. Our tiny apartment was furniture-free. I had to make a dinner table out of cardboard, which wilted if the plates were too hot. We had no chairs, so we sat on the floor at the table, Japanese-style.

The work was easy. I just had to hop around the construction site with my surveying instrument, and plant rows of sticks showing the height to which earth graders had to pile the subbase gravel. The doofusses driving the dump trucks had fun careening roughshod and regularly snapped whole rows of my precious work, so I had to start all over again. I figured *that* was my job security.

I hired my old childhood friend Bruno to serve as surveying rodman—this is the guy who has to stand still with a rod in his hands while the surveyor takes his readings. Bruno was the son of a gruff balding Italian immigrant from Campobasso. At the family dinner table, Bruno and his brother Carlo were likely to get whacked upside the head for whatever Papa deemed a good reason. I don't think you needed a high school education to be a rodman for Armand Sicotte, but Bruno had one. I think. Moreover, in his favour, he always had some good hash.

In November the construction work was halted for winter, and everyone was laid off. Basically we were screwed. The site headquarters—a farmhouse in the middle of nowhere—was to be boarded up until spring, so I got the bright idea that Joss and I would be the house sitters. At least we wouldn't have to pay any rent until spring. I brazenly got them to kick in an extra $50 a month for our "trouble", but still, we couldn't live off that.

Bruno passed by to visit. I confessed we were broke and couldn't invite him to dinner. He said "let's go shopping," so we followed him to a nearby shopping mall with a supermarket. As we walked through the place he said "watch this". He picked up an Adidas sports bag, ripped the price tag off and kept walking. We entered the supermarket and had trouble keeping up with him as he raced through grabbing expensive steaks and lobsters and shit, stuffing it all into the bag nonchalantly as he went along. As we exited the place he turned around and flashed us a big grin and a peace sign, as if to say "*that's* the way it's done". So that evening we indeed had ourselves a thoroughly satisfying repast, complete with wine.

⇌ The house was exposed to the freezing winds, and the water pipes soon froze. In the middle of winter I now had to fetch pails of water on foot from our only neighbour, a half mile down the road. We took showers only when visiting my parents in Montreal—which now had to be every weekend.

Then the heating furnace blew up. We had no money to fix it. It was time to get the hell out of there. So I found a cheap $80 per month one-bedroom apartment in crappy Montreal North, and soon landed a comfy office job at Doucet & Associates—a small engineering firm on McGill College Avenue corner Cathcart, across from Place Ville Marie.

When we returned to the farmhouse to pick up our stuff, we were shocked to discover we'd been broken into. If you ever think you're poor and have nothing, wait till you get robbed. They stole all of my precious vinyl records I'd been collecting since age 11. About 200 records. All of my original Stones, Beatles, Hendrix, Cream, Mothers of Invention, Zappa, Bowie, Roxy Music, Sparks, and more. Our crappy stereo was also gone. Other than that, their pickings were pretty slim. Oh right, I forgot. *They stole the fucking fridge.*

As we were making a mental inventory of the damage, we saw a pickup truck slow down in front of the house. When they saw someone was there, they took off. They were probably coming for the goddamn *stove* now. We eventually learned it was the white trash "family" I'd also hired as rodmen over the summer. Many a time I had them over for pizza and beer: the two brothers—the younger's nickname being *Ti-Za*[1]—and their tall, skinny, creepy dad. He had a greasy thinning duck-tail haircut, sported a pencil moustache, wore white socks in tan loafers, and snickered like a cretin while sucking on a toothpick. I felt sorry for them and gave them a break, hiring the starved cocksuckers, and that's how they paid me back.

It turned out our criminal hillbilly Dad & Sons team broke into many houses and cottages in the area. The cops found the stolen goods stashed in their barn. Years later I heard the weasel ringleader dad died of a heart attack in prison. Good riddance.

⇋ It was 1976, the Montreal Summer Olympics were going on, and I couldn't care less. I was working long hot hours outside, supervising the construction of Bell Canada manholes and miles of phone line conduits buried by concrete poured in trenches. After a typical ten-hour day I'd come home, eat, and collapse to sleep.

---

1. Pronounced "Tsee-zah"

That dreadful year was the very bottom pit of my life. I was 21 and didn't know what I wanted to do with it. I had zero culture, no vital spark, I was soulless, felt alone in the world, shared no common bond with people around me. Manholes. How appropriate. I was the man with a gigantic hole in him. To add insult to injury, on the radio Peter Frampton was asking me if I felt like he did. Well, *NO!*

Sundays often found me and Joss sitting with her white trash family watching TV, yawning and picking at their crotches unseen. Her surly uncle, aunts and owlish granny *Mémère* sat there grunting and communicating in terse monosyllables. How trashy were they? How about Joss' brothers and their girlfriends slathering on *Valvoline motor oil* as suntanning lotion at the beach?

Her aunts coughed and retched while chain-smoking, and drank coke after coke like it was beer. They actually looked like Marge Simpson's sisters, minus the foot-high beehives. One of them had a beer belly from the cases of coke that filled her fridge. She worked in a factory and once cut short her union-decreed summer vacation, returning to the shop sobbing "I missed you guys!" Not too bright. Of course, to them I was the one who was the weirdo—not that I used "big" words or anything—I was considered weird because I wasn't *one of them* and they could smell it.

That fall, with a letter of recommendation from my employer, I was accepted back into McGill Engineering. The idea being that after a sweaty year discovering the sober realities of a diploma-less paycheque, I'd learned my lesson.

⇜ And so started an intense period of being a full-time student, while also being a full-time employee. You heard right. I'd get up at 6, start work at 7, then walk up the street to McGill to attend the day's courses from 10 to 2 PM. Then I'd return to the office and work as a draftsman until 7 PM. Then a sandwich and guess what—homework! I'd stay at the office and do my engineering assignments until late at night. I'd get home at 11 or midnight, drop to sleep and start all over again. I did this for two whole years. That's not a life. That's not living. Lucky for me, my job was just off campus down the street, or I never would have been able to pull it off. This insane worka-study-holic "life" I sorely wish upon my best frenemy.

The little free time I had was spent moping around Dutchy's Record Cave, flipping through all the Prog albums that bored me. Then one day, in the upstairs bins at Phantasmagoria, tucked away from their Prog clientele sight, there began appearing cheaply made black and white sleeved singles by new bands with strange names: Slaughter & The Dogs, The Radiators From Space, Hammersmith Gorillas. I settled on an EP of Eddie & The Hot Rods—*Live At The Marquee*. The manic beat and stabbing guitar jabs of their brutal take on *96 Tears* floored me. Something new was going on here. Rock was finally waking up again. *That* started recharging my Life Battery, which was currently redline flashing at 1%.

Even if Glam had lost its glitter for years, I hadn't stopped checking out magazines like *Rock Scene*, *Creem* and *Hit Parader*, plus France's *Rock Folk* and *Best*. They kept talking about this thing called "Punk", and I was intrigued by the photos of a dishevelled Debbie Harry mugging with Joey Ramone.

The first genuinely punk record to hit the shelves here was *Damned Damned Damned*, and I bought it out of curiosity. As soon as the record player needle kicked off the breakneck-throbbing bass line of *Neat Neat Neat* I was hooked. But what really did it for me though, was the raw intelligence of The Sex Pistols' glorious *God Save The Queen*. And Steve Jones' amazing wall of noise made me want to pick up a guitar again and DO something. I'd given up playing guitar since entering CEGEP[2] at age 17, but now the musician in me was rousing from his Rip Van Wanker sleep.

I was getting the music itch again.

---

2. Quebec's two-year pre-university phase, between four years of high school and three of university

3

MONTREAL PUNK

The first punk band I saw were The Vibrators at The Hotel Nelson that October. We didn't know it, but many luminaries of the future Montreal scene were in attendance that evening.

England's '77 Summer Of Hate turned into 1978, and at the end of spring I wrapped up that semester's studies. When Elvis Costello's *This Year's Model* came out I was utterly demolished. It felt like an insulting gauntlet flung at my feet: if such a dweeb could put out an album, well then so could I! I bought myself a guitar, slowly dusted off my chops, and out of nowhere I immediately began writing songs—something I'd never been able to do. The songs poured out of me. I soon became obsessed—I had to write at least a song a day, or else my life was a total disaster. I was writing a lot of crap, but that's ok. Practice makes poison.

I was getting antsy and craved to get going in music already, but didn't know what to do. Finally, I got up the courage and put an ad in the paper, seeking musicians who were into everything I was. I got an answer from Chuck F—Charles Foucrault. The lucky bugger already had his own band—*Narcisse*: Serge Giguère[1] on bass, who could pass for a Ramone, and Richard Lacoste on drums. Chuck was the rhythm guitarist, and also sang. In French. They had a practice space, they had equipment. Wow. I had nothing. They were more into The Stranglers than the Pistols or Costello. Close enough.

I started hanging out at Narcisse's practice space, which was

---

1. Pronounced "Sair-juh Jhee-ghair"

12

shared with none other than Quebec's première neanderthal blues band Offenbach. The piles of two-fours[2] were taller than their Marshall stacks.

The Narcisse boys graciously lent their services, backing me while I worked out my songs. The owner often complained about the noise, and the cops offered us several final notices to cut it out. We shrugged 'em off. Chuck and I had more important matters to discuss. Such as "Is Punk dead, now that the Sex Pistols broke up?"

On a hot day in July Charles asked me, "You wanna go to a punk show, with local bands playing? There's one in Old Montreal this Saturday."

I couldn't believe it. "What?" I exclaimed, *"Punk in Montreal?* You mean there are *others* into that here?"

We went down to the 364 St. Paul—"The Store Front"—in our leather jackets. I was carrying a ghetto blaster with a tape of songs I'd recorded. We stopped to talk to local svengali Marc Durand[3], whom Charles knew. He was always pestering Durand to be their manager, and soon we crouched in a gravel parking lot for him to hear my tape. He was not impressed. Then we walked into the 364. There were smashed acoustic guitars and assorted trash glued to the walls. It was a scene of total energy and chaos—a packed horde of jostling leather-clad kids yelling atop the din, and every so often there was the sharp crinkle of beer bottles being shattered against the floor, punctuated by loud "Fuck You's".

I fought through the crowd to go see what the hell was going on. It was a couple of guys yelling unintelligible stuff into a microphone, hovering over a reel-to-reel tape recorder playing back some more unintelligible stuff. The punters were just as impatient as I was to get on with it, let's hear some goddamn music already. More exasperated "FACK YEWWWS!" rose from the audience.

"Fuck You!" was the primal unchained melody of sudden liberation, the only way inarticulate kids had to express the explosion of

---

2. Case of 24 beers
3. Pronounced "Mark Doo-rah"

sheer joy Punk gave them—like prison doors miraculously blown off their souls.

The Normals jostled in through the crowd—nervous sensitive David Byrne/Norman Bates look-alike Robert Labelle on guitar, Tracy Howe at the drums—looking like Jean Genet just out of jail—and deceptively thuggish-looking sweetheart Scott Cameron, trying to strap on his bass amid the bodies pressing in around him. There was no stage. The band played surrounded by the pimply multitudes. They launched into *Noisy Neighbors*, sung by Scott. The song was interrupted several times by fighting and taunts—"You can't play! You don't even know how to fucking plaaaaay!!!!"—then Tracy took over the vocals for *Work To Rule*. The chaos was indescribable, and time became meaningless— a minute seemed to last a century and a decade could be compressed into a millisecond. For the first time in my life I felt really alive. It was as if all of a sudden the shackles of world history had dropped their dead load onto the floor once and for all. I was finally part of ... *something*. Here was a roomful of young kids who felt like me and who wanted the same thing I did and had been looking for all my life: Total Freedom.

After the show, the shattered beer-bottle crinkles and "Fack Yews" tumbled onto the street. I crouched in a nearby alley and blasted my cassette to add to that night's talent show. A curious crowd assembled. I had my first audience.

⇜ I went back to work the following Monday, and the fall semester soon started up at McGill. In the Engineering Graphics class one day— given by the improbably-named Professor Szombor Murray—I saw a guy with John Lennon glasses and sandy hair climb over the rows of desks to talk to a friend. He looked like Andy Warhol and wore a Ramones badge on his tan buckskin jacket. What? An engineering student wearing a Ramones badge? Couldn't be.

There was a Halloween show that fall at the now-legendary 364 St Paul, founded by a certain Robert Ditchburn. For the occasion I dressed up like Dave Vanian of The Damned: slicked-back hair, whiteface makeup. I was wearing a red waiter's jacket festooned with badges and safety pins linked by rusted old jewellery chains and others I'd made out of paper clips linked together. The guy with the glasses who looked like Andy Warhol was there and wanted to take a picture of me. I went over to a drum kit and placed my head on the floor tom like a head about to be chopped off, and he snapped the photo, grinning in delight.

The Widows played, followed by the 222's with Louie Rondo at the microphone. Their original singer was Jean Brisson[4]—arguably Montreal's first punk. He went around with green food dye in his hair and called himself Johnny Frisson[5]. Subbing for the drummer that night was Angel Dust—or Angel Calvo[6]—who later wound up in my bands. The notorious Chromosomes also played, but I don't remember any details. Too many years, too many dead braincells.

The atmosphere was chaotic beyond belief. The very air itself was crackling with explosive energy. It was charged, as if only one tiny spark was needed to blow the place. When the din evaporated during merciful lulls between bands roaring power chords through the speaker cabinets, your tintinnited ears heard "FACK YEWWS!!!" all over again, screamed randomly in the still electric air, punctuated by the occasional "POK!" of a full bottle of beer exploding its contents all over the floor. Which was sticky. With sweat. With beer. And the thrill of finally finding your tribe, your people, and the soundtrack to your own life. "YAAAAAHHHHH!!!!" someone yelled ecstatically. And then the next inept band stepped up to lash out the next barrage of welcome noise.

There were no selfies back then—just kids rejoicing in the glorious moment. Someone with a camera was a rarity, and even frowned upon as an intrusion. Documentary evidence is hard to find, but we came and came often, and if you weren't there, you missed it. You had to be there, and I sure was.

After the show we stuck around to listen to the DJ play dozens of great records I was hearing for the first time: *Shadow* by The Lurkers, The Buzzcocks' *Spiral Scratch, Oh Bondage, Up Yours!* by X-Ray Spex,

---

4. Pronounced "Juh Bree-so"
5. Pronounced "Johnny Free-so"; Transl: Johnny Shivers
6. Pronounced "Ahjel Calvo"

Sham 69's *Borstal Breakout*. Out of nowhere suddenly came forth a limitless supply of new bands with outrageous names: The Buzzcocks, Revolting Cocks, The Slits, Subway Sect, 999, U.K. Subs. The 45's had everyone pogoing ineptly, jostling into one another with cartoon buck-tooth Sid Vicious grins.

⇆ To me, Punk was the thrill of creating a new universe to live in where we could breathe. It was the sudden release of pent-up energy accumulated over the years of societal boredom fed by ultimately point-less jobs and studies. We were the Struggling Class. Struggling for total freedom. Instead of "No Future", to me Punk meant *No Bullshit*—a punk speaks his mind bluntly, gets to the heart of a matter, and tells you what's what. Which is the exact opposite of polite social conven-tions and "being diplomatic"—which is shorthand for bourgeois hyp-ocrisy. The primordial takeaway of the bourgeois attitude is worrying about appearances and "what will the neighbours think?" Punk was the liberating upending of all that for good, or at least the possibility that such a thing could be carried out. It was the sound of the crucial quest for the complete liberation of the individual.

⇆ Things were hopping now. Just two days after the crazy Halloween show at the 364, we were treated to the landmark show put on by DEVO at El Casino. They had their Minion-like yellow boiler suits and industrial goggles on, and flailed around jerkily banging out spastic riffs on guitars. Mark Mothersbaugh ended the show singing a mawkish lament in a baby's crib while wearing his creepy *Booji Boy* mask. It was worthy of Eraserhead.

When the show was over the house lights went up, and I was too stunned to move so I just sat there. Mothersbaugh and Jerry Casale lingered around after the place had emptied, and sat down to chat. I asked them what it was like to have Brian Eno produce them. They groaned and rolled their eyes. "We didn't need him," they said. "We knew what we wanted and he was just in the way." Mark and Jerry were very nice and friendly indeed, but seeing the groupies starting to close in, out of courtesy I figured I should leave, and allow them to move on to their evening's more pressing denouement.

⇝ Then the Screamers rolled into town. They played at l'Éveché[7] of the Hotel Nelson, with The Normals as the opening act. They were from Los Angeles and had been invited to Montreal by writer and translator Susanne de Lotbinière-Harwood.

The members of The Screamers filed out one by one and silently took up their positions: Blond, James Dean look-alike K.K. at the drumkit, then Tommy Gear and Rio at distorted electric piano and synthesizer.

Something was wrong here. Where were the guitars? There *were* no guitars in *this* band. What, I'd just started getting into Punk, and it was already over?

Singer Tomata du Plenty came out and just stood there, glaring at us menacingly. There was a long, angst-inducing pause. Then he declared "Welcome to The Eighties," and the band proceeded to thrash out *Vertigo*, with Tomata doing a demented spastic puppet dance while shaking his head, moving his hand sideways rapidly in front of his face[8]. Then he covered his mouth making big surprised Shirley Temple eyes, like he was as shocked as we were. While the keyboards and drums pumped out a deafening barrage of raw noise, he suddenly lunged at the audience, threatening to assault us, but stopped short and spat the lyrics in our face.

The Normals broke up shortly after their opening stint. Musician/cartoonist Rick Trembles recalls: "I remember Rob telling me after that show that they felt so old-fashioned after seeing The Screamers."

Tracy and Scott got together and soon evolved into the superb five-piece Heaven 17, and gave a show at the McGill Ballroom. In addition to Scott and Tracy they now had Roman Martyn from the *Young Adults* on guitar, and new faces—Kim Duran, and the luscious Lysanne Thibodeau[9] on keyboards. The new songs were outstanding: *Sister In The Navy, Tony Walker, Sinking*. The level of songwriting had taken a quantum leap from the days of aping the raucously primitive Clash style.

---

7. Pronounced "Lay-vay-shay"
8. For a demonstration, see https://www.youtube.com/watch?v=Z0-w0hUnhpI
9. Pronounced "Lee-zann T'see-budd-dough"

As for me, I was soon laid off, and after my fall semester exams in December, I had one more term to go before getting my goddamn diploma.

So I dropped my studies. I was tired of reading *New York Rocker*[10] part-time. I wanted to be a *Montreal* Rocker. *Full* time.

---

10. New York's premier music weekly

4

MONTREAL NEW WAVE

Montreal is a town basically split in two, by the street that runs North-South—St Lawrence street—also known as *The Main*. The richer, more reserved anglophones stick to the West side, while the poorer, livelier francophones keep to the East side. This cultural cleavage also applied to the bands.

Rock is anglocentric, and the punk/new wave scene in Montreal wasn't any different. There were two distinct clans: the bands made up of anglophones who sang in English, and the bands made up of francophones who *also* sang in English. But apart from Danger[1] and Narcisse, no punk band sang in French yet. We didn't really notice or cared, as long as the guitars drowned out the lyrics.

The first proper punk band in Montreal were the 222's. In '76 they opened for the already-established Danger—who were more of a straggling New York Dolls—but without the makeup or girly clothes. After Brisson left, the 222's became more bubbleglam than punk. Around the time they got the *very* young slinky gay-jailbait Chris Barry to front them, I befriended Pièr[2], their spike-haired scary-thin incandescent guitarist.

In the spring of 1979 I dropped by his basement apartment on de Chambly below Hochelaga, which was close to my childhood home. Pièr looked like a young punky Ron Wood and enjoyed wearing outrageous outfits onstage, such as a pair of dayglo orange feathery plush

---

1. Pronounced "Duh-jhay"
2. Pronounced "Pierre"

pantaloons that made him look like a demented Big Bird. Their first single was out: *I Love Susan*. He took it out of the sleeve and put it on the turntable. After a few seconds he angrily zipped the needle off, grabbed the 45 and threw it across the room like a frisbee, exclaiming, *"Le son est pourri!"*[3]

I loved Pièr because he was an authentic no-bullshit mean streets offspring, who trashed conventions to a different drummer—himself. He dressed and even looked like James Williamson circa *Raw Power*, and peeled off smoking riffs just as hot. He regaled me with great stories of the 222's early days:

"I booked one of the 222's first shows at my old high school Antoine de Saint-Exupéry. The line-up was me on guitar, Angel Calvo on bass, Louie Rondo on drums, and Johnny Frisson (Jean Brisson) at the mic, in all of his glorious punk decadence.

"The auditorium was packed. Kids were even sitting on the floor in the middle aisle. A week before the show, the organizers got permission from the school administration to put up posters of the band. The next day, the principal, teachers and students were shocked when they saw the posters screaming JAILBAIT, showing a 12-year-old girl with bound arms and wrists bleeding. (This violent image of sexual abuse was a bit too much for the times, and it's unthinkable especially now.)

"The administration had all of the posters taken down promptly, but for the rest of the week leading up to the show, everyone was talking about the band. The 222's were broke and couldn't rent a good PA system, so we rented two huge Cerwin Vega speaker cabinets from Marrazza on St. Hubert.

"The day of the show, I arrived backstage, and the first person I saw was Johnny Brisson, sitting in front of a large mirror flanked with light bulbs. His head was mustard yellow, and so were his hands. Being penniless, he had the habit of dying his hair with food dyes. But there was no sink backstage, so he couldn't wash his face or hands of the dye. Plus, he'd forgotten to bring his hair dryer and he was about to go on.

"So Johnny stepped onstage like that in full punk mode, with a

---

3. Transl: The sound sucks!

mustard head. His hair was still wet, and under the heat of the spot-lights the dye on his face mixed in with the sweat and melted down his neck, while his wet hands smeared the slippery mic.

"It didn't take long for the outraged prog-friendly audience to start heckling us. Angel, who was always the first one ready to step up and protect the band members, stopped playing in the middle of a song and sternly warned a heckler, glaring and wagging his drumstick at him in anger. The kid calmed down and we resumed the show, which lasted only slightly more than half an hour. Johnny had to shuffle back home, still caked with the yellow dye.

"The following day, a car couldn't be found to return the goddamn Cerwin Vegas to the rental store. Since no one in the band had a solution and the rental was in his name, poor Johnny had no choice but tó bring back the huge cabinets by himself. He pushed one of the wheeled cabinets from our rehearsal space downtown on Beaver Hall, all the way uphill to Marrazza—a distance of over 7 kilometers. Then he had to go back for the other unwieldy cabinet and do it all over again."

⤳ The Hotel Nelson Grill in Old Montreal picked up where the 364 left off. Some bands played at Station 10, but The Nelson was the choi-cier watering hole for local punk/new wavers. I was always there to catch the local acts, as well as great bands from out of town: Teenage Head, The Viletones and Arson[4] from Toronto, The Mods, Bureaucrats and RAF from Ottawa, plus The Brains from Atlanta, Georgia.

On the slow week nights when no band was playing, the DJ used to put on exciting new singles. Like *Rock Lobster*, by a certain band based in Atlanta, Georgia called the B-52's. Punk violinist Natalya and I loved to dance to this instant camp classic. She had a brush cut and was only 17, but had a huge crush on me and used to make me strange propositions: "Do you want to fuck me, with Sylvie at the same time? I give music lessons and can get you little boys if you want!" Sorry sweet-ie, but me no pedo. I *do* owe her thanks however, for turning me on to

---

4. Hear their excellent *Love On a Leash* at: https://www.youtube.com/watch?v=k0I2k4uV0j0

the iconic French musician/writer Boris Vian[5], via his delightfully nasty song *Fais-moi mal, Johnny.*[6]

⤳ The Nelson Grill cemented the coalescing music scene. The man who made it all happen was Spike—a smooth-talking, lanky 6-foot-plus ambassador of cool. He looked like the Prince of Punk, and he actually *was* one. His name was John von Aichinger, and his father's family was from Austria. They were related to Ludwig III—the last king of Bavaria—and were the Austrian equivalent of the Vanderbilts, Astors and Rockefellers. John was registered as a knight and a baron and his family could be traced back to the 9th century.

After spending a couple of years on the Toronto punk scene, Spike came back to Montreal and discovered that aside from a few haphazard shows at the 364 St Paul, there wasn't really much going on. In the summer of '78 he was part of the punk art gallery Studio Z on St. Denis, as well as a performer in many cutting-edge performances and videos at the Véhicule Art gallery on St. Catherine near St. Laurent. In addition, he was also the drummer of the previously mentioned Widows, who along with Nikki Nightmare, Gigi Duval, and Jean Brisson played shows at studio Z and the memorable Halloween show at the 364. Spike says "I missed that gig because I was in jail along with Dave Rosenberg of the Chromosomes—the one who baptized me Spike. They caught us selling 100 hits of LSD."

Dave got out of jail just before Christmas '78, and asked Spike to become the singer of the Chromosomes. Though Dave was a good friend, the Chromosomes were too fucked up (well, they were actually junkies who robbed drugstores), so Spike decided to concentrate on opening a new venue and start producing shows instead.

Spike chose the Nelson Grill for a variety of reasons. "It wasn't easy," he says, "I had to spend a couple of months clearing out the old clientele—bikers, mainly—before I could put on a first show at the beginning of March '79." After that, he produced a different show three nights a week every week, until June.

---

5. Pronounced "Bo-reese Vee-unh"
6. Pronounced "Feh m'wah mal, Johnny"; Transl: *Hurt Me, Johnny*

I got tired of watching other bands play on stage and was itching to finally give it a shot. A quick chat with Spike over a beer and I had a gig. So yeah, the guy that gave me my first break in showbiz was Spike. I still didn't have a band, but Chuck F and his Narcisse buddies obliged by agreeing to back me up. My first gig was set for May 11th and 12th, under the name Alan Lord & The Marauders.

A few weeks before the show I brought the boys to a small studio in Côte St Paul and cut a five-track demo, two of which featured lead solos by my pal Pièr of the 222's. When I sat him down to add his parts, he whipped off searing melodic riffs in one take on the spot, never having heard the songs before. And *that*, my friends, is pure musical genius.

In the meantime I'd also struck up a friendship with Ivan Doroschuk, whose nascent Men Without Hats I'd invited to open for me at the Nelson. So yeah, I was the one who gave Ivan his first break in showbiz. Cheque please!

While rehearsing for the show in Narcisse's garage I was looking for an amp to plug in my guitar. We weren't supposed to touch Offenbach's equipment. I ignored the unwritten rule that says you never plug a guitar into a bass amp. I plugged my guitar into Breen Leboeuf's bass amp and promptly blew out one of the twelve-inch cones. Big mistake. That's like tipping over a Harley Davidson parked in front of a biker bar. I was in deep shit. I called up Monsieur Leboeuf and explained the situation, shaking on the phone. "Yes sir … don't worry … I'll have the cone replaced before your next rehearsal."

For the Nelson gig I pasted up my own posters that asked the burning question: "Who is Alan Lord?" Indeed, who the hell was he? I sure wanted to know, I was still looking for him.

Come showtime, the Marauders and I put on a decent performance, and at the end Pièr joined us onstage for his two songs. When you're the front guy you can't hide, so I resorted to the rocker's choice nighttime accessory: sunglasses. Some said I looked like Ric Ocasek of The Cars. Well, I was just as rail-thin.

Coming offstage on my second night, I noticed this funny-looking guy wearing black horn-rimmed glasses, who definitely outdid me in the schnozz department. He'd been watching my show accompanied by this delicate sultry porcelain doll that just oozed sex. The girls back then used to dress up real sexy: miniskirts, black stockings, spike heels, topped off with a cute leather jacket. They all looked like Ramones' girlfriends. They wouldn't have been caught dead in a lumberjack shirt and army boots. They were feminine as hell, and you wanted to bang them all.

So the fella with the sex pot babe and prominent proboscis said he liked my songs, but that they were missing something. "The songs are like, only the skeleton," he said. He told me he had a Minimoog synth, and my eyes lit up. His name was Bernard Gagnon[7], and he wound up putting the meat on my bare bones. We became musical partners and fast friends to this day.

A certain Matt Radz called me up and said he wanted to drop by my place to do an interview for *The Montreal Star*, one of the two major English-language dailies. Great! It came out in the fat Saturday edition, and I rushed over to the dépanneur[8] to buy several copies. Wow— the article took up a whole page, and there was a tall picture of me in it. I held it up for the dépanneur guy to see. "Look!" I said," … it's ME!"

I ran back home, and while I didn't exactly sit by the phone, I *did* expect a call from CBS Records offering me a five-album record deal. I waited. And waited. Nothing. *The Montreal Star* even folded a few months later.

It's always the rabid music nerds who start fanzines that promote and nurture underground music scenes. Legs McNeil and John Holmstrom did it with *Punk* magazine in New York, Mark Perry with *Sniffin' Glue* in England, and here the bubbling new scene was covered by *Surfin' Bird*. It only ran three issues, but that was enough to document the short vital span of Montreal's punk/new wave explosion.

Surfin' Bird was put together by Bill Varvaris and David Sapin— the Andy Warhol guy who took my picture at the 364. We finally got to meet, and actually became lifelong friends and collaborators, as you will see. He too was a McGill Engineering dropout.

Bill Varvaris sported a skinny tie and punk badges pinned on a Mod's jacket. He looked like a young pudgy Roy Orbison without the

---

7. Pronounced "Bear-narr Gaw-knee-oh"
8. Pronounced "Dih-pan-eurh" ; Transl: Bodega, 7/11, corner convenience store

shades, and had long oily black bangs he was always sweeping back. His erstwhile girlfriend Sue Ducharme also wrote for *Surfin' Bird*, under the pen name of S'who, as well as local musicians such as Dave Hill, Ivan Doroschuk and Rick Trembles of Electric Vomit. The latter two provided the great cartoons, and in the second issue David Sapin illustrated an Elvis Costello parody I'd done. They also printed a letter I'd sent to staid newspaper *Le Devoir*, lambasting journo Nathalie Petrowski for disparaging the landmark Devo show. The snobby rag had elected not to print it, so *Surfin' Bird* obliged. In the letter I said: "Nous sommes tous Devo. Y'a même du Devo dans *Le **Devoir**.*"[9]

⚡ David Sapin lived in the filthiest apartment I'd ever seen, on St. Mathieu just below Ste. Catherine Street. You literally had to wade your way through all kinds of shit piled ankle deep: empty beer bottles & crates, crumpled sheets of paper and posters, torn newspapers, dog-eared magazines, vinyl LP's & singles out of their sleeves getting scratched, McDonald's, Burger King wrappers & bags, pens and brushes, X-Acto knives, open bottles of hardened glue, cigarette butts and spilled ashtrays.

The kitchen sink overflowed with crusted-over dishes that hadn't been washed in ages, and to top off this amazing ungodly mess, the forks and knives at the bottom of the sink *had started to rust*. He soon moved into an apartment split with Dave Hill on Prince Arthur street in the McGill ghetto, and I started hanging out there a lot, listening to records and swigging beers. I was still mourning the demise of the Sex Pistols, but when Dave Hill put on John Lydon's first single *Public Image*, featuring Keith Levene's mesmerizing swirling guitar[10], I nodded "okay". Things would be just fine.

⚡ I also started hanging out with Ivan Doroschuk. It was the first time *this* Hochelaga-raised kid was traipsing around upscale Outremont. There was a Steinway in his parents' stately house—*the* telltale mark of bourgeois privilege. We hung out in his basement and he turned me on

---

9. Transl: "We are all Devo. There's even Devo in *Le **Devoir**"
10. Hear it at: https://www.youtube.com/watch?v=JjzkNOzFVtg

to strange records like The Residents' *Santa Dog* and Robert Wyatt's eerie *Stalin Wasn't Stallin'*. Adventurous stuff indeed—not exactly *Pop Goes the World*.

Life was good in my Summer of 1979. I could fully devote my time to making music because back then the cost of living was ridiculous. The unemployment insurance I was getting used to last *two whole years*. No one bugged you to look for a job, the rents were ridiculous, and life was cheap. Joss and I went out every night, always had money for beer and hash, and I even had a car—an ugly green Chevy Nova my father'd given me when he bought a new cab. We lived on nothing, yet everyone threw parties all the time. Even *we* held parties, cramming people into our small 3½[11].

The choicest hobnobby parties were at Outremont socialite Mia's parent's house on Mcdougall. *This* working-class louse felt out of place, but enjoyed the chance of suddenly being able to crash the class that was slightly upper than mine. The first of those parties I attended was advertised by a poster done by Ivan—who that night was also furnishing the live entertainment with his Hats.

Natalya was often at those parties, and Joss suspected I was nuzzling and smooching her in the corners. Which I was, but you could convincingly blame it on crowd jostling.

At a late summer party at Mia's, the front door was open and we watched horrified as a stumbling drunk Ivan was having a hard time making it from the sidewalk to the door. One step forward, two steps back, and a few sideways. We gasped, and whispered how sad it was and how pathetic he'd become. He drank too much, his music was floundering, and what a waste of talent. We were seriously worried about him. Well, he sure showed us.

11. One-bedroom apartment

5

FROM NEW WAVE
TO POST PUNK

I n early May I was an Elvis Costello clone, but by June I had a new band doing synth-driven numbers bearing odd titles such as *DNA, Silent Inertia, Hybride* and *Programmed To Rock*. I went from New Wave to Post Punk in less than a month. What happened?

There'd been an avalanche of new and adventurous music pouring out: Public Image, Siouxsie and The Banshees, Tubeway Army, The Flying Lizards, Thomas Dolby, *Warm Leatherette*, plus New York's *No Wave* scene: James Chance & The Contortions, Teenage Jesus and the Jerks, and Mars. It sufficed to kick my ass a quantum notch higher. I tired of simplistic punk rock and also wanted to do something more experimental.

Barely days after my Nelson show I called up Bernard Gagnon— the guy with the Minimoog and the babe—to get together and see if something could happen. He invited me over to his practice space above a Chinese restaurant, which was a huge to-die-for loft with panoramic windows that wrapped around the corner of St. Lawrence and Dorchester[1].

After a few jams we saw things gelled between us. I sang and played rhythm guitar, Gagnon played Minimoog on half the songs, then switched to lead guitar for the rest. We recruited Phil Nolan on bass, Angel "Dust" Calvo on drums, and I christened the band *Alan Lord & The Blew Genes*.

---

1. Now the Boulevard René-Lévesque—named after a Quebec premier and key separatist figure.

Bernard Gagnon was the first bona fide genius I'd ever met. He read Baudelaire, de Sade, Lautréamont and Nietzsche, knew Wagner inside out, understood Boulez and eventually managed to decipher a Schönberg score that had been daunting him for weeks. His mentor was the illustrious Quebec composer Claude Vivier[2], he studied composition under Xenakis, and even got to jam with John Cage. In our band he was the Hendrix of the Minimoog, and could easily switch over to playing a mean guitar solo on par with Jimmy Page. Plus, whenever necessary, he could also blow a mean Delta Blues harp. Gagnon later wound up composing award-winning works of contemporary music, but for now he was making a living by working in the parking garage building of The Bay, in the unheated entrance gatehouse booth, whose roll-up doors were open even in winter. He started working there in 1976 when he met his knockout girlfriend Micheline.

Joss and I spent many an evening at Gagnon and Micheline's place downtown on Baile street, smoking tons of hash, and listening to Throbbing Gristle, Gagnon's fetish *Metal Box*, and The Residents' *Third Reich n' Roll*.

My Blew Genes gave a single show at the Hotel Nelson Grill on June 9th—which also happened to be the last show of the Grill. Spike explains: "The hotel had been struggling to rent rooms and its bar was always empty. When I started producing shows, the Grill was so successful it kept the hotel alive. What I didn't know however, was that sometime before I showed up, the owner had applied to the federal government for a $200K grant to turn the hotel into a youth hostel. The grant came through towards the end of the spring and the owner appointed a hippie asshole to administer it. He just hated me and my punk staff, and used every little pretext to make a case for the owner to get rid of us. It worked, and the fucker pulled the rug from under our feet."

Just as this was going on, Tracy, Scott and others from the local bands showed up at the Nelson to ask Spike what the summer schedule was going to look like. He had to break the news to them about closing the Grill, and that he'd negotiated for one last night. It was to be a

---

2. Pronounced "Clode Vee-v'yay"

festival called the 3-3—meaning that it was to be held from 3PM to 3AM. The bands that played at that last gig were Electric Vomit, The Eighties, Heaven 17, Lorne Ranger & Go. My Blew Genes were last on the bill, which means we had the dubious honor of closing the place.

The Nelson Grill may have lasted only three months, but those three months were utterly crucial. It gave us all a place to go, hang out, meet new faces, exchange ideas, and grow as artists. It changed the musical scene, it changed people, it changed Montreal. Without the Nelson Grill the nascent scene could have been strangled at birth. So a big *Thank You John* to Spike. Without him I would have been nothing, I would have remained a frustrated office slave with his pipe dreams quickly dashed.

After our show, Tracy Howe of Heaven 17—who'd been under-standably unimpressed by my weeks-old Marauders incarnation—flipped out and jumped onstage to vigorously shake my hand, enthusi-astically congratulating me on my radically new musical direction. David Sapin, Joss and I bought some six packs, drove up the mountain, and continued the celebration yakking in a field until dawn.

⤌ The Nelson's Last Stand was covered in the third issue of *Surfin' Bird*, which also featured new pieces by Joss and yours truly. I egged her on to write an article about the colourful Quebec bands that were the French pop *yé-yé* answer to 1964's British Invasion: Les Classels, all dressed in white and with white moptops—the Hou-Lops, also with white hair—answered by Les Excentriques dressed in pink satin—then César et ses Romains, dressed up as Roman soldiers—the Bel Canto with FOUR guitars, count 'em—Les Sultans with their sultry singer Bruce ... Every week on TV you'd see a new band dressed ridiculously —like Les Gendarmes, in French cop getups, keeping the beat with truncheons clicked together. It was a crazy period, and totally exciting for a 10-year-old kid like me.

Together, Joss and I met some of the by-then paunchy, balding, retired-from-showbiz stars for an interview in their tacky suburban homes with creepy chirping parakeets in standing cages. Such as Gilles Girard of Les Classels. Were they big? Why, they got to play on Ed Sullivan! When pitching them to Ed, stereotypically shlock manager

Ben Kaye explained the brilliant strategy behind the name he'd given them: "Class sells ... get it, Ed?"

⇗ On Sunday mornings Joss and I used to listen religiously to a radio show on CKOI-FM called *Rock en stock/Francoeur en chute libre*[3], that played the great garage stuff from the Sixties: The Young Rascals, Tommy James And The Shondells, The Troggs, The Kinks. The DJ was Lucien Francoeur[4]. I turned to Joss: "Why not interview him for *Surfin' Bird*?" After all, he *was* the only true precursor of Quebec Punk—coming along before Danger.

Lucien Francoeur was sort of our local Lou Reed. He'd disappeared after releasing a few milestone albums with his band *Aut'Chose*[5] in the mid '70's. They put out a single that was just as cool as any Stones single—*Nancy Beaudoin*[6]. Their first two albums remain Quebec's best to this day, and incidentally Beck Hansen favourites.

After *Aut'Chose* broke apart, Francoeur made a solo album in 1978, but hadn't been heard of much since. Not only was he a singer, he was a *poet*. Having attended English Catholic school in Montreal, poetry to me was boring stuff like Longfellow and Rudyard Kipling. I was surprised to find in Francoeur's books *Snack Bar, 5-10-15*[7], and especially *Le Calepin d'un menteur*[8] something that finally spoke to me. Also, I really dug his cockiness and natural-born fuckyou punk attitude[9].

I went to his place in the suburb of Boucherville, where we chatted amid a jumble of pinball machines, a working jukebox and various Aut'Chose memorabilia. We gabbed about music and all sorts of things, and quickly struck up a friendship. He told me he was collecting material for a next album, I told him I was a musician, and that I might

---

3. Transl: Rock In Stock/Francoeur In Free Fall
4. Pronounced "Lew-see-yay Fruh-kirr"
5. Pronounced "Oat shows"; Transl: Somethin' Else
6. Pronounced "Nancy Bo-d'way"; see the clip at https://www.youtube.com/watch?v=KV9HB5pNH60
7. Transl: Dollar Store
8. Transl: Diary of a Liar
9. See Appendix A—Selected Texts for a sample song lyric

have a few songs for him. For the *Surfin' Bird* article I cut out snippets from his poetry books and songs, and pasted them over a picture of him, radially arranged like gun blasts shooting out of his mouth.

⇄ The highlight of that summer was the Ramones show on July 13th at the *Pretzel Enchaîné*[10] club on Clark below Sherbrooke, in what had once been the 50's beatnik haunt *El Cortijo*. Everyone was anticipating that show feverishly—including me, Joss, Serge Giguère of Narcisse and his girlfriend Hélène. We danced madly to *Rocket To Russia* in their basement apartment in our pre-show warmup.

It was the best show I saw in my life—and I've seen plenty. Everyone in the local music scene was there. The place was packed tight, but I certainly didn't mind being pressed up against Heaven 17's luscious Lysanne Thibodeau. It was hot and steamy and our hair was wet and limp from all the sweat. We grinned at each other with big gleeful smiles dancing without a care in the world, bouncing and flailing to *Cretin Hop* and all the other *"WANN TWO CHREE FAOW!"* hits chained in a row.

I pushed through to the front and stood at Johnny Ramone's feet, leaning my elbows on the stage. I looked up at him and marvelled at his frenzied downstroke-only guitar strumming. Ooh! He dropped his pick! I scrambled and grabbed it fast. It was white and on it was printed RAMONES. Of course, I lost it since. Or rather, swiped by a "friend".

⇄ After the Nelson Grill show, Phil left us and went to form Ulterior Motive, and we no longer had a bass player. I changed our name to the simpler *Vex*, and in July we recorded our seminal song DNA at tiny Studio 1741 in Verdun. As well as playing the lightning guitar riff of the song, I composed the music and lyrics—which were written as the cheeky board game instructions accompanying a kid's home lab DNA tinkering kit[11].

Bernard supplied the Minimoog flourishes, as well as the solo in the middle, which consisted of a tape loop superimposing layers of his

---

10. Pronounced "Pretzel Ah-shay-nay"; Transl: The Linked Pretzel
11. See Appendix A—Selected Texts

sweeping motifs, giving the song a Wagnerian grandeur. It was an avant-garde tour de force that far surpassed anything else being done at the time. DNA was released by the German label *Anna Logue Records* in 2008, on the vinyl LP *Echoes From Our Past*. The liner notes called the song "a truly pioneering work". It was also released in 2020, kicking off Quebec's *Nome Noma* compilation[12], and online comments showed it was overwhelmingly the clear favourite out of the album's thirteen tracks.

⇜ Dave Hill was recruited on bass, and on July 27th we gave an outrageously chaotic show in our fabulous practice hall. It was a mini festival cum benefit, to raise money to put out the next issue of *Surfin' Bird*. I remember what happened to me *after* the show, but as for the show itself, nada—it was sheer pandemonium both in the place *and* my head.

Here's Gagnon's recollection of that illustrious evening: "Several other groups played that night: Ulterior Motive—with Phil—as well as Lorne Ranger and the 222's—who started their set with The Sex Pistols' *Holidays In The Sun*. We (Vex) were the last ones to play. By the end of our show, there was only Angel who continued playing his drums. You (Alan) started playing guitar lying on the floor with your head hanging off the stage, while Dave was running after people, swinging his bass at them like an axe. I felt tired and started to doze standing at my Minimoog. I woke up, and was wondering where the synth sound I heard was coming from … it was my arm leaning against the keyboard. Later I was in the men's room peeing in a urinal, and punkette girls with hacked haircuts like Joan of Arc came in and fucked around; they grabbed my ass while I tried to pee. Then at a certain point everyone rushed to the windows to see a woman—victim of a hit-and-run—being dragged by a car westward along Dorchester. This had nothing to do with the show; it was just the last cherry of craziness on top of the sick cake of a weird evening."

All I remember is when everyone piled onto the sidewalk of St. Laurent after that apocalyptic soirée. We were all plastered from too much booze and drugs. I started bickering with Joss, when out of nowhere I received a punch in the face. It was from Johnny Graham—

12. Hear it at: https://soundcloud.com/user-55178726-221949985/vex-dna-1

guitarist of The Blanks. He broke my nose, which now pointed to the left side of my face, instead of straight ahead. Dave Hill drove me to the emergency ward of The Montreal General Hospital, which was a bit of a drive. I was greeted there by an angelic Lysanne Thibodeau—of Heaven 17—who was on her night shift as an orderly. She comforted me by gently stroking my head, with her comforting boobs serving as a pillow. I was finally in heaven! After a few minutes, another orderly in green scrubs approached us. It was Ivan Doroschuk, also on his night shift.

⟨ What was the reason behind the mass insanity that reigned that night? This orgy of blotto creativity was the final crashing of the Punk/New Wave that had been welling up for over a year. It started with the musicians, but now the immense wave had caught up with the public, and the sensation of being unshackled had also finally overwhelmed *them*. People everywhere now pitched themselves headlong at their life's desires in abandon, without thinking about "The Future" or their social status. There was no concern to maintain a cool front at all costs. The moment was so hot that nobody had time to stop and take stock shots. There reigned a "fuck all" attitude that was very liberating, especially for us artists, musicians and poets.

Yet for all that boil and trouble there was never to be a fourth issue of *Surfin' Bird*. Things also broke down for Vex: Angel and Dave left, and there was only me and Bernard. After such heady trips, the down is always brutal.

⟨ That August, Joss and I decided to take a trip to New York. After taking pictures of the tall buildings like any stupid tourist we slummed around St. Mark's Place, ducking into Trash & Vaudeville to look at the by-then standard cheesy punk fare on display: studded leather chokers, Doc Marten boots and posters of a snarling Sid Vicious. I bought records at the great Bleecker Bob's: Cabaret Voltaire's *Nag Nag Nag, Do The Mussolini (Headkick)* and PragVec's *Bits* EP among other things. I also got to visit CBGB's on the scuzzy Bowery, which back then was a hellhole of misery—you had to tiptoe around the bums passed out on the sidewalk.

That night, the Patti Smith Group was playing. Meh. I bought the single *Because The Night* when it came out, but other than that I wasn't a big fan. I was playing the pinball machine in the corner near the bar and heard Patti's voice, but I couldn't see her. I plowed my way through the crowd—people were packed in the tiny club. As I approached the stage, to my astonishment I saw her crawling on all fours toward the edge of the stage, stammering her yelpy poetry in a trance. Or at least a good simulation of one. In front of her, a pair of emaciated hippie Patti clone devotees brushed back their long stringy hair nervously and wept with excitement, screeching at her with arms outstretched, feverishly hoping to touch their idol with trembling fingers. I was mortified by the embarrassing spectacle. I took a sip of my Rolling Rock and got back to my pinball game.

Before leaving the Big Rotten, I rummaged through a remaindered book bin on Bleecker Street and picked up *Jack's Book*—a book about Jack Kerouac. I'd heard the name before, but I didn't know anything about him. Back home I placed it on the shelf, and meant to get around to reading it. One day.

⇜ In October I got a surprise call from Montreal's *other* svengali Marc de Mouy—who'd taped my Marauders show at the Nelson[13]. He was looking for a band to open for the B-52's at the Pretzel, and thought of Vex. You bet your ass I accepted. For the gig we had to call on a friend of Bernard's—Réjean Garneau—who played bass, and I also called up my old Marauder drumming pal Richard Lacoste. He says we played 45 minutes, but I don't remember much, except that Bernard's amp head wasn't plugged into the loudspeaker cabinet, so we couldn't hear any of his guitar playing.

That show was the last one for Vex. Afterward I devoted myself to working with my new pal Lucien Francoeur on his next album, which took us into a new year, and a new decade.

---

13. The tapes got lost, natch

6
THE RETURN OF
JOHNNY SHIVERS

L ucien Francoeur was Quebec's Lou Reed, except he didn't play guitar and couldn't sing. He talked his way through the songs just like Lou. And it worked. Because his lyrics were striking, it was obvious he was a poet. A *Rock* poet. His big influence was Jim Morrison, and it approached fetish level. He even printed a limited edition luxury book of Morrison's poems called *Dry Water*.

I gave Lucien a demo tape of my songs, from which he chose two for his album. One of them was a James Bondish riff, which became *l'Espion*[1]. The other was *Nowhere Beach*—an inspired Brian Ferry rip-off gem I had lying around. Lucien proposed I produce his album. Hot diggity. Phil Spector, here I come.

Lucien and I became fast friends, not only during the recording of the album, but throughout the rest of the year. In fact, we were inseparable. After spending a whole day together, we'd continue yakking on the phone for hours in the evening, as well as on weekends. Like girls with pink Princess phones. It was a "bromance"—something I never experienced before or since. There reigned between us a mutual respect and a certain unspoken complicity—often much to the chagrin of people around us.

I felt it my mission to bring him up to speed in music. I made him mix tapes and turned him onto the great new sounds of the day: Public Image, Siouxsie, Joy Division, Cramps. In return, he wised me up to *good* poetry. He bought me the complete works of Rimbaud—which became

---

1. Pronounced "Less pyoh"; Transl: *The Spy*

my *livre de chevet*[2]. He told me: "Alan, all you really need is Rimbaud and Burroughs." Cool! Who's *Burroughs*?

⇄ At Lucien's place one day he started complaining about being broke, unable to pay his bills. I asked him how much his rent was. He said $600 a month[3]. I said, "are you nuts? I'm only paying $85—you gotta get *out* of here, man!" He froze in the panic revelation. "You're right!" he balked.

As it happens, he was also in the process of breaking up with Yolande, and moving in with new girlfriend, the poetess Claudine. Her apartment was small, so he asked me to help him move his pinball machine, huge juke box and stuff to his friend Coco's place. This was none other than Jacques "Coco" Mercier, leader of the Devils Disciples, one of Quebec's many rival biker gangs—Satan's Choice, Popeyes, Hot Pistons, and of course Hell's Angels. Coco had done ten years in jail for the attempted murder of two Popeyes. Lucien met him when he'd invited Aut'Chose to play in the Institut Leclerc[4] prison, where he reigned as virtual boss. Even the frickin' *screws*—prison guards—were deferential to Coco.

After carrying the heavy pinball machine and juke box up the stairs at Coco's place, I collapsed onto the couch, dead exhausted. It was noonish and I hadn't had breakfast. My stomach was empty. Coco brought out some beers for us, then loaded up a pipe with a ton of tobacco, and crumbled chunks of hash on top. He lit it up, took a deep drag, then in a coughing fit passed it on to us. Feeling it wasn't a good idea to brush off Coco, I breathed in a lungful. It was strong shit as hell, and soon the room started spinning. I bolted to the bathroom just in time and stuck my head in the toilet bowl, hurling violently whatever little curdles of last night's meal were still in my gut.

⇄ I wanted to make Francoeur's album as punky as possible, and got to punk up a song Francoeur wanted by '60's French rock star *Antoine*, called *Les Élucubrations d'Antoine*[5].

---

2. Pronounced "Lee-vruh duh sheh-veh"; Transl: bedside bible
3. $2000 today
4. Pronounced "Aye-stee-tew Luh-Claire"
5. Transl: Antoine's Rants

As the artistic producer I conducted the rehearsals, coached the musicians and coordinated the recordings from January to April, at Studio Pélo in the south shore suburb of Longueuil[6]. Michel Péloquin[7] was the sound engineer. It was an 8-track studio, but that was enough for us, and we never needed to "bounce" anything to free up more tracks. I did all the guitars and the occasional bass and synthesizer parts. Lucien's faithful companion Jean-François Saint-Georges (JF for short) played keyboards and synths. Future Quebec rock star Marjo came in to do backing vocals on the song *Fascination*. Back then she was painfully shy and insisted on doing her vocals in the dark.

Throughout the recording sessions Lucien and I joked around and laughed like loons. I cracked him up with my Fat Elvis imitation, clicking on the talkback mic: "I'm The King, Mama—could you fry me up a batch o' donuts sprinkled w' pills? Thanks, Mama." During the sessions I was up to smoking a pack a day to calm my nerves. Cough cough.

The drummer was an alcoholic, and he played with two *grosses molles*[8] parked next to his hi-hat pedal. I taught that old dog how to do Paul Cook's signature skippy beat[9], as well as other tricks. Eventually he had to be fired because he was too drunk to play. Or even bother to show up for the sessions.

⇄ During the mixing of the album, the sound engineer spent most of his time on the phone. He twiddled the sound board knobs with his head cocked, cradling the phone on his shoulder. Lucien was getting pissed off. He complained, "Pélo's mixing the goddamn album *on the fucking phone*, fer chrissake!" The mix was becoming a muddy mess, so Lucien had to call in a fixer, a real sound pro—Billy Szawlowski.

Billy zoomed into the parking lot in his red sports car, and hunkered down right away in dead seriousness at the mixing console. We all got out of the way, and everybody was real quiet. You could've heard

---

6. Pronounced "Loan-goil"

7. Pronounced "Pillow-quay"

8. Tall Molson beer bottles

9. The Sex Pistols' *Did You No Wrong* (at 0:24 & 0:30): https://www.youtube.com/watch?v=niaIRGZFMdU

a pinhead drop. He checked all the gear and wiring from top to bottom, grilled Pélo and told him what to do. "What's that buzz?" he inquired. "Why do I hear a buzz whenever I turn on this switch?"

There was a mystery buzz that was messing everything up, and it had to be eliminated before Billy could even start mixing. It turned out the buzz came from the security system of the bank above the studio. Producer Paul Lévesque[10] managed to convince the bank manager to disable their security system so we could mix the bloody album already.

Billy carefully listened to each track of each song, one by one. Worried, Lucien asked him "Billy, can you save my album?" After a long pause, Billy told him: "Yeah, I can do it. We won't have to re-record any tracks."

☡ In retrospect, I now appreciate that recording the *Johnny Frisson* album—even if it was only an 8-track studio—was a priceless *analogue* experience—something no longer possible. I pity young musicians today who fiddle with computer sound plug-ins and never experienced recording in a real analog studio, hearing the accelerating *flup flup flup* of rewinding tape, then the *dzyoot!* of a tape reel braking to a sudden stop. We didn't have the luxury of adding limitless tracks for minor corrections. We had to time "punch-ins" properly on existing tracks, and any "cut and paste" editing was accomplished *manually*, by splicing tape ends together using Scotch tape.

Back then, making an album in a studio was also *glamorous*. In this wonderful digital age, anyone can make an album on a laptop, in their kitchen, in their skivvies. That's all well and fine, democratic and inclusive, but where's the *glamour* in that?

With the album finally under our belts, we needed a good title for it. We scratched our heads over that one for a while. It was his comeback album. It was the return of The Original Punk. I turned to Lucien: "Johnny Frisson! Why don't we call it *Le retour de Johnny Frisson?*"[11] Sold!

10. Pronounced "Lih-veck"
11. Transl: *The Return Of Johnny Shivers*

⤳ On one of the first warm days of April, a sunny Saturday afternoon, Francoeur and I stopped off to check out the brand new McDonald's at the corner of Papineau and Mount-Royal. As we exited from our regal Clown Meal, we ran into a rail-thin dark-skinned guy coming down the sidewalk, hands tucked in the pockets of his red leather jacket.

"Tiens, salut Mario!"[12] Francoeur greeted him. "This is Mario Campo," he turned to me, adding nonchalantly, "he's a poet." He said that matter of fact, as if it were the most natural thing to say about anyone. *"He's a poet ..."* as normal as saying "he's a plumber". I was taken aback. The guy was roughly my age, and *a poet* ... I mean ... somehow, I thought only people *older* than me could be poets. I was astonished.

Along with the other writers of *La Modernité*—Quebec's '70's generation of writers and poets Jean-Paul Daoust, Claude Beausoleil, Yolande Villemaire and Paul Chamberland[13]—Mario was one of the guests invited to the poetry festival *La Nuit de la Poésie '80*[14] at UQUAM[15]. Francoeur would be accompanied by the band I was to lead.

JF remembers: "The whole affair was disorganized and there were a lot of people reading, so we finally got to play only at 6 AM, after having a bite to eat at the Green Garden on Ste-Catherine, around 5 AM—the time when all the hookers and trannies finished their shifts."

But first we were regaled by a fistfight backstage between Francoeur and his great rival, the poet Denis Vanier[16]. Looking like a cross between Howard Stern and the Flemish *chanteur* Arno, Vanier had his first book of poetry—*Je*[17]—written at the age of 13—published by none other than the firebrand union activist—and all-time working-class hero of mine, Michel Chartrand. At the age of 16 Vanier ran away from home to New York City, where in 1965 he wound up working at Ed Sanders' famed Peace Eye Bookstore. When he came back he wrote his landmark book of poetry *Pornographic Delicatessen*.

---

12. Transl: "Hey, hi Mario"
13. Pronounced "Juh-Paul Da-ooh, Clode Beau-so-lay, Yo-lund Vill-mehr, Paul Shaw-bear-law"
14. Transl: Night Of Poetry '80
15. The University of Quebec in Montreal
16. Pronounced "Duh-knee Van-knee-yay"
17. Transl: "I"

As soon as Vanier spotted Francoeur, he lunged at him, flinging out a typical litany of Catholic Quebec curses: *"mon hostie de câlice de tabarnak de saint ciboire…"*

Francoeur grabbed Vanier's sweater by the bottom and tugged it over his head, over the shoulder-length mass of black frizzy hair, exposing his bare back. Vanier tried to swipe punches left and right blindly, and they struggled in the hallway, legs and arms flailing. After the initial shock had passed, a few of us dove in, and struggled to separate our twin distinguished laureates from each other.

And that was my initiation into the ethereal world of Quebec poetry: Put two poets together, you get a Poetry War.

When it was his turn to go onstage, Mario Campo walked up to the mic, holding a sheet of paper. Instead of reading from it, he violently scrunched it into a ball against the mic—which gave loud crinkly sounds coming out of the speakers. He then tossed it at the audience and left in disgust—to howls, hoots and whistles of approval *and* disapproval.

I was gobsmacked. *He was my man!* From then onwards Mario came to all our shows and hung out with us backstage. We became fast friends, and he remained my best friend ever since. We became punk brothers, post punk brothers, soul mates of the anarcho-nihilist mind. Mario was the brother I never had, the brother I kept asking my mom for, the brother my parents had a quack abort on the kitchen table of our Clark Street hovel—the brother whose remains dripped off the tip of a blood-soaked wire hanger.

⚹ Another poetry festival followed—*l'Après-midi de la Poésie '80*[18] at Rosemount College. After that one, Lucien and I, Claude Beausoleil, Jean-Paul Daoust and Yolande Villemaire piled into their literary watering hole—the Saint-Sulpice[19] restaurant on St. Denis—and sat down for drinks and dinner. Mario didn't get past the drinking stage. We watched him come down the stairs, then trip and tumble the rest of the way down.

---

18. Transl: Poetry Afternoon '80
19. Pronounced "Say Sue-l'piss"

"Don't worry, Mario," Lucien cracked, "no one saw that." Without a word I went over to help him up. I spent the rest of *his* life picking him up.

Mario wasn't a poet who drank. He was an alcoholic who wrote. Given the choice between the two, the booze always beat the words.

⇜ Kébec Disc released *Johnny Frisson* in May, and it also came out later in France. It still holds up today, and even became a favourite of The *Dead Kennedys'* Jello Biafra. When I finally got to hold the album in my hands I looked all over it for a picture of me. I mean, there'd been a band picture on Lucien's last record. This time there were only pictures of Johnny Shivers in various poses. Well, at least my *name* was there. In small print.

I rushed over to my parents' house and put it on the old TV cabinet record player, to proudly display my several months' work. "He can't sing!" they announced, to my profound dismay—"all he does is talk!" It was pointless for me to protest apoplectically "But Ma, Pa, *he's a Rock Poet!*"

⇜ Nevertheless, I was starting to enjoy my new status as a minor rock celeb. I ran into Ivan Doroschuk at the Glace—the dance club that had replaced the defunct Nelson as *the* hangout spot. The Glace was instituted by ex-222's manager Pyer Desrochers. Among the club staples being played by the Glace DJ were *Mirror In The Bathroom* by The English Beat, and Joy Division's sublime *Love Will Tear Us Apart*—shortly before the singer hanged himself.

Drink in hand, Ivan came up to me and declared, "It's me and you, Alan"—meaning we were the only two "success stories" to have emerged out of the Montreal punk scene. I asked him if he wanted to play keyboards for the Francoeur shows coming up. He said: "No thanks, I'll stick with my Hats." Smart boy. Ivan got his dad to co-sign him a $15,000 loan[20], went out and bought synths, sequencers and drum machines, and put out his EP *Folk Songs Of The 80's*. See how it helps to be born into a proper boojwa family?

---

20. $50,000 today

And what was the rest of the old Nelson gang up to? David Sapin was now doing layouts for *Blow Up*—a brand new hip mag that mimicked Warhol's *Interview*: chichi articles and fluff pieces of cooldom. It didn't last long.

↗ The album launch of *Johnny Frisson* took place in a bar on Dorchester, across from the Radio Canada[21] tower. I was relaxing in the kitchen before we went on, my back propped against the big brushed-metal fridge. Among Lucien's guests was Coco. Uh oh. He came up to me and grabbed my head by the ears, pulled it toward his face and gave me a big disgusting slurpy sloppy walrus-mustached biker's smooch, smack on my mouth. That was a good reminder never to wind up in jail. Where is he now? They found him alone on the floor of an empty apartment. He'd been dead for two days. Either murder, or a drug overdose.

Lucien got a call from famous impresario Donald K. Donald. He was offering us the opening spot for The Ramones. Lucien asked me, "Should we do it?" I exclaimed: "Are you fucking kidding me? The Ramones? They're my idols! *Of course* we're gonna do it."

I was going to meet my heroes! We rehearsed for the show the night of Quebec's referendum on independence. During breaks we looked with a jaded eye at the results tallying up on TV. The final vote was to stay in Canada. Fine, whatever. *Next song.*

The show was at Le Plateau, an auditorium in Lafontaine Park. After our mid-afternoon soundcheck, I was hanging out with some guys on the fire escape landing, when Dee Dee Ramone saunters up the stairs. I said, "Hey Dee Dee, how are you man?" Dee Dee asked, "Does anyone have any dope?" Now I was the only one present who knew that when a Noo Yawker talks about "dope", he means smack. "Sorry Dee Dee, I only have this," I said, whipping out a skinny little hash joint I had in my pocket. I handed it to him. He grabbed it, said: "Wow, cool, thanks!" and disappeared. I was disappointed, thinking I could've smoked the joint with him. But hey—*I gave Dee Dee Ramone a joint!*—put *that* on my pet sematary tombstone.

Before going on, we were entitled to the buffet dinner laid out for

---

21. The French-language CBC

the Ramones backstage. It was a macrobiotic feast as specified on their rider. Not a slice of pizza in view. What the hey? Were they indeed the Buddhists they kept telling reporters they were?

Backstage, the Ramones were very nice, and allowed me to be photographed with them—both individually, and in group shots—just like those pictures in *Rock Scene* and *Hit Parader*. And wouldn't you know it, I lost those goddamn pictures of me with Joey, Dee Dee, Johnny and Marky. Or more likely, Joss ripped them up and stuffed them in the trashcan in revenge when we broke up years later.

Fellow guitarist Al Gunn, who was in the audience in the middle of the 8th row, remembers our show vividly: "It was good. Lucien was being spit on quite intensely. At one point he slipped on the accumulating slime and fell on his ass. After getting up he pointed at the back of the room, shouting 'come and help me!' ..."

Poor Lucien didn't know that spitting was the punk sign of affection.

꒳ Backstage after our show, we went back to drinking and smoking as we did before we went on. It was a helluva shock for us to watch— with beers and cigarettes in hand—the Ramones doing warm-up exercises before *their* show. Johnny and Dee Dee were furiously strumming their unplugged guitars, and Marky hammered the sofa arm with his drumsticks like a maniac.

Instead of drinking, smoking and joking around like us idiots, these Olympian punk gods were warming up like serious athletes! I was ashamed of myself, and of all of us two-bit Montreal "rock stars". *These* no-nonsense working-class boys from Queens made sure to warm up properly beforehand, to hit the ground running. It was a hell of a punk lesson for me. In the end, the Ramones weren't musicians—they were impossible and improbable beings, almost superhuman—Blitzkrieg Bop's unstoppable Nazi shatze shock troopers.

꒳ After the Ramones show JF dropped out of the band, wishing a saner and more stable life working at Delisle Yogurts. We were to go on tour across Quebec, and I was dissatisfied with the remaining uncool dudes we had. I wanted a band with guys *my* age, and with similar musical tastes. So I thought of recruiting Bernard Gagnon, Angel, and

Dave Preston of The Blanks on bass. I went to Gagnon's place and pitched him the idea. He liked, and said he was in. Micheline added, with sparkling eyes: "And I could play the *whip*."

In the end, the "tour" turned out to be a show at the Café Campus in September, a week's residency out on a wharf in the boondocks of Sept-Îles[22] in October, and a six-night residency at the *Imprévu* of the Hotel Iroquois in Old Montreal in November. Gagnon had given up his job at the parking garage for nothing, and I still feel shitty about it to this day.

Meanwhile, the album wasn't selling, no songs off it were playing on the radio, and Lucien complained about being snubbed by the Quebec public. Whaddaya want, back then Quebec was at least three years retarded—there were still beards, long hair, and gals wore long peasant skirts to drink their herbal tea. Macramé reigned on apartment walls.

During our Café Campus show in Quebec City, a couple of gaunt stringy-haired hippies got up and walked out on us, waving us off as crap. They didn't like the smart-ass new wavers giving their sacrosanct Aut'Chose the Post Punk treatment.

Being some 600 miles from Montreal, Sept-Îles was pretty much the ass end of the province of Quebec. That's where the St Lawrence River yawns to become the *Gulf* of St Lawrence, and nothing much memorable ever happens there, apart from a memorable fish catch. So *we* were the big attraction for miles around, in the only bar for miles around.

Our wonderful road trip up the flat coast to nowhere included a car accident. Gagnon remembers "we were all in the same car, and at a certain point we lost control on the icy road and landed in a ditch."

The owner of the bar provided us a big apartment we all lived in, which was quite a distance from the bar. Gagnon brought along Micheline, so naturally they had their own room. Dave and Angel probably had to share theirs. The days before showtime were long and boring, and we just sat around in the kitchen or the living room. What the hell is there to do in Sept-Îles except drink? Answer: get stoned.

---

22. Pronounced "Set ill"; Transl: Seven Islands

Dave Preston had a Master's degree in Philosophy and a junk habit. One evening I saw him preparing to shoot up. Figuring I had nothing better to do in Sept-Îles than to scratch *that* off my bucket list, I asked him to also prepare me a shot. Knowing my system, I told him to give me *half* of whatever he thought was an appropriate dose.

Dave shot me up. I immediately felt woozy and started teetering. "Uh oh," he said, "maybe I gave you too much." Exactly what I *didn't* want to hear. I collapsed onto the couch and felt happy as a cooing Tribble. I was fine. The great feeling you get on heroin is like sinking into a warm bubble bath and enjoying it eyes closed, a happy mollusk in the suds. Right then I knew I should never get into smack, because that was the only thing I'd ever need in my life. Then I threw up a little retch. Every twenty minutes an unpleasant little retch. Well *that* nailed the fun out of Junkie Life for me.

⤜ During one of our afternoon rehearsals in the bar I got a call from Joss. Montreal's prestigious engineering firm TGL (Trudeau Gascon Lalancette)—was offering me a job. Wow! I'd tired of my glamorous penniless rock star life and had been sending out resumés for months. I was 26, and talk about *No Future!* Well now I finally had a job to go to. Boys, I'm *outta here*! For this momentous occasion there was even a Francoeur song with a ready lyric for me: "At the moment, there's someone happy to have found himself a job."

Our last engagement was the six-night residency at the *Imprévu*, which turned into a near-riot. Campo's girlfriend Susanne—the one who booked The Screamers in Montreal—gushed in a Québec Rock article "the club was packed to the gills, the band assaulted our senses— Angel, Bernard, lil' genius Alan and heartthrob Dave—it was all leather jackets and champagne … a living theater in red, total anarchy, and the last night the band couldn't play their last set cause it was busted by the cops. It was a live Rolling Stones movie."

Lucien felt so inspired he squeezed his feet into a pair of women's red high heels and teetered around the stage on his lady stilts.

After one of the shows, while Francoeur held court in the dressing room, the boys and I sat down at a table in front of the stage to enjoy a post-show beer. A Brit who was still hanging around came up to us raving, "You guys are *fucking GREAT!*... but you should get rid of the *singer*!" Well *that* sure had us in stitches.

≷ In the final analysis, I owe Francoeur everything. And I owe him nothing. I owe him nothing because I was always my own man and worked my ass off for him, pretty much for free. And I owe him everything in the sense that thanks to him I got to open for The Ramones and meet them, I got to record a *real* album, plus he exposed me to Rimbaud, poetry, and the great names of the Quebec literary world—then also Burroughs—the future Rosetta Stone of my intellectual life. But most importantly, he introduced me to Mario Campo, who became the brother I'd been wishing for all these years.

7

MARIO

Just like me, Mario Campo liked the Damned, the Clash, Johnny Thunders (his next guitar hero after Keith Richards), the Cramps—and The Ramones. They were *his* four brothers. Mario Ramone, why not. His favourite punk single though was The Vibrators' mawkish *Baby, Baby, Baby*—which he played to me a few times too many.

In his writing, Mario was always rebellious and railed against the powers that be. It was typical of the countercultural leanings of early '70's Quebec cutting edge poets, whose writings could be found in the seminal periodical *Hobo Québec*. Nevertheless, he succeeded in getting his books *l'Anovulatoire* and *Coma Laudanum* put out by established publishers.

Francoeur said "Campo's *Coma Laudanum* is an incredible and ineffable inner journey—a dreamlike and unfathomable writing that I loved so much and that I have always read and re-read either stoned or straight, smoking a joint or smack. Campo was a poet of inner excess, his writing was strewn with diamonds and irrefutable, his poems jewels in precious words."

⇘ But Mario found his true voice and identity in the Punk and Post Punk era. In the tradition of punk 'zine Sniffing Glue he self-published a stapled xeroxed poetry 'zine called *Insomnies Polaroïde*[1]. He illustrated it with photos of Patti Smith, and of himself wearing punk

---

1. Transl: Polaroid Insomnias; See leftmost bottom download link, at https://mario-campo-poete.com/mariocampo-recueils.html

shades while carrying under his arm the first Public Image album. There was a poem titled *Blank Generation* and others made of cut-out ransom note words in Sex Pistols fashion. Some texts were magnificently integrated within graphic layouts: cassette tapes, computer screens, and mirrored stencils[2].

It turns out that Mario, Gagnon and I grew up in the same area—Hochelaga west of Pie IX. They were a bit older than me, so on Saturdays they went to *Les p'tits bals Yéyé*—sock hops for kids where you could see the great mid-Sixties bands previously mentioned: Tony Roman, Les Hou-Lops, Les Classels, etc.

Francoeur says: "I got to know Mario when I was 20, with Laurent Tourigny—brother of the poet François. We used to meet in Laurent's parents' basement in Repentigny to drink red wine, smoke joints and listen to albums. Mario said: "We put on The Doors and Francoeur would mimic Jim Morrison, grab a lamp by its stand and croon at the lightbulb like a microphone."

Around this time Mario began to write, but showed nothing of his writings. He painfully finished high school in the year of revolt 1968, left home at 17 and rented a lousy room. He survived by begging, selling plastic flowers he made, and also occasionally by selling drugs. He then left for Greenwich Village in New York, where he discovered the Beat Generation, hung out at the Peace Eye Bookstore, and saw The Velvet Underground. He then left for Vancouver, became a junkie, and wound up at the Woodstock festival.

Mario took the slogan *Free Love* quite literally. He smoked hash and participated in orgies where he freely licked, sucked, groped and penetrated whatever was at hand. Then during the androgynous Glam Rock days a few years later he used to dance at the Golden Café and went to Peter's dressed as a cheap slut: leather miniskirt, high heels, fishnet stockings, lipstick. He squirmed on a bar stool striking sexy poses and caressed his thighs, exciting the businessmen nursing their paunches. Mario lived Glitter to the max.

---

2. See "textes choisis" (chosen texts) at my Mario Campo memorial website: https://mario-campo-poete.com

〜 As a teenager Mario's idol was Brian Jones. And he boasted that his first girlfriend looked like "Brian Jones with big tits." With the decadent blond Stones as his ideal of male anatomy, this explains the undertow of self-hatred that coursed throughout his life, which maybe fueled his quest for the transcendence of reality through poetry.

Campo loathed himself. He was never comfortable in his own skin. Which was brown, thanks to his Sicilian grandfather Giuseppe. He looked like an ancient Egyptian scribe, but he wanted to look like his heroes Sid Vicious, Johnny Thunders or Keith Richards. Just like Keef, Mario squinted from the smoke of his cigarette dangling at the corner of his mouth, and his movements were jerky and uncoordinated. But *this* Drunken Stone was penniless.

When I met him, Mario looked like a skinny brown Jiminy Cricket with punk shades and close-cropped Brillo Pad hair. By the end of the decade, after he'd progressively inherited his father's bald pate, he looked more like a *surprised* Jiminy Cricket, with Three Stooges Larry's frizzy hair sticking out sideways. He now had good reason to despise himself: here was a bug-eyed incarnation of Kafka's *Metamorphosis*. But this self-loathing is the trigger that pushes some to become poets.

〜 In the late Seventies—before I met him—Mario traveled a lot with his girlfriend Danielle. They visited Mexico, including the Mayan sites, and also Italy. They visited the Greek Islands, and ended up in Egypt after a stopover in Cyprus. At the time they were decadent epicureans— he weighed 200 pounds, while she weighed well over 250.

When they landed in a small town in Cyprus, nympho Danielle took off and got busy getting shtupped by the whole village. Meanwhile, our hero lost weight, and became a skinny sexy punk dandy walking around in tight black jeans, pointy boots, red scarf, cut-sleeve T-shirt, black mascara and lipstick. He soon wound up being chased through the streets of a seaside town in the night by a carload of randy Turks trying to catch this choice piece of ass. Looking the way he did, he could only be "another fag tourist cruising for a rough gangbang."

Our erstwhile gay lothario made it to a restaurant and frantically knocked at the door, until he woke up the patron and the guy let him in. The car with the Turks was parked on the other side of the street.

They were waiting for him. They stayed there till dawn, and didn't leave until the patrol car started its rounds again.

⊅ Mario and Danielle met up in Cairo. The Arabs were so in love with the voluptuous Danielle that during the mandatory tour of The Great Pyramid of Giza in a camel, an Arab businessman offered Mario on the spot four camels for his wife. Back at the hotel in Cairo, Mario told the story to the manager shaking his head, laughing at the crazy proposition he'd just been made.

"*FOUR* camels! And you refused?" asked the incredulous manager, "Normally, a woman is not worth more than a *single* camel!"

Mario and Danielle visited the Valley of the Kings, then went their separate ways. One last bus ride together. With his dark skin, the old ladies mistook him for a local and chatted him up in Arabic. He nodded back smiling.

Mario returned to Cairo and smoked hash all the time. He swears the policemen's eyes were red from also smoking hash. He dressed in a djellaba with a turban and answered the Muezzin's call, entering a mosque at prayer time. He fit right in, and our decadent Infidel of Infidels joined the masses kneeling down to bow in prayer.

His day started in Cairo, and ended in a bar in East Berlin.

⊅ Mario got to visit East Berlin when it was still an open-air communist museum. As with any Western tourist, he was required to first buy a stack of worthless *Ostmarks*—the East German DDR currency. Except in East Berlin, there was nothing to buy. Unless you wanted *The Complete Works of Erich Honecker,* or else cross back to the West at Check Point Charlie with a trail of sausage links dangling out your back pocket.

Mario wanted to meet and talk with the locals, so naturally he made a beeline to the nearest bar. It was also a chance to finally get rid of those damn Ostmarks. He wanted to buy a round of drinks for everyone present, but problem was, he was such a welcome curiosity that everyone started buying *him* drinks. He finally solved his Ostmark dilemma by hiring a taxi, telling the cabbie to drive around the city aimlessly. It was a drab, shabby place of endless drab, shabby block towers, festooned with slogans egging on the hapless *Ossies*[3] towards a bright Socialist future.

Mario then took the subway and experienced time travel: the subway car slowed down as it entered a station, but didn't stop. Before the train sped off again, he got a good look at a station left intact since 1945.

Years later in his astounding novella *Le Délire*[4], Mario talks about an 18-year-old prostitute called Ulla who fell in love with him and wanted him to stay with her in West Berlin:

"Ulla told me maybe we could live together, she'd practice her craft while I'd write; she could even find me an occasional gig writing porn for the yellow press. Ulla had a present for me. I opened the package. It was a studded belt. 'For a rebel writer,' she said. We ordered drinks. Ulla was in a happy mood. She was radiant. As for me, I felt rather sinister. She noticed. 'What's wrong?' She asked. I froze, unable to answer her. After a few drinks, I finally unveiled my story: 'I'm leaving for Paris in two days, that's it.' She didn't want to believe it. 'Why, *why* my love?' 'Because that's how it is,' I said, 'because you gotta move, change places.' Her face said it all. She was completely demolished."

ℤ Emulating his archetype—the *other* booze-loving writer Malcolm Lowry—Mario headed next for Mexico, where he soon found trouble in Villahermosa. Not under a volcano, but under his bed.

In Spanish, Villahermosa means "beautiful villa", but in reality it's an industrial town, the hub of the Mexican oil industry. What the *chingada* was Campo doing there, pray tell?

One evening he decided to have a beer in a rough cantina full of tough oil workers and pistoleros. It took no time for the swarthy patrons to start giving the little gringo punk the evil eye. One of the *bad hombres* got up and started toward him. Mario quickly downed his *Dos Equis* and bolted back to his dirty hotel room, where the cockroaches were as big as Snickers bars. He barricaded himself by standing up his

---

3. Transl: East Germans
4. Transl: *Delirium*; See Appendix A—Selected Texts for a translated excerpt; the entire novella in French can be downloaded at https://mario-campo-poete.com/mariocampo-recueils.html

rusty iron bed against the door, piling up against it dresser, table and chairs.

But Mario didn't have to travel that far to find trouble. Usually he found it in the biker dives of Montreal or at Peter's, where he liked to go get beaten up. Or else in a drunken fit at home, smashing his toilet door, throwing beer bottles at the wall or down the corridor of his apartment building, bringing the cops at three in the morning.

From the time I met him onwards, Mario settled into a simple life of shabby nicotine-stained, one or two bedroom apartments, with the same round orange plastic patio chair, and a forest of empty cider bottles under the sink, with a few still rolling around on the cruddy carpet festooned with cigarette burns. Wherever he chose to live always looked the same, always smelled of stale beer, smelled of poverty. On the wall there was always a scotch-taped picture of Rimbaud, or Mario's all-time literary hero Baudelaire.

He was poor, he was on welfare, but he lived exactly the way he wanted. No one was up his ass in some crappy corporate cubicle. In the morning he took long baths reading Baudelaire, with Bach or Chet Baker playing on the stereo. Jeff Bezos could never permit himself such luxury, that only poverty can bring. Mario lived his poverty very well. And I *never* heard him complain.

I loved my fucking brother so much I could cry.

Nearly two decades after his death, I'm still trying hard to grasp why Mario meant so much to those who knew him and why, after his death his work still strikes such a deep resonating chord in all of us. Was it because he threw himself head first into life, diving in to the point of no return? Mario was one of those few select individuals who must fall and crash to reveal to us life's essence. Maybe such deep knowledge can only be transmitted through the flames of the poet being consumed by his own burning life.

Francoeur summed him up best in his epitaph: *"Mario ... this dear, sensitive and so fragile being ... he alone could testify to the loneliness of the poets that was his, and to the lifelong malaise that inhabited him and inhabits me and sequesters me in my incurable melancholy ..."*

It takes a poet to know one.

8

A BRIEF RETURN TO REASON

fter a couple years of my precarious, chaotic lifestyle earning peanuts on the music scene, it was a novelty and a relief to have a steady paycheque. For the first time in my life I had a *real* income and could afford things. Like furniture. More importantly, I savoured the quiet, drama-free sanity of working in a no-nonsense engineering firm.

Hard to believe, but throughout my whacked-out life in the music/art underground, I managed to have a sporadic life as a civil-structural engineer. The couple of recessions we had—in 1982, and later in 1994 —also contributed substantially to the holes in my career cheese.

When hired by TGL[1] in the fall of 1980, I still didn't have my diploma and was officially considered a technician. I started out manning the pen plotters that drew the stress lines of costly Stardyne structural analyses of the Olympic Stadium's tower, but they soon gave me engineering design tasks beyond my pay grade, thus getting a bigger bang for their bucks. Some of the work consisted in back-calculating the prestress losses in the Olympic Tower spine's post-tension cables. During the construction for the 1976 Olympics they'd run out of time, and the tower was left at half-mast for a decade. There were other problems, but this isn't *Builders Bloopers*. In any case, I was relieved to finally be over the starving music bum thing, and enjoyed the sanity of going to work every day.

One morning though, as I entered the subway station and stepped onto the escalator, there was an ominous feeling in the air. The Beatles'

---

1. Trudeau, Gascon Lalancette—now Tecsult

song *In My Life* was playing—which was highly suspect. And it felt sadder than usual. As I got to the bottom of the escalator, I passed by the subway dépanneur and glanced at the stack of newspapers sitting in the rack. The big black headlines screamed *John Lennon Shot Dead*.

According to Gagnon, Lennon's death was the tipping point after which things started being fundamentally wrong with the world. He had a point. After that came AIDS, Reagan, Wall Street wolfs and the tyranny of personal computers for starters ... then, every decade since has been worse than the previous one: 9/11, Bush and Cheney, Trump, Putin, COVID, runaway climate change and social media cretinisation ... while billionaires play with rockets and Orwellian nightmare fascist China installs *its* Greater East-Asia Co-Prosperity Sphere around the world.

ζ I was also happy to be working because the music scene had become boring once again. The incredible creative explosion from 1977 to 1980 had petered out, and now began the reign of serious young men taking themselves seriously, frowning under severe haircuts behind expensive synths. There were all shapes of *New Romantics* with outlandish poodle quiffs and silly pretentious band names. How now, *Bau Hau Haus*?

So yeah, music had become Poodles, Synths n' Snobs—a sudden 180-degree whiplash against yobby Punk—just like the stylish revolt of the *Premier Empire*, once the *sans-culotte* riff-raff of the French Revolution had met the last heavy metal blade drops of the guillotine.

The shameless turning back of the clock smelled to me like Neo-Prog, but now drenched in pricy perfume to hide the stench. I wanted no part of it, and was happy to toil seriously at *my* machines: the number-crunching mainframe computers and whizzing pen plot printers of my trade.

ζ One evening in March Joss and I invited David Sapin to dinner at our place. Joss was at the stove stirring a big pot of spaghetti sauce. The phone rang and she answered, cradling the phone on her shoulder while stirring the bubbling sauce with a long wooden spoon.

Suddenly she shrieked and threw her arms in the air, splattering the kitchen walls and ceiling with tomato sauce. David and I looked at each other. What the hell happened? Did she get a shock from the stove's faulty wiring?

She ran off to the bedroom and collapsed on the bed, sobbing uncontrollably. Her brother Richard had just died. He'd been hit by a drunk driver swerving into him from the opposite lane, just as he was getting into his car. It was a Sunday afternoon—on the first warm, sunny day of spring—perfect for an outing with his girlfriend. She was there and saw the whole thing.

Ronald Reagan was shot on March 30th. I remember this distinctly, because at the time I was shopping for a suit to wear at the funeral, and the breaking news came flashing on the haberdashery's TV.

The poor girl never recovered from the devastating shock of losing her brother. It was hard to keep her busy with distractions. There was a Van Gogh exhibit coming up in Toronto, and I suggested we fly over to catch it.

The exhibit at the Art Gallery Of Ontario was *Vincent Van Gogh And The Birth Of Cloisonism*. The term referred to Van Gogh's style of separating painted areas by borderlines, or *cloisons*. After that we did dumb tourist shit like play a giant pinball machine and feel stupid at the top of the CN Tower.

David in the meantime had moved to Toronto, to make it big as a graphic artist. "I'll have my Mercedes by the time I'm 30," he declared. We met up and he took us sightseeing on Queen Street, then we slid into a booth at The Bloor Street Diner, one of the new snazzy spots that were starting to gentrify Hogtown. There's a picture of him in bow tie and tuxedo, perusing the foot-high menu under the lazy cool warbling of Billie Holiday.

~ For our work on the Olympic Tower they moved us into the basement of the stadium, where I got to rub shoulders with a skewer of no fewer than six PhD's. Among those heavy hitters were my old Prestressed Concrete McGill professor Denis Mitchell, and the father of Toronto's CN tower—the eccentric, pipe-smoking Swiss Franz Knoll—who wore thick tan corduroy pants, along with wool socks and sandals. In winter.

ℤ That summer my father was one year short of retirement age and was suspended from his job. The cops caught him driving his cab past a yellow school bus with the red flashing lights and STOP sign out. They took away his driver's licence for several months, and he was fairly despondent. Being a solvent adult now as well as a dutiful son, I decided to pay him a trip to Spain, and took out a loan for $3000[2].

In a further attempt to get Joss' mind off her brother's death, I decided we should join up with my dad, and took her on a vacation in Spain that August. Fueled by the pain of Joss' loss, we spent most of our three weeks and 4000 kilometers[3] in Spain drinking. A hell of a lot. We mostly sat at terraces in Madrid and Barcelona, and ordered serial gin tonics. Of course in Spain, as in the rest of Europe, there was no shortage of churches and cathedrals. All along the trip, Joss just wanted to go into a chapel, light a candle and kneel in prayer. Then we'd drink some more.

I brought her to the Prado museum in Madrid, Gaudi's architectural marvels in Barcelona, and dragged her along on *my* pilgrimage of Dali's landmark Cadaqués, the fantastic *Teatre-Museu Dali* in his home town of Figueres, and lastly his house in Port Lligat.

ℤ That fall I went back to McGill to complete my last semester and get my engineering diploma already. Yet in the sacrosanct bowels of academia I was educating myself again more in the things that mattered to me than my boring engineering studies. I roamed around the wrong library stacks, and wound up reading books on Picasso, Duchamp, Rauschenberg, and dusty late 19th century French newspapers for word of Rimbaud. One of the publications I stumbled upon that intrigued me the most were the Semiotext(e) journals *Schizo-Culture, Autonomia, Polysexuality*, and *The German Issue*—with a nurse attending a Cold War console in front of a hospital patient. This one was about the Baader Meinhof Gang, the artist Beuys, and East German playwright Heiner Müller. I devoured those tomes, happily neglecting my "real" studies. A professor at Columbia University called Sylvère Lotringer

---

2. $9000 today
3. 2500 miles

was the culprit disseminating this exciting subversive stuff. I can say in all honesty that *he* was the one who ripped my mind open to crucial new ways of thinking and seeing things. And I can only thank him eternally for that.

⇆ Out of boredom I also picked up *Jack's Book* from my shelf and started reading it simultaneously with *On The Road*, switching from one book to the other, fact and fiction, each step of the way. Sure, it was *Jack's* book, but for me, the two people who clearly stood out above the crowd were Huncke and Burroughs—men of heart and mind, respectively.

In early November I caught Burroughs live on SNL, doing his *Dr Benway* routine[4]. For me it was one of those life-changing moments again, like when you saw the Beatles on TV for the first time. Or The Stones. Except *this* satanic majesty was something else entirely. I ran out and bought his new novel *Cities of The Red Night*, and was blown away.

After the SNL bit I became a rabid superfan, and never stopped reading and collecting every bit of Burroughsiana I could lay my hands on—both in English and French. Because the French have always been serious students of all things Burroughs.

Apart from the books, I remember being especially affected by listening to his *Last Words of Hassan Sabbah*[5] on the album *Nothing Here Now But The Recordings*. It was a treasure trove of Burroughs' sonic experiments put out by Genesis P. Orridge of Throbbing Gristle. This signal piece expressed all the rage I felt, but at the time could not yet articulate.

To my great surprise, I soon vomited 35 pages of crazy prose in one sitting, something I'd never done before. It was bad, but all first efforts are.

⇆ As if discovering Burroughs wasn't enough, one evening on the Vidéotron cable TV channel I saw a strange video of a guy strapped to a wall doing a series of bizarre rituals. He drew a semi-circle over his head on the wall with a liquid and set fire to it. Then under the arc of dancing

---

4. See it at: https://www.youtube.com/watch?v=aTl6xVMbJ6Y
5. Hear it at: https://www.youtube.com/watch?v=gvbz_kKJcqU&t=32s

flames he began singing the song *Enter Into Eternity*, increasingly hysterical, accompanied by someone playing a cheesy Casio in the background.

It was a guy named Monty Cantsin:

> *Enter into Eternity*
> *Cosmic Urban Eternity*
> *Enter into Eternity*
> *Eternal Immortality*
>
> *Total Freedom of human Life*
> *Total Freedom of human Brain*
> *Total Freedom of human Will*
> *Total freedom of human Love*
> *Total Freedom, Total Freedom*

Total Freedom? I'll have some of that!

Instead, I got a different kind of freedom: in November I was laid off, starting a lifelong trend that would regularly see me shorn of a paycheque right before Christmas. My engineering "career" had so many holes in it, it's a good thing I never built any dams. Nevertheless, after all these years of academic struggle and self-inflicted setbacks, I finally got my McGill University Bachelor of Engineering degree.

I graduated smack into The Great Recession of 1982, with diploma in hand.

9

RENAISSANCE PUNK

nemployment oblige, 1982 was a crucial transition year for me—the year I timidly started writing, the year the art bum in me took flight, the year I became a Renaissance Punk. It was a pivotal year when I explored brand new domains of artistic expression, and left pop/rock music behind.

Bored with music, I started making collages I called *Zerographs*: hijacked ads from magazines, to which I added cheeky titles. I also started fooling around with language: writing experimental concrete poetry, manipulating text using matrix methods from mathematics, and working out a new Pop Art Poetry style. I also plunged into the world of Kerouac, reading most of his work. Here was a writer who was perfect for a lost 27-year-old male, whose bottom had also dropped out of his life, and who was seeking a way out toward his inner core.

After digesting Kerouac, I spent the rest of the year devouring Burroughs' books, and spent quite a few hours in McGill's MacLellan Library researching and photocopying various rare works of his, including magazine articles and interviews, which I collected in a thick binder. Yes, I had become quite the serious Burroughsian. Yet in the course of kicking around texts of my own, I became more interested in the experimental aspect of his writing, as demonstrated in *The Third Mind* and *Electronic Revolution*. When I got a pocket computer I started writing computer programs to cut up texts, and experimented with word permutations.

⚡ Joss and I lived up north in the St Michel area but we were always downtown, and getting sick of the long bus and subway ride. I wanted to be closer to all the artistic activity, so we decided to move into a bigger two-bedroom apartment on Champlain street just below Sherbrooke.

A scrap of paper I recently found says: "We have lived here six long years. We hate this place. But in that space of time a miraculous transformation occurred. I came in here having nothing, being nothing, and now depart having become an engineer, musician, artist, and poet. I firmly resolve never to slip back into the darkness from which I finally emerged."

Our new place was right across from the gray steel rollup door of Notre-Dame Hospital's loading dock, where hearses went in to pick up the corpses.

That spring Francoeur decided to put out a 45 rpm single. I wrote the music for both songs, played the guitar and synths, and again directed the studio recordings. The single wasn't too convincing, played a few times on the radio and then promptly disappeared. But not before getting slapped with a court injunction—we'd lifted a popular AM radio station's traffic report without permission and used it to intro the song on Side A.

As summer came around I tried putting a band together for Francoeur all over again. I auditioned future *French Bastards* keyboardist Jean-Robert Bisaillon in a studio rented on Plessis street. After a while I told him: "Listen, forget it, let's call it a day."

My heart wasn't in it anymore. I was done with Johnny Shivers. I felt empty, I was sick of being his sidekick, and wanted to go back to being my own man. I wanted to put out my *own* stuff—like Ivan.

After that, apart from a couple of random encounters, Lucien and I pretty much lost sight of each other for decades. However, we rediscovered each other in 2010, and became close friends again. He even acted as a real godfather to my teenage son, and I helped his accomplished daughter with English translations of her academic papers. The yin and yang of karma sometimes works in wonderful and unexpected ways.

◄ I wrote a song for a solo project and asked David Sapin to do a mock-up sketch for a maxi 12" sleeve. It was called *Too Much Money*. It went nowhere because I *had* no money. After that I was determined to be more radical than commercial. I rented and fooled around with a Korg synthesizer, and when I picked up my guitar again, I adopted a more experimental *Noise Guitar* technique, using phase delay, flanging, and a shiv to scrape the strings.

Mario told me he was putting on a theatre-installation at this cutting-edge gallery called Véhicule Art, and he wanted to film me playing guitar. The video would be projected during the show. I said "sure".

At the time, Véhicule Art was run by a triumvirate of notorious performance artists: Bernar Hébert[1], Michel Ouellette, and Monty Cantsin—the guy I saw strapped to the wall on cable TV. With a shock of thick black hair standing straight up like Eraserhead's Henry atop close-cropped sides, a shaved patch in the shape of an "X" on one side of his head, plus his thick caterpillar eyebrows, Monty looked like a punk Rudolf Hess. His thing was a Fluxus-like anti-art movement he called "Neoism".

As I came in lugging my amp and guitar into the gallery to tape the guitar performance, Mario was rushing around installing the theatre sets nervously. He kept worrying about this Neoist *Kiki Bonbon*[2] character who could suddenly show up any minute and destroy his installation.

Our mysterious Kiki Bonbon indeed enjoyed a notoriety that was well-founded. He'd walked into a Véhicule gallery show of typically complacent mediocre art—a Quebec specialty—and promptly tore it off the walls, stomping on it in a rage. *"Hey, my kinda guy!"* thought I. Monty kept reassuring Mario that he had nothing to fear from the abominable Kiki.

⇁ For my Noise Guitar performance I started out with an Andalusian-sounding motif, then proceeded to do a howling feedback solo. All the while I manipulated the delay settings, thus obtaining different effects to which I improvised. I then took out a 10-inch switchblade and started scraping the strings, making eerie sounds which would have made a

---

1. Pronounced "Bear-narr Eh-bear"
2. Pronounced "Kee-kee Boh-boh"; *Kiki* came from Kiki de Montparnasse, and *Bonbon* = French for candy

great horror movie track. I started banging and hacking at the guitar, and it wound up flat on the floor. To my horror I saw blood spattering the guitar, and realized I'd cut myself inadvertently. So I worked that into my performance, bleeding over my Les Paul and wiping the blood around the white pick guard. I ended the performance by completely sawing through all the strings, threw away the shiv and walked off[3].

≷ Inspired by his visit to Berlin, Mario called his production *Berlin Blocus Haemoglobin*, and put up a wall that split the gallery space into "East" and "West". As you entered the show you were given a "passport" and entered "West" Berlin, which was set up like a typical Berlin discothèque playing the post punk music of the time. My guitar performance was shown on a video screen, and Mario spliced in scenes of himself shooting up with a syringe. Spectators then stepped through a door in the "Wall", where dour officers in grey uniforms grilled them and stamped their passport, after which they found themselves in "East" Berlin.

The première was a success, and several of us went to an after-party at Bernard Gagnon's place to celebrate. Gagnon says "We smoked hash and I played tapes of my new band Cham Pang. Suddenly, we realized Mario was gone. I went outside and found him in the backyard. He wanted to kill himself, and that created quite a stir."

It wouldn't be his last attempt.

≷ Hanging around Véhicule Art I started talking with Monty Cantsin, and told him I'd been impressed by his performance on cable TV. The next event he was curating at Véhicule was *Art Par Ordinateur*[4], and I asked him if I could take part in it. He agreed immediately.

So for ten consecutive days in November, I output texts and graphics using a Sharp PC-1500 Pocket Computer, which had a tiny four-colour pen plotter that printed on a paper scroll, like that of a cash register. I made the tape crawl along the gallery wall, and the goal was to have the scroll join back on itself to complete a continuous loop on the last day of the exhibition. I advanced the tape by hand and held it by little magnets

---

3. See the clip at: https://www.youtube.com/watch?v=hOr-hJHaUpk
4. Transl: *Art By Computer*

arranged along the wall. On the day of the "vernissage", everyone gathered around to watch me press "Return" on my little machine.

Among the text and graphics spit out were poems by Mario Campo that I illustrated[5], texts by Rimbaud and Burroughs cut-up together live—called *Rimburroughs*, live random phrase permutations, mini one-inch square digital Jackson Pollocks I called *Random Tableaux*, and a tiny reproduction of Jasper John's *Flags*. I also compressed Rimbaud's *Season In Hell* into a *Week In Hell*, then a Day, a Minute, and on down to a *Millisecond in Hell*.

The tape inched its way along all day, and day after day. I used all the tricks and tips I'd learned from the Burroughs and Gysin book *The Third Mind*, and invented some of my own. The most elaborate was *Sozialtriptych*: a Corporate Fascism Simulator, which randomly picked words from 3 sets of 33 manipulative verbs, social institutions and corporate buzzwords each, combining them randomly to generate endless permutations of three-word social indoctrination slogans, such as:

Create Future Competition   Develop Elite Care
Choose Parent Skills   Use Career Benefits
Decide Manager Goals   Choose Home Ideas
Win Food Rewards   Orient Election Goals
Create Manager Values

Gee, it sounds like great slogans readymade for the Chinese Communist Party now—stack up your Social Credit scores, folks!

The software code I used was BASIC—a brilliantly simple programming language invented by Bill Gates, which took you no time to master. I wrote the programs continuously during the exhibit, then at home at night, in order to have programs ready to advance the paper scroll the following day.

On the last day the 300-foot-long paper scroll looped back on itself, and I glued the ends together. I stood back to marvel at my postmodern Bayeux tapestry, and what I'd achieved. To me, this exhibit was the

---

5. See middle bottom download link, at https://mario-campo-poete.com/mariocampo-recueils.html

summit of my lifetime expression as an artist. For the first time I felt completely centered as a creative human being, finally doing something only I could do. It was totally unmarketable, and *that* was my idea of Art. There is never any money in what really counts. *Art par Ordinateur* was my highest high ever, accomplished on coffee and cigarettes.

⤢ The other "computer" art on display in the gallery was crap—butterflies and owls, now drawn by a computer-controlled Spirograph instead of macramé. Another thing on exhibit was just the AT&T logo being generated by computer—a portent of the sinister corporate co-opting of the personal computer to come.

The last day of the exhibition ended with an evening dedicated to music made using computers, and chairs were laid out in the gallery for the audience. At my suggestion, Gagnon agreed to take part in the event. Like me, he'd gone back to McGill the previous year, but to record his electronic compositions. One of these—called *Gwendoline Descendue!*[6]—which employed a complex self-regulating system—won a Radio Canada prize and played in Germany. Gagnon has since become the Marcel Duchamp of Montreal's contemporary music scene, and developed the same ambivalent attitude toward his precious art, even.

For his part, a dapper fella called Tristan Stéphane Renaud—in white shirt and black tie tucked into his shirt—played *Neural Nets* off his Apple II computer. He had the severe Filipina beauty Carolyn Fe Trinidad dancing to his music in a long black slit dress and black opera gloves, using violent karate-chop motions with her hands.

It was a very inspiring evening, and to top it off, Jean-Luc Bonspiel —the so-dreaded Kiki Bonbon—joined Tristan and sang his sublime *Mondmächen*[7], which Tristan had programmed on the Apple II.

⤢ The day came to take down my exhibit at Véhicule. This Funny Guy Frenchman was in the gallery talking loudly to Monty and gesticulating animatedly. When he was through, I went up and introduced myself, and for some reason I launched into a routine, speaking in the

---

6. Hear it at: https://www.youtube.com/watch?v=nwQ0I70_aFY
7. Hear it at: https://www.youtube.com/watch?v=lB299JlQV5Q

exaggerated syllable-stretching style of Salvador Dali. He answered me perfectly in the same manner without skipping a beat, rolling his eyes like Dali—I had finally found a kindred spirit! His name was Pierre Zovilé, but called himself Boris Wanowitch[8]. He was one of Monty's Neoist compères.

I started carefully rolling up my scroll of paper off the walls. It was a long process, and this other artist was getting impatient. She wanted to take pictures of her stupid computer butterflies n' owls on the walls, and my scroll was ruining her so important shot.

At a certain point I got fed up and started running around the gallery ripping my paper scroll off the wall in a frenzy, yelling and swearing in frustration. I bunched up the ticker tape and punched it into a big ball with my fists, then crammed it into a garbage can, wiping my hands in triumph.

Monty's pals Tristan, Boris and others were there and cheered me on, clapping and yelling "bravo!"—my totally spontaneous performance had greatly impressed them. And that's when the bond was formed among us.

I invited my brand new Neoist friends to an after-party at my place. I was high on the significance of the moment and mimed skits and outlandish accents that didn't fail to dazzle. Tristan declared me *The Greatest Neoist of them all*. I gathered I'd been wholeheartedly accepted within their clan. Boris sealed my deal by lobbying Monty, saying "Lord's an *engineer*—he's disciplined, he gets up and goes to work in the morning ... *he gets things done!*"

⇒ Meeting Monty Cantsin was a pivotal event in my life. Montreal's avant-garde multimedia art center of the moment—Véhicule Art Gallery —attracted me more than the Club Soda. I wanted to hang around more around art spaces than goddamn clubs.

I was thrilled with my new friends. They were all insanely creative individuals, and I finally had equals with which to converse. There was no furniture where Boris lived—it looked like some sort of arts lab, with computers and audio and video equipment on industrial shelving.

---

8. Pronounced "Van-o-veetch"

He sat at his Apple II and dedicated his whole time to creative projects. He held an architecture degree, but didn't feel like repeating the same mind-numbing window detailing expected of him while patiently climbing up the architectural career ladder.

It turned out Boris' father was a louche art dealer in France and had to escape because he was involved in the fake Dali prints scandal and other shady art deals. But Boris had several *real* Dali prints locked away in a bank vault. We became fast friends and he treated me to a tape he had of Jean-Christophe Averty's superlative documentary on Dali called *Autoportrait mou de Salvador Dali*—or, in its Orson Welles-narrated English version—*A Soft Self-Portrait of Salvador Dali*. Boris was always a hoot. Plus, any activity with him led invariably to a pipe stuffed with hash.

As for Bonspiel and Tristan, they had a band together called *Boys du Sévère*[9]. The name was derived from the opening words of the master Surrealist writer André Breton's *L'amour fou*[10]. So you could see where *these* boys were coming from.

⇄ I soon graduated to the Commodore 64 computer. Wow. Imagine how much you could do with a whole 64KB of memory! In addition to text, I could now make art using 16 colours, plus you could make music with it.

On December 26th, *Time* magazine gave its *Man of the Year* award to the personal computer, calling it *Machine of the Year*. I bought the issue and ran to show it to Monty and Boris.

Back then, personal computers were an exciting new tool in the hands of cutting-edge artists like us. With our primitive machines we were exploring the use of advanced technologies through a futurist determination to break with the past, and saw no other possible use of personal computers other than as a tool for the arts.

But Bill Gates and co weren't listening. We never imagined the geek gods would take over and turn our lives into a living daily tech

9. Listen to their *Party Kat* at: https://www.youtube.com/watch?v=DyQ-QOmEn9s
10. Pronounced "Lamb-moor foo"; Transl : *Mad Love*

hell. Soon enough they became the stultifying instruments that have cretinized humans ever since.

1982 gave us AIDS and the personal computer. In my mind the two were somehow linked—The end of carefree human sex—and the beginning of anxious inhuman workaholism.

10
ATTACK OF THE NEOISTS

The Neoists were a loose collective of musicians, writers, artists, filmmakers, video artists, art provocateurs and innovators, a bunch of incredibly creative individuals grouped around the performance and video artist Monty Cantsin. They were consumed by a total pursuit of raw artistic expression while crusading against social norms by carrying out disruptive public "actions". They sacrificed themselves for their quixotic visions with little regard either for personal health, comfort or rewards. For them, money was a rare and bizarre resource largely unavailable at all times.

They were the contemporary reincarnation of the Dadaists and Surrealists, the difference being that there were no wealthy arts patrons to finance or promote them. Which ensured that their efforts were short-lived, threadbare, and largely dissipated—a few posters, tracts, photos, writings, and disintegrating audio and videotapes are all that remain. I was interested mainly in the Montreal branch of Neoism, which I was allowed to join by logical osmosis.

Meeting the Neoists in the fall of 1982 was a crucial moment in my life. Until then I thought I was alone in the world with my peculiar view of things. Now I could suddenly converse with a wonderful peer group of like-minded Art Fuckers. Likewise, they appreciated the new addition to their ranks.

What exactly *was* Neoism? The perfect example to illustrate what it was all about was a poezine they put out called *Salut Les Riche*[1]: The poezine cost $1, *but a two-dollar bill was glued to the inside back cover.*

---

1. Transl: *Hail The Rich*

If you don't get it, there's no chance you could ever be a Neoist. Not everyone could be a Neoist—it took a special mindset.

⤳ The apartment Monty shared with Boris on Lajoie street in Outremont was the Neoist Embassy, while my place on Champlain became the Neoist Consulate. I was a latecomer, so a lot of Neoist lore preceded me: *The Burning Barbie Q Dolls, the Flying Cats, Peking Poolroom.* But first, there was Monty Cantsin, who came up with the idea of Neoism, after a first stint as The Neon Boys with Montreal artist Zilon[2]—aka Lion Lazer—whose performances early on centered on lacerating himself with razor blades.

Monty Cantsin—whose real name was Istvan Kantor—was a Hungarian folk singer who branched out into the avant-garde in the manner of the anti-art movement Fluxus. He hated the oppressive communist party and escaped Hungary, where as a schoolkid he was forced to recite poems and sing songs praising Comrade Stalin. As a Young Pioneer he had a summer job in a chicken factory, where he furthered the Communist Ideal by killing baby chicks born with genetic errors like having two heads or four legs. Monty says "I waited for them at the end of the conveyor belt, and as they rolled down I had to pick the mutants and kill them with a little push on their tiny necks with my thumb."

He fled Hungary in a meat truck, hiding under the bloody carcasses of pigs, and breathed through a thin tube. He was wrapped in a cotton sheet soaked in pig blood and guts so no police dogs could sniff him out in case of a stop n' search.

He arrived in Montreal in September 1977. Monty says: "First I was a bit frightened by the place—it seemed to be a desolate land, but then I realized it was the perfect situation to start something new, I was finally out from the oppressive ambience of Europe, that fucking History that controlled everything. I had no idea what I was going to do, the government put me in a language school for immigrants and I took a job in a factory—I called it the Plastic Brain Factory—they made plastic toys and all kinds of cheap pressed plastic things, sort of dollar store stuff. I worked night shift, went there after school. I was a

2. Pronounced "Zee-low"

machine operator, pressing on a button, opening and closing a sliding door, plastic things would fall out into boxes, at the end of a session the machine had to be cleaned, the rest of the plastic had to be emptied on the floor, this created brain shaped forms, for me it was great art. I kept lots of them, and also took pictures of the machinery and my co-workers, mostly refugees from Chile. I was one of the workers under a total capitalist rip-off management, getting paid way under the minimum salary—we got something like $2.75 an hour, ha ha."

⇁ Like Andy Warhol, Monty was a magnet for gifted disturbed individuals, and attracted an ungodly collection of highly creative misfits and genius miscreants. "How did I meet everyone in the Montreal Neoist gang?" he asks. "By hanging out late night in new wave clubs, by meeting people at Véhicule Art, by walking in the streets. I first saw Kiki at Daniel Guimond's studio at the launching of his SCRAP 'zine. I went for a walk with Kiki afterwards, and it was either he or Zilon who introduced me to Tristan and Napoléon."

The following couple of years were amazingly rich in subversive activities for the Neoists, and one of their signal activities was holding the occasional "apartment festival"—events organized in their homes, to which the public was invited.

I felt a kinship with these weirdos. First and foremost, there was Jean-Luc Bonspiel—aka Kiki Bonbon, aka Kazimir Strassman. He was big-boned, barrel-chested and strong, as per his Mohawk and Scottish roots. He was one of the brightest, most complex people I've known in my life. He was a troubled, yet witty and charismatic character, larger than life, but erratic and undependable—couldn't hold a job longer than a couple of months. He was a charming penniless Falstaff, always a girlfriend away from being homeless—when he had one. Otherwise, without the benefit of girls he easily conquered through his wiles and smooth talk, he survived on the largesse of friends, including Monty and myself. Throughout his nomadic wanderings he nevertheless managed to compose great music, and fill ceiling-high stacks of abandoned notebooks disdainfully tossed into a corner for posterity to discard. He had a wonderful deep radio voice, and his specialty was coming up with brilliant repartees ad-libbed on the spot for any and all occasions.

He could've been a contender, a somebody, but there was always a merciless civil war going on in his head. Finally, in 2019 he had two books of poems published to instant acclaim, notably a full-page feature in *Le Devoir*[3].

⇜ Tristan Renaud—aka Zbigniew Brotgehirn—was a well-dressed, pleasant-looking, good-natured fellow, who could easily have been a Philip Glass had he cared enough. Hearing this, of course he'd let out one of his deep resounding sarcastic laughs. What I liked most about him was his admirable *désinvolture*[4]—a refreshing cavalier attitude toward *EVERYTHING*—just like Breton's much-idolized war pal Jacques Vaché[5]. He also held a job at the SAQ[6]—and I always had a higher respect for artists who pulled their own weight.

⇜ And then Alain-Napoléon Moffat was our resident Sartre. He lived for literature and philosophy—both reading and writing it—yet was loathe to get published. The few pamphlets and broadsides he managed to bother tossing about were absolutely brilliant, and always mentioned among us reverently: *l'Indice, Le nerf obscure, Progressivement*[7]. Hopefully, these will one day be rescued from oblivion.

He also made remarkable short films, notably *Framed*—a black and white film of a tape deck, its reels slowly spinning in front of a window with a view on a street, accompanied by a voiceover of Napoléon's gripping poetic reflections. Tragically, as with Campo, alcohol was Napoléon's best friend, and many an embarrassing incident was witnessed. Details will be spared.

⇜ Other Montreal Neoists worthy of note included Eric Filion aka TTP[8], the excellent artist François Mignault[9] aka Moondog (we called

---

3. See Appendix A-Selected Texts for a few samples of his poetry
4. Pronounced "Dih-zeh-volt-tour"; Transl: Casual irreverence
5. Pronounced "Vah-shay"
6. Quebec's liquor board
7. Transl: *The Index, The Dark Nerve, Ongoingly*
8. An inversion of PTT—the French Telephone and Telegraph company
9. Pronounced "Frah-swah Mee-n'yoh"

him Fred), as well as his younger brother Jean-Martin, whom we called JM. He became quite adept as a digital percussionist, and was in demand in all our bands. Just like Zilon, the Mignault brothers hailed from Pont-Viau—a neighbourhood in the brain-dead northern suburb of Laval. Their understandable thirst for stimulation—artistic, or of any kind—led them to gravitate to downtown's bohemian hangouts.

Asked about how the Mignault brothers came into the picture, Bonspiel recalls: "We met the Mignaults at Véhicule Art after a performance of Boys du Sévère / Zilon. It was a memorable evening for many reasons. My first performance was stamping the word D-E-A-T-H on a canvas. I had prepared two other canvases with the words "Stay Comatose" and "Have a Relapse". I had a big school classroom type clock strapped around my hips, facing forward. At the end I removed the clock, screamed "Time OUT!" and threw it out the window. At the very end, the Mignaults mysteriously came up to us, groupie style, and gave Zilon gifts. I guess they had been following him since they were all from Pont-Viau. I remember a green latex glove stuffed in an empty ink bottle particularly clearly. After the end, we were wrapping up and wondering how to deal with a sheep's brain we had displayed under a glass dome. My eye was drawn to a drunk man in a really bad polyester suit on Ste. Catherine street below. He was swaying and trying to hail a cab. Grasped by the demon of perversity, I snatched the sheep brain and threw it out the window. It hit the drunk guy square on the lapel, smashing to smithereens. I will never forget his look of ultimate dejection as he looked down at his jacket, looked up, and got into a cab."

⇘ Bonspiel, Tristan and Napoléon were Neoists *avant la lettre*—that is, they popped up organically, before there existed a term to describe their common natural penchant for brainy troublemaking. Among this trio reigned a bitter will to break violently with the past and embrace a technology-led rush to possibilities beyond *The Now*, much like the Futurists. To them, punk new/wave was already an embarrassing anachronism. Their hair was close-cropped, and despite their dire poverty were neat in appearance, wearing jackets, crisp white shirts and ties—or in the case of Napoléon—a pleasant little bow tie. All picked up at the Salvation Army, of course. Theirs was mainly a diet of André Breton and the Surrealist writers congregated around him, plus precursors Jacques Vaché and Arthur Cravan. Lastly, Samuel Beckett was their common god.

Then add to this very original unholy trinity of the Mignault brothers and Zilon. Together they wound up making music, holding performances, defacing sleepy Laval with graffiti, and causing mayhem in various permutations and under the briefest of names, such as *Neonzz* and *Urbanzz*. This all happened before they even met Monty.

JM recalls: "Napoléon's parents were away on a trip once, so he held a party at their place. Tristan had bought goldfish, put them in a bowl at the entrance, and to get in you had to drink a glass of water with the goldfish in it. Then you'd feel it in your tummy. That was the concept of the party. The bathtub had also been filled with Sangria. I pretended to swallow the goldfish, but most of the guests gulped it right down. Bonspiel lived with me for years and I guess I supported him, but I didn't mind, because I knew nothing and he knew everything, so I learned a lot from him. I've always had a tremendous amount of respect for him."

Soon the locus of gratuitous havoc shifted to Bonspiel and Tristan's notorious lair *The Peking Poolroom*[10]. At the time it was a filthy rundown hovel, and the squalid living conditions allowed for the cheapest rent in town. Bonspiel recalls: "There was very little money at that time, and basically what we had to do is steal food in order to eat. We would put on heavy winter coats. We looked like street bums, except that we ironed our clothing, which all came from the Salvation Army. We would go to grocery stores and buy a loaf of bread and hide various flat cans of food in our pockets. Or we would boil huge amounts of rice and chicken liver."

The Flaming Iron was invented by Tristan, and in a grainy black and white video filmed at Peking Poolroom he can be seen setting fire to an iron and start waving it around, yelling "Austérité! Sévérité!"—which was the brutal cry of an impoverished young man, a shriek calculated to provoke people and rouse them out of their sleepwalking mediocre petty artless existences. Evidently, given their dire subsistence conditions, the boys were not in the mood to brook any manner of self-indulgent

---

10. Today the Burgundy Lion pub on Notre-Dame West's now gentrified strip

evanescent artistic musings. They demanded more intellectual rigor-ousness.[11]

Peking Poolroom went up in flames. Or nearly so. JM remembers: "On the evening of the fire, there was Adrénaline who was there—who was like, Bonspiel's girlfriend, but unrequited if you will. She was in love with Bonspiel, he respected her a lot, and she was never far from us —a very beautiful woman. So there were Bonspiel, Adrénaline, my broth-er Fred and me. We went to bed around midnight or one in the mor-ning, everyone on the floor in the living room. Then Bonspiel decided to go make himself some fries during the night. He put on the oil to heat it up, then went back to bed and fell asleep. He was the one who woke up, but he was on the top floor—the Peking Poolroom was a two-story building. So he started yelling "Fire! Fire! Fire!"—the kitchen was pretty much all on fire by then—the kitchen cabinets, the ceiling. Bonspiel and Fred managed to put it out. I went outside because every breath of air we took felt like a dagger in your lungs. The next day we surveyed the extent of the damage. Peking Poolroom was a business that didn't pay the rent, or the bills either. At that time all the businesses were boarded up—everything in St. Henri was dead, it was a blighted area. So our "landlord" wasn't too difficult—Bonspiel and Tristan lived there a long time without paying rent. Basically, it was a squat."

⚡ As for how Boris Wanowitch came in the picture, Bonspiel says: "I remember seeing Boris for the first time in the bathroom of Véhicule Art, a vernissage night Tristan and I had decided to terrorize the artist Stella Sasseville[12]. We had made copies of a manifesto and were going to do an action. Tristan and I went to the bathroom to smear our two clothes irons with rubber cement each. Once we had done this, we real-ized our hands couldn't free themselves, so we asked Boris—a stranger who was washing his hands and minding his own business—to light our irons. Plus, we needed someone to give out the manifestos, which

---

11. See Appendix A—Selected Texts—*Sample Neoist tract*
12. This is the famous destructive action that caused Kiki Bonbon such notoriety.
    Bonspiel reveals: "She made more money off the gallery's insurance than anything she managed to sell."

we enlisted him to do. We learned to only flame one iron per person from then on. Fun fact: I had novelty sparkler matches with which to light the irons, which amused Boris even more." While we're on the subject of things going up in flames, it's time now for *Boris' Burning Barbie Q Dolls*:

➤ During a conference called *ART and SOCIETY* in Quebec City, Monty was invited to talk about his *Blood Campaign* (don't ask) and the activities of the Neoist Research Center. He invited Kiki[13] and Boris, who brought in a big oil drum filled with water, and placed it in front of the people in the theatre seats. Over the drum were some Barbie Dolls hanging by wire. Boris poured oil onto the water, then using his skills as a firebreather, spit out a spray of flame at the Barbie Dolls, barbecuing them. Naturally, the dolls melted and dripped fiery globs into the drum. The fire got progressively bigger, and huge flames soon started lapping at the ceiling, creeping toward the curtains. A few feminists shrieked—since of course the flaming Barbies represented "typical male violence towards women". Luckily, the organizers who had a more pressing task on their hands managed to put out the fire.

➤ Among Monty's other memorable "Neoist conspirators" was Gabor Toth—also from Hungary. His "art" consisted of making these funny little stickers he'd slap everywhere, with anti-art slogans such as:

SORRY, NO ART TODAY
ARTISTS GO HOME!
IT IS ONLY ART
I AM NOT RESPONSIBLE FOR ART

Back home in Europe, Gabor placed the sticker **I COULD HAVE ALSO DONE THIS** on museum paintings of landscapes or quaint European towns with church spires. He stayed at Monty's Neoist Embassy a few weeks, but Monty soon tired of him, finding he was too much of a sedentary pipe-smoking rocking-chair pappy, lacking proper

---

13. Monty always called Bonspiel "Kiki"

Neoist zeal. Why hell, compared to the intense, overdriven Monty, *everyone* was.

⇁ I was thrilled beyond belief to be with these remarkable fellows, finally people who shared my indefinable disgust and disdain for conventions and conventional people. They possessed this indefinable quality which I call *surrintelligence*—a kind of higher, unquantifiable intelligence, beyond the banal IQ-Test sort, that surpasses any conventional criteria bent on quantifying it.

Surrintelligence implies being well-read and having a solid knowledge of art and history—but more importantly, the key element was to possess a wry wit, a naughty playful attitude, a readiness for spontaneity, and a withering contempt for stifling things like money, worldly ambitions and social status—but especially the unquestioning morons who gobbled it up whole, including pious, undoubting, self-satisfied "intellectuals". People sitting around discussing Kant or Derrida in all seriousness invited snickering eye-rolls from us. The unwritten gentleman's agreement was to at all times be glib, dismissive, witty, and make the other fellow laugh.

Surrintelligence also meant maintaining a simultaneous ambivalence toward the very art they practiced, and feeling utter disdain for exploiting it for the pursuit of a proper career. As Bernard Gagnon said, "It's the dullards who build themselves careers."[14] The surrintelligent person is content with what he or she has done, and moves on without leaving a trace. "The production of an era can only be a reflection of its mediocrity," said Duchamp. That's why Céline Dion is a household name, and not Alan Vega.

Rest assured though, being surrintelligent was no inoculation from doing dumb shit and getting in trouble. And unfortunately, self-sabotage and self-defeatism also formed part of the surrintelligent equation.

⇁ You had to keep an eye on Bonspiel and Tristan, especially when they were together. They were thick as thieves, they were Nitro and

---

14. In French: "C'est les niaiseux qui se font des carrières."

Glycerin. Once at my place we drank and caroused all evening, until we ran out of booze around 2 AM. I wanted our hair-raising intellectual fever party to go on forever. I went to my father's place and my dad caught me trying to sneak out a couple of jugs of his home-made wine from the basement. I got one out and returned to my place. The discussion turned to World War III and Tristan howled: "We're doomed! We might as well draw fat targets on our heads and get it over with!" He bowed his head and pointed to it, saying: "Come on, Lord, let's shave our skulls and paint a big red X on our heads—*RIGHT NOW!*" He gave a maniacal laugh but was totally serious. I almost fell for it, then realized I had to go to work in a few hours. I said: "Ok Tristan. But *you* go first."

ζ It didn't take long to convince Mario Campo to join me, and we both plunged wholeheartedly into this Neoist madness, taking part in crazy activity that mainly served to freak people out. We all met to concoct our world-changing art revolution conspiracies at a tavern on Ste. Catherine, that served the cheapest beer in town. Ideas flew faster the more we drank. The *6th Neoist Apartment Festival* was coming up at the end of February.

With electronics wiz Bill Vorn handling the music, Monty was putting out recordings of his great techno songs on YUL Records— *Blood And Gold*[15], *Mass Media, Fake Science*—and led us on propaganda campaigns gluing posters all over town while singing his Neoist songs and slogans:

> "One two zero ... modern hero!"
> "In any situation, take your complete liberty, and never respect
>   the spotlight's burning heat, heat, heat!"
> "Life is boring, let's have fun!"
> "In the blue endless sky a flaming iron flies; mommy says get
>   up daddy, your breakfast is ready ..."

---

15. Hear it at: https://www.youtube.com/watch?v=57T3vvv9cJE

This last line was taken from his song *Catastronics*[16]—from a previous club performance of the same name. The title was a conflation of his prescient prediction that "The Future" would consist of two things: catastrophes and electronics.

It was all good fun like being in the boy scouts, which I'd never been in. Even better, it was the *Dada* Scouts. It was the first time in my life I fit anywhere and liked the people I was with.

⇒ The 6th Neoist Apartment Festival was inaugurated at Phillips Square, across from The Bay department store downtown, with all of us waving flags and flaming irons at arm's length (an example of such a Neoist intervention can be seen here[17]). We handed out the festival program and yelled "Severity! Austerity!" to puzzled shoppers and harried office workers on break.

Soon a car stopped, and the legendary Neoist and American artist tENTATIVELY, a cONVENIENCE disembarked, straight from the US border. He wore a beany cap with rotating propeller, trousers made entirely of zippers sewn together side by side, and from his belt hung a cassette player that played a loop of constant applause. "Because," he explained, "it's the wish of all artists to have an approving audience clapping them, so I carry mine with me at all times."

He chose his name to point out the fact that a name was a mere convenience, tentatively. We'll call him "Tent" for short. He lived in Baltimore, and for a time called himself Tim Ore, so that the name of the city would serve as a subliminal message to the ladies: *Ball Tim Ore*.

Tent is the most radical and inventive artist I've ever known. One of his favourite hobbies in Baltimore was to be driven around the city, tied to the roof of a car like a bagged deer. It never failed to annoy the police, who couldn't figure out what ticket to give him for such an outrageous affront to normal behaviour. Tent also took Marcel Duchamp's declaration "The great artist of tomorrow will go under-

---

16. Hear it at: https://www.youtube.com/watch?v=Fd1SUu8dypM&t=54s

17. Scroll to the clip at the bottom of the page, at: https://mario-campo-poete.com/mariocampo-photos.html

ground" quite literally, and held performances in the subterranean canals of Baltimore.

On his otherwise bald head, Tent shaved out ten mustaches, because he wanted to be "ten times more normal than any upstanding cop, firefighter or security guard." His slogan was "Kill Normality Before It Kills You". Another one was "Anything Is Anything"—which remains the perfect repartee to counter and completely demolish anyone's deeply held theory or conviction.

乙 Joining us for the 6th Apt Fest was also Gordon W. Zealot from Toronto: a pleasant-looking round-faced whirlwind of a man, excellent cook of Eastern flavours, and lapsed Hindu monk who preferred alcoholic and sexual debaucheries to pious asceticism. Gordon W was a master maker of yummy *chapatis*, an unleavened flatbread originating from the Indian subcontinent. He was also never without his tabla drums, which he dragged around and played for any and all occasions, much to our delight.

Permission was obtained to build an igloo out of a big snowbank in a parking lot at the corner of Cherrier and Saint-Denis. We all built the igloo together, at the direction of architect Boris, who'd studied the method and demonstrated it to us. When the igloo was completed, we gathered for the inauguration. Boris set his homburg hat on fire—another specialty of his—then poured rubber cement over Monty's shoes and set them on fire. As the flames danced off the tips of his shoes, he regaled us with his new song *Dorogoj Dracula*.

That night we all slept in the igloo, in sleeping bags. It was very comfortable, warmed from the heat of our bodies. There was the occasional drip drip of melted snow, but nothing to worry about in the sub-zero cold.

乙 The next day I assisted Bonspiel for the action he was planning in front of the Place Ville Marie office complex entrance on Cathcart. It was called *Lousy Luggage*, and he dragged along a heavy beige cardboard suitcase which he deposited on the sidewalk. We blocked the way, and very annoyed secretaries and shoppers had to step around us.

Bonspiel suddenly jumped on the suitcase and started stomping on it angrily, until it was eventually bashed open, revealing its secret cargo: *live poultry.*

He calmly walked away in the most dignified manner, leaving our shocked fellow citizens with an entirely unexpected setback in their daily schedules. I also stood there completely stunned for a moment, then scrammed the hell out of there.

> *"The injection of irrationality and craziness and disorder*
> *into the ordered life is what regenerates life in general"*
> —David Rattray[18]

Mario gave us *Brainwashing*—a performance-theatre in his new apartment in the Castel Rosalie building. The cramped 2½-room apartment was swiftly packed. Mario played a husband coming home from work to his wife—played by his ex, Danielle—to sit in front of the TV and complete his brainwashing. The video alternated between sequences from the series *Dallas* and the mask of a human face being scrubbed by suds behind the porthole of a washing machine. At a certain point the phone rang unexpectedly. This wasn't part of the performance. Gordon W picked it up and said "telephone!"—everyone broke up laughing.

For the musical portion of the festival, TTP showcased his electro-acoustic music in his apartment, and there was a two-night gala concert of music and videos at the *Pleine Lune*[19] club on Park Avenue. Monty was on, as well as Bonspiel and Tristan's Boys du Sévère. My noise guitar video from Mario's *Berlin Blocus Haemoglobin* at Véhicule Art was also shown.

≷ More significantly, the festival had a "first": at my place we held *The 48 Hour Computer Drill*—a live demonstration of art and music using computers, that indeed lasted 48 hours. Tristan and Bill Vorn made music, while Boris worked on his computer graphics. He created funny

---

18. You'll be meeting this amazing American poet much later
19. Transl: Full Moon

outlandish fat bit pixelized computer drawings and animations on his Apple II, using klunky "paddles"—the computer mouse didn't exist yet.

Using my new Commodore 64, I generated *Machine Paintings*—kind of 16-colour digital Mondrians—made of vertical and horizontal stripes of lengths, colours and placement chosen randomly. The stripes kept adding onto and erasing each other, thus generating new "paintings" that constantly evolved.

For his performance called *Frame The Flesh Tint* at Véhicule Art, Fred Mignault had lined up grey paintings along the walls, the whole length of the gallery. He then ran from one to the other spraying a developing powder upon the prepared canvases, and thus revealed a hundred Fast Art paintings in 15 minutes.

At my place I performed *Think Tank*, with Mario assisting me. I'd adapted my Sharp pocket computer's *Sozialtriptych* program from *Art par ordinateur* for the Commodore 64. Now, the three-word corporate fascist commands generated randomly were being displayed live on a TV hooked up to the Commodore. Furthermore, at the same time an audio tape of Bonspiel reading random *Sozialtriptych* phrases previously recorded was played simultaneously.

The computer's TV was stacked atop two other TV's which ran industrial training videos. As soon as plant personnel wearing hard hats appeared on the screens, I blotted their heads out with liquid corrector fluid I applied on the screen. Gordon W, who meanwhile was preparing chapatis in the kitchen, threw me small balls of dough spontaneously, which I also used to block off the industrial heads.

By the end of the performance, the liquid corrector and dough covered most of the screen, and you could hardly see anything. I finished the performance using a demagnetizer to distort the on-screen images in waves of colours like the Northern Lights, which also destroyed the TV's electronics.

After Think Tank was over, Tent gave us a Blow Dart demonstration in my apartment. He put up life-sized human targets on the wall and started spitting darts at them, explaining the procedure in English, while Mario translated into French. The audience started getting worried when Tent suggested a volunteer try it on one of the guests.

⇌ Lastly, the festival program announced that our eminent natural born philosopher Napoléon Moffat was to deliver his lecture *Technological Monk* at the Olympic Basin on Île Sainte-Hélène[20]. It's not clear whether it happened or not. Bonspiel says: "Was I at the Olympic Basin? I very much doubt it. Many of these titles were just that, nothing actually occurred."

Yet I wouldn't at all be surprised had Napoléon indeed given a lecture all alone in the blowing arctic weather. If it happened, this marvelous quixotic gesture would yet again exemplify the unique spirit that fired up our small group. And if not, it still makes for a good Neoist joke on all, including us.

⇌ Please keep in mind that all of this wonderfully creative zaniness was accomplished with no money, no arts grants, no sponsorships. We had no rich benefactors, no *Comtesse de Noailles*, no Peggy Guggenheims, no Gertrude Steins, no nothing. Very few of us had jobs, and even these were iffy. We were artists whose palettes and brushes had become the personal computer—meaning we made nothing we could sell. Or would even want to.

> *"When you're old, make art. When you're young, make trouble"*
> —Nam June Paik

---

20. See Appendix A—Selected Texts

11

BRANCHING OUT

W hile I was fooling around ... er ... *exploring novel modes of artistic expression* ... with the Neoists, plenty other things were happening.

I continued with my Sharp PC-1500 pocket computer experiments, and started producing booklets of poems integrated with graphics. I cut the output strips into four-inch lengths, stacked them up and bound them for a booklet called *International Spleen*. It was displayed at the *Media Byte* computer art exhibit at Concordia University, and I mailed off copies to a few people, including Burroughs and Ginsberg. Tristan was also at the exhibit, playing his music. All of my *Art par ordinateur* and *International Spleen* outputs are glued in a big scrapbook I called *Early Subroutines*. One copy only, folks.

On the music side, a tape of my Noise Guitar experiments was played at the *Muzak, Noise, Sound* show at Véhicule Art.

I was also starting to get stuff published here and there: one of my Pop Art Poems in *Blow Up*, and various texts in the literary magazine *Rampike*, as well as a plethora of publications: *Ose* (Paris), *Esse, Last Issue, Xero*, and *Lèvres urbaines*[1]. I'd also started keeping a journal of my surrealistic dreams, later collected as a book called *Dreamscans*, from which a few were published in the magazine *Dreamworks*. I loved American Pop Art of the early Sixties, was inspired by Warhol's book *Popism*, and wanted to apply that aesthetic to poetry. So in April, David Sapin helped publish my tome of Pop Art Poetry called *Silver*

---

1. Pronounced "Lev ur-ben"; Transl: *Urban Lips*

Amusements, which consisted of nonsensical haikus functioning solely through the plastic beauty of pop ad lingo[2].

Dave produced the beautiful art deco silkscreened artwork that graced the book cover. He also reproduced that artwork on a series of 18" × 24" mirrors that were taped up on the wall during the book launching, which was well attended by my Neoist friends and other hipnescenti.

When Dave and I opened the boxes from the printer, the books were stuck together—when we tried prying them apart, the covers ripped off. Dave had forgotten to instruct the printer to slip in a sheet of paper between the freshly silkscreened ink of the front and back covers. So it was a very "limited edition" indeed—only a few dozen books survived intact.

Suddenly we heard a large crash and turned around. The whole wall of mirrors had come tumbling down, fracturing into a jumble of jagged splinters scattered across the floor. Good thing no one was near. I guess the doubled-up tape wasn't enough.

❧ The Neoist meetings taking place now increasingly wound up being drunken shouting matches directed against Monty. Or at one another. But Monty had a brilliantly effective way to end acrimonious fighting between two people: he asked each one in turn to say the nicest things he could think of about the other. It worked.

Monty's new brainchild was *L'Arche de Noé*[3]—a Neoist intervention in the town of Sherbrooke slated for early summer. The controversial happening consisted of being towed away in a used car—*Noah's Ark,* you see—accompanied by a procession of police patrol cars with shrieking sirens and flashing lights. We paraded through the bumpkin capital chanting slogans and singing Neoist songs.

Bonspiel, Tristan and Napoléon chose not to participate in this latest outlandish extravaganza. Campo and I were now the sole remnants of the Old Guard still waving flags and flaming irons atop the car. The "Neoists" that were left surrounding us were Monty's latest dull recruits.

---

2. See Appendix A—Selected Texts for examples
3. Transl: *Noah's Ark*

When we got to a field on the outskirts of town we got out and proceeded to smash the car with sledgehammers and crowbars, then set the sacrificial car on fire. Which contained half a dozen of Monty's little friends—red-eyed white lab rats. He later protested to shocked reporters that he'd carefully rescued all of the rats before the fire was set. The event was controversial because Monty *planned* it so. His never-ending publicity-seeking stunts had become an end in itself. And I'd had it.

⇄ So, as with all things, my adventure with the Neoists came to an end. I bailed because Monty's rote histrionic slogans started sounding stale and getting on my nerves. I was also sick of serving as an extra in his serial narcissistic wackopaloozas. As the poet Jules Laforgue said, the destiny of an artist is to be enthusiastic and then disgusted with successive ideals.

My involvement in official Neoist projects may have lasted only several months, but I continued collaborating throughout the Eighties—and beyond—with my comrades in arts Bonspiel, Zilon, JM & Fred Mignault, Boris, Tristan, and latecomer Jack Five. In fact, most of my future bands were to feature Neoist alumni. The Montreal Neoists have always been the people I feel closest to. It was our singular *attitude* that united us. There was always an instinctual complicity among us that remained unspoken.

So what, pray tell, would I have done without meeting all these fine odd gentlemen through Monty's auspices? In truth, Monty was one of the scant handful of people in my life who gave me a break, who always encouraged and pushed me forward. And thanks to him I met all of the people I needed to make art and trouble, and shape the rest of my tumultuous decade into a very interesting one indeed.

⇄ We must have been out of the Great Recession by now, because I was offered a job by Roche—another of Quebec's top engineering firms. Again, it was to work on that damned Olympic Tower. This time however, it was to do the structural analyses that served to buttress a counter-suit against the French architect Roger Taillebert[4], who was

---

4. Pronounced "Tahyi-bear"

suing the City of Montreal to obtain a greater fee for his costly Olympic Stadium.

I brought in my trusty little PC-1500 pocket computer to estimate the prestressing losses of the Olympic Tower, as well as complicated concrete "creep" calculations (don't ask) for Armin, an engineer with a PhD. He was amazed to see this tiny machine spitting out on a ticker-tape the crucial diagrams he needed.

I then lugged in my Commodore 64 and plonked it on my office desk, along with a black and white countertop TV, and the Commodore's "cassette drive"—disk drives didn't exist yet. Everyone gathered around to see this amazing novelty. Printers didn't exist yet either, so I had to flash the output on the screen using a "do loop", then jot down the results on a sheet of paper. I don't know of anyone else who was using personal computers in civil engineering in Montreal at this time.

Armin was blown away. Without knowing it, I'd just established my lifelong career as a sought-after computer-savvy structural engineer. It was to serve as my lifeline, both to feed myself and my future family. It was also a newfangled pair of shackles. Unwittingly, I was also Montreal's first Engineering MicroSerf—a fucking technological rick-shaw-puller.

In the end, it took our expert team no time to nail Taillebert on a major design flaw: the huge front tower bearings had been crushed by the weight of the tower, which was already past its full design weight at only half-height. The result was a stalemate in court, with both antag-onists forced to withdraw their respective suits.

After that gig, I got to do my first building as a bona fide struc-tural engineer. Well actually, it was only to add a floor to the Quebec Bar Association building. A good start, nonetheless.

⮜ So if you drew a Venn Diagram of music, poetry, art, computers, engineering and drugs, smack in the middle, you'd get … *moi*. Sure, I was stoned most of the time between the age of 15 and 35, but I still finished high school in the top five and went on to university. And I never did any drugs on the job, your honour. My buildings were as sober as the next dweeb's.

Our boss at Roche was another PhD named Jacques Proulx. He was Armin's mentor back in his student days, and a brilliant man. We were adding a floor to a building, fine. But the owner also wanted an interior building column knocked out at ground level, to accommodate a new amphitheatre. This column supported the weight of several floors. What to do? Proulx's solution was to grab the top of the ground floor column and run unbonded prestressed tendons right up to a new truss on the roof, punching through all floors on each side of the columns. The ground floor column was then removed, and voilà. Brilliant. I also got to design the steel truss on the roof that held those tendons.

⧫ In June, Monty called me out of the blue, asking if I could organize a reading for the American poet Bern Porter. He couldn't do it because he was busy with something else. Bern was a wacky pioneer concrete poet, lettrist, and overall wild man of fringe poetry: "Found" poems, "Found" sound, inventor of Mail Art, anything, and everything[5].

I'd never heard of him. Of course I said yes. So I hastily organized a night at the Café Commune bar in the McGill student ghetto, which was attended by only my twin Ex-Neoists-in-arms Bonspiel and Tristan. Maybe there were one or two other stragglers present.

Bern—then all of 72 years of age—decided to call it *THE POETRY RIOT SHOW*—and makeshift posters and handbills were hastily pasted up and distributed.

His audience may have been tiny, but he held us in thrall and cracked us up with his crazy poems. He had us in stitches when rattling off absurd titles of fake pop songs he'd made up, such as "If You Love Me So Much Baby Then Why Won't You Wash My Socks".

In between reading poems and snippets of stuff, he banged a salt shaker loudly on the table, going "LO, LO, LO, LO, LO!" and pretty soon we all joined him also banging salt shakers on the table, chanting "LO, LO, LO, LO, LO!"

Bern stayed at my place, and Joss made us a meal, which he promptly

---

5. Discover Bern Porter at: https://www.moma.org/interactives/exhibitions/2010/lostandfound/

devoured. He regaled us with great stories, but also a gruesome anecdote about his recently deceased wife. He loved her very dearly, and after she died, he put some remnants of her cremated bones in the fireplace, and kept poking at them until they turned to ash. To him this was a great sign of affection, but I remember Joss and I being pretty creeped out and unsettled by his macabre story. We breathed a sigh of relief when he finally left.

It may have been a small event, but it turned out to be a key moment in my life: it was my debut as a curator of arts events—an activity I'd stumbled onto by chance, but which was to occupy a fair part of my life for the rest of the Eighties.

⪦ Bonspiel had been squatting for a while at the Neoist Embassy, and by summer he had overstayed his welcome. Boris complained he'd caught Bonspiel cleaning his toes with the eraser at the end of a pencil. "What are you doing?" Boris yelled at him. "I put those things in my mouth when I'm working! By the way, when are *you* going to get a job? Look at Alan—*he* works! You think it's interesting for *Le Lord* to get up every morning and go to work? No! But he *does* it!" Boris was frowning as he told me this, adding ... *"c'est un clodo!"*[6]

Boris kicked him out and I took him in. Bonspiel lived with Joss and I for about a month. He'd decline to join us for dinner, then at midnight while we were asleep he'd cook himself a pound of hash meat and eat it right out of the frying pan. He also drank my aftershave for its alcohol content. When I got up in the morning to go to work, I had to daintily step around his hulk on the living room floor, where he'd fallen asleep with a blanket covering his face. I'd turn off the TV which was still on, the grey electronic snow softly going *shhhhhh* ...

Bonspiel and I were so close, we even experienced an unmistakable case of telepathy. We were both thinking of words to input into my Apple II computer cut-ups program. I was about to suggest the word "obviate". He turned to me and asked: "What does *obviate* mean?"

One day Joss told him I was coming back from work pissed off, and

---

6. Transl: "He's a homeless guy!"

Bonspiel mistakenly took that as a clue to vamoose from the premises. Well, maybe it was a good idea by then too.

≷ People now either forgot or don't know how unsettling this period was, especially for the young. In the summer of 1983 there was a mini Cuban Missile Crisis. Reagan wanted to install Pershing missiles in Germany and Italy, the nuclear arms race between the US and the Soviet Union was at its height, and in *Time* magazine and newspapers there was constant talk of surprise Soviet attacks on Europe, with articles on how many millions could be wiped out in a "limited" nuclear exchange. People were rattled and there were marches in Germany with banners and papier-maché effigies deriding Reagan as a rocket-riding cowboy. Reactionary bosom-buddies Reagan and Thatcher were reviled by any self-respecting artist or musician, and this was often reflected in their art. It makes me laugh now to see Reagan worshiped as a saint in America, even by supposedly "liberal" Democrats.

With the ominous Orwellian year 1984 fast approaching, there was a greater fear of an imminent WWIII happening, due to Reagan's aggressive military buildup and sabre-rattling against the *Evil Empire*.

So in the tradition of Neoist happenings, I decided to hold an end-of-the-world party called *Goodbye 1984, Hello WWIII*. I shoved all of my furniture into a room and walled it off with huge wooden packing crates. Then I topped it off with long strands of barbed wire that Dave Sapin found in some abandoned lot and dragged all the way over.

I decorated the whole apartment with a military theme, in barbed wire. Drawings of tanks, planes, missiles and mushroom clouds I made were photocopied in stacks, cut out and pasted across the walls. And in the entrance hall, the guests were greeted with posters announcing *Goodbye 1984, Hello WWIII*.

Gordon W was in town, so we got him to provide catering. During the party the place was packed elbow to elbow. As soon as Gordon set the food out on the table and pushed it into the living room, the ravenous partygoers attacked it and left it bare like ferocious piranhas. I took pictures of the installation beforehand, but no one took pictures of the place when it was packed with people. We weren't selfie-minded back then.

➤ Bonspiel decided to put a band together called Electro-Luxe[7], and invited me to join on the guitar. He sang and programmed a Roland TB-303 Bass Line, linked to a Roland TR-808 drum machine that was manned by JM, and Zilon provided bleeps and bloops on his EMS AKS synthesizer.

We played a total of two shows at the Revox club on Rachel, across from the Parc Lafontaine. Funny thing is, the machines had limited memory, so in between sets, while we were enjoying a beer and yakking with the guests, Bonspiel was busy backstage punching in the programming for our next set. We lasted the summer. Another of our short-lived bands, playing at another short-lived club. It was a relief too, because it wasn't too thrilling for me to play live along with pre-programmed machines.

➤ In November there was a small film festival going on at the Polish Hall on Prince Arthur. I picked up the program and saw *Burroughs: The Movie*. It was a feature documentary film by a certain Howard Brookner. Wow, what an unexpected heaven-sent gift from the nether world!

Joss came with me and we sat down for the screening. I was thrilled beyond belief. Howard was on stage to introduce the movie, and after the film I bribed him with drinks to ply me with stories about my great literary hero. During our conversation I mentioned that by some funny quirk we were going to Manhattan the following day. "I'm going back also," Howard remarked nonchalantly. "Would you like to visit The Bunker?"

Huh? Had I heard right? I couldn't believe it. Here was an invitation to visit Burroughs' legendary abode—the chance of a lifetime! Joss and I flew down to New York the following day and I called at The Bunker—222 Bowery. Howard was to join up with us later, but Ira Silverberg was there manning the fort.

I was waiting in a nearby bar and Ira hobbled in with a cane and leg in a cast, wearing a black leather vest atop a white shirt with rolled-up sleeves. He had movie-star good looks—much like a young Richard

---

7. Hear us at: https://www.youtube.com/watch?v=mz73xGj6l1o

Gere. He was later to become Burroughs' and then Kathy Acker's publicist, then moved on up to prestigious Grove Press and beyond. Joss arrived and he took us in to explore Burroughs' inner sanctum.

I didn't know it then but John Giorno—whom I later got to know—lived on the floor above The Bunker. I was very much impressed with the heavy iron gate of the downstairs entrance—the whole medieval urban padlock mentality. Ira very graciously gave me a tour of The Bunker. "Bill's left for Lawrence, Kansas," he explained, "but his stuff is still all here."

And there it was, laid out before me: all the objects I had become so familiar with, perusing the countless classic photos: the chunky typewriter atop the army-issue desk, the long table that served for all the illustrious dinners in Victor Bockris' *With William Burroughs*, the gun-practice targets riddled with bullet holes. I even got to sit in Burroughs' famed Orgone Box. I closed my eyes and waited patiently for the Orgones to tingle my energies. Nothing. Going through the place, fingering Burroughs' things, at the same time I felt thrilled and shitty. I was the ultimate voyeur, desecrating Bill's secret lair. Howard took my picture. "Stand in the urinals," he motioned to Joss and I, "close your eyes and fold your arms across your chest to look like a Pharaoh inna sarcophagus."

I emerged from the Bunker completely bowled over. The least I could offer Howard and Ira was to buy them dinner. During the conversation it came about they were organizing the festivities for Burroughs' upcoming 70th birthday on the 5th of February 1984, which would coincide with the release of his next novel, *The Place of Dead Roads*. Naturally, I had to be there and finally get to meet the man. To my relief they graciously obliged.

⇍ In early December Monty had a big show at the Spectrum called *Opérat Blanc*[8], and asked me to make a guest appearance as guitarist on a couple of songs. How could I refuse an old comrade? While he sang with mic in hand strapped to an elevated board, I played the strains of *Restrictions* on my Les Paul, and also his song *No Escape*, for which I

---

8. Transl: *White Operat*

composed the music. The song was put out on one of Monty's obscure vinyl releases. His new backing band was called First Aid Brigade, and backstage that evening I met his bassist and fresh Neoist recruit Jack Five. He invited me to an event he was putting on which he called *"une épreuve"* [9]—taking pains to explain "it's *not* an art performance." I passed. Getting up early every morning to go to work was already sufficient of an ordeal for me.

↗ The Christmas holidays were coming up, and boss Proulx insisted I attend the office Christmas party, which was at Roche headquarters in Quebec City. I groaned and tried to get out of it. He insisted I come. So I took the long bloody bus ride to Quebec City. Took me three hours and a quarter. In the middle of the party, with drink in hand he says, "Alan, come and step into my office." Since it was so important for me to come all the way there, I expected a raise. Or a Christmas bonus. Wow! I followed him and sat down expectantly. On his desk was this neat Napoleonic-era cannon, made of a Cognac bottle laying sideways on a wheeled cradle.

Proulx had big bushy eyebrows and looked a lot like Robert Oppenheimer—the father of the atomic bomb. He looked at me with a wry paternal smile and said ... "Alan, I have to lay you off."

I was stunned. I said, "What? You made me come here all the way from Montreal just to *fire* me? You couldn't have told me that *by phone*?" He raised his fuzzy caterpillar eyebrows in hurt surprise and explained: "I wanted you to come to the office Christmas party!"

I stared at his fucking Napoleonic cognac cannon. I felt like grabbing it and bludgeoning him to death with it.

I left without a word, made my way out of the building, took a cab to the bus terminal, and looking out the bus window I cried all the way home. It was the *third* time these bastard engineers fired me right before Christmas—a favourite psycho CEO tactic. That could explain why I seriously started getting into violent Noise Guitar.

---

9. Transl: An ordeal

12

BURROUGHS, HUNCKE, NEW YORK, THE FOUFOUNES

For some reason, Joss couldn't make it to Burroughs' birthday party in Manhattan, so I enlisted Fred Mignault, and we got to work on our special gifts for Uncle Bill. Not only was he an accomplished neon sculptor, Fred invented his ingenious *Verre Luminex* display, which consisted of an etching done between two-foot-square plexiglass plates held in a metal frame, with the etching illuminated from below by a neon tucked into the frame. He did several of them, and the one chosen for Burroughs was that of a couple of kids playing baseball.

Learning from Fred, my gift was a smaller sheet of plexiglass illuminated by a neon bolted behind it. For the image, I chose the silhouette of Burroughs from a famous photo of him in Paris, where he's walking away from the Beat Hotel along Rue Gît-le-coeur.

For the flight to New York I placed my sculpture in a big soft rubber bag plastered with FRAGILE stickers, but like an idiot I stowed the neon away in the plane's baggage hold. When I retrieved the bag off the carousel and unzipped it, the neon was of course smashed to pieces. So I unbolted the plexiglass drawing and was left with *that* as a gift to give Burroughs.

In New York, Fred stayed at a friend's house, and thanks to Monty I slept on the concrete garage floor of the workshop of his artist friend Michael Keene. Over my head dangled a work of his hanging off chains—a car door splattered with paint.

ℤ Howard and Ira held Burroughs' 70th birthday bash at the Limelight club on the Avenue of the Americas at West 20th Street. Formerly an

Episcopal Church, it was now Manhattan's hottest club. A huge crowd lined the sidewalk, and lots of limos came and went, depositing the celebrity guests.

Those familiar with Kerouac's work will remember that Herbert Huncke was the Pope of 42nd Street in New York. And those familiar with Burroughs will know Huncke was one of his early shoot-up junkie buddies.

As Fred and I approached the Limelight, from across the street I recognized Huncke making his way through the crowd. Someone yelled "Hey Huncke!" and he briefly turned, waved and quickly ducked inside. Fred and I jostled our way through the thick crowd, I handed the doorman my invitation card, and we walked into the impressive digs.

"The name of the game is fame" was the New York mantra, and Ira and Howard always wore suits now. It had become a New York thing in the Eighties, like riding limos unashamedly. And *they* were still in their twenties. When they greeted us they were discussing a friend who was freaking out because he was turning 30. Suddenly, I felt ancient at 29.

Ira led us to the VIP room, where I noticed Peter Orlovsky milling about in the A-list crowd. He stood regally with his huge lion's mane of salt and pepper hair down to his shoulders. I didn't have time to crane my neck looking for Warhol and other big fish—I followed Ira to *The Man Himself*, who was sitting on a plush sofa in the middle of the room.

Ira introduced me to Burroughs, saying: "Alan came all the way from Montreal to meet you, Bill."

"Oh my, yes, yes ... *Montreal!*" Burroughs turned to greet me. He was very gracious, and spent a fair amount of time talking to me. He was especially curious about the ongoing linguistic problems in Quebec, and I brought him up to speed.

I gave him my plexiglass drawing, explained the busted neon, and he thanked me. We then walked him, Ira and Burroughs' manager James Grauerholz over to see Fred's *Luminex*, which he'd plugged in and hung up in the room. It was a big hit, they all loved it.

So I finally met the man whose books I'd practically all read. Wow. I came away very impressed. Burroughs was the perfect gentleman, and treated *this* Canajun bumpkin like frickin' royalty.

◄ The festivities surrounding Burroughs' 70th birthday included the release of his new novel *The Place Of Dead Roads*. The book launching was at B. Dalton *In The Village* bookstore, corner of 6th Avenue and West 8th Street. Inside was a long line of waiting fans, some of them carrying stacks of dog-eared paperbacks of *Naked Lunch* and whatnot for poor Bill to sign. Over in a corner I spied the tall, lanky Ric Ocasek of The Cars talking to Grauerholz. Later that night a huge party in Burroughs' honor was held at the Congo Bill lounge, which was on the fourth floor of the Danceteria club on West 21st Street. The place was packed, you could hardly move, and it was *open bar*. It was impossible to get to the bar for a free drink.

Huncke suddenly turned up next to Fred. Fred didn't know much English. They didn't speak to each other, but a knowing glint in their eye signaled that the race was on to see which of the two would get to the bar first. Away they went plowing through the crowd; I caught up with them at the bar and introduced myself to Huncke. "I was standing there at the bar," Huncke said, "you know, kind of surveying the scene in general, when this dashing guy slides up next to me."[1]

Huncke and I hit it off, and he invited me to drop by his place the following day. When I asked Fred: "So, who won the race to the bar?" he said, "Oh boy, Huncke was sure hard to beat. I think in the end it was neck and neck. The bar only served you one drink at a time, so every twenty minutes it was back to square one. We repeated racing each other to the bar several times during that evening—plenty of revenge matches! Boy, did we have fun. We got on like a house on fire. I had no idea who he was, so I wasn't nervous talking to him. I think he appreciated that."

◄ Huncke was staying at R'Lene Dahlberg's place, a beautiful high-ceilinged apartment on Third Avenue, above 25th Street. It had large front windows that gave on Third Avenue and was rent-controlled, costing a ridiculously affordable $150 per month. The Dahlbergs were away on vacation, and we had the place to ourselves. I brought along beer and whiskey, and we gabbed the day away. He gave me a signed

1. From the biography *Herbert Huncke*, by Hilary Holladay

copy of *The Evening Sun Turned Crimson*—which remains one of my favourite books.

In his book *The Great Antonio,* Quebec writer André Trottier[2] offers a rather unflattering image of Huncke: "Sunken eyes in a horror-movie head, and moving sideways stiffly like a crab through the apartment." It's true, Huncke looked like a spectre straight out of a Murnau film, but the wracked shell of his body was soon forgotten when this lively spirit warmed up to you.

We left the apartment and Huncke told me the story of his life as we walked up Fifth Avenue, with the Empire State Building towering over us, its huge red, white and blue lights at the top waking up at dusk. I was completely aware this was a very special moment, and took it all in ecstatically as we strode briskly uptown.

I was on my way to the New York avant-première of Brookner's *Burroughs* film at Carnegie Hall. By the way, it's now in the prestigious *Criterion* collection. For some reason Huncke didn't go, and we bid each other goodbye. When I got to Carnegie Hall I found Fred in the lobby, and we sat down to watch the movie I'd already seen. Fred was particularly struck by the pathetic story of Bill Burroughs Jr, whose sad death is the most emotional moment of the film.

乙 Before returning to Montreal I bummed around the clubs a bit and wound up striking a conversation with Jana Jagendorf, a Manhattan socialite. She ran *On The Wall Productions* with partner James Bacchi, and told me they were putting together a group show of artists in a club called Visage that June. I told her many of my friends in Montreal happened to be great artists. "Well then why don't you bring them down to participate in the show," she said. I was still flying on the buzz from the Burroughs hoopla, so I guess my exposure to such excitement boosted my desire to curate events. I said: "Great, why not?" And so was born *North By Northwest,* an "Exhibition and Celebration Honoring Montreal and New York Artists". Now I couldn't wait to get back and start telling all my friends I was going to launch their art careers in the Big Apple!

---

2. Pronounced "Awn-dray Troh-t'yay"

The first thing I did when I got back home was to set up a little Burroughs shrine on my library shelves, adorning my Burroughs books collection with everything I'd gathered during the trip: movie and book launch posters, invitation cards and flyers.

ಒ Zilon initiated his *Urban Primitive* soirées, and I joined in for the fun along with Bonspiel, Fred, JM, and Napoléon. We roamed the night, a mobile graffiti art action team, spray-painting abandoned buildings and redecorating the soon to be filled-in Park Avenue pedestrian tunnel[3]. We made campfires in an abandoned viaduct directly under a fire station and hammered out industrial concerts on building pipes, sheets of metal and concrete walls, chanting like postapocalyptic possessed friars.

Tired of her dead-end job as a bookkeeper in the garment industry, Joss decided to become Joss Designs, and fancied herself a clothes designer. Oh the countless hours did I have to suffer at Fabricville, while she took her time choosing cutting patterns and bolts of cloth. Her dream was to wind up at New York's Fashion Institute of Technology. The mere moronic concept of that moniker never ceases to throw *me* into FITS of laughter.

She had no talent, really. Whatever she made turned out looking like a differently misshaped potato sack. *Of course* I encouraged her— what thoughtful boyfriend wouldn't encourage his girlfriend in such self-delusion? We got the idea to team up Joss and Zilon for a Graffiti Fashion Show at the upcoming Visage club gig. Fashion models would wear Joss' white potato sack dresses, and Zilon would spray-paint drawings onto them live.

Leading up to the Visage show, I returned to New York for a couple of coordination meetings with Jana. How could a guy living on unemployment insurance cheques afford going to New York so often?

Laker Airways. In the early Eighties it was the cheapest airline ever. You took a bus from Montreal to Burlington, Vermont, then hopped

---

3. The scene of many a rape, this piss-laden underpass at the foot of the grotesque *Sir George-Étienne Cartier* monument was eventually closed off and backfilled.

on a plane to New York. The fare was generally $35, but it depended on the number of passengers. Once in the air a steward rolled a cart down the aisle, punched in the attendance on a small Sharp pocket computer just like mine, and you paid him cash. Once, a flight out of New York cost me a jaw-dropping $17.50—less than my cab fare to La Guardia! Of course it was too good to be true, and it didn't last. Laker Airways folded soon after.

⇒ Each time I was in Manhattan Ira suggested the latest eating hot spots. For lunch we met at *America*—a high-ceilinged cavernous restaurant in the Flatiron district, that had a massive Statue Of Liberty mural. The food was representative of the 50 states, and the floor was chaotic with lots of tables and commotion. It was the place Ira went to watch people and to be seen. He also suggested I check out *Bayamo*— which I did—a new Cuban-Asian fusion resto in Noho, where I tasted my first *Ropa Vieja*. But my choice eating spot was the cruddy *Life Café* off Tomkins Square Park, where I dug into my habitual *Chicken Chimichangas,* washed down with a couple of Rolling Rocks.

The center of the art universe is forever shifting, and in the early Eighties the center of the universe abruptly shifted to the East Village. The art explosion happening there was astounding, amid a riot of extravagantly-named art spaces and galleries: *Civilian Warfare, Fun Gallery, P.P.O.W., Gracie Mansion, New Math, International With Monument, Limbo, Nolo Contendere, Sensory Evolution, Piezo Electric, Semaphore East, Vox Populi, Area X.* The most ingenious among those crazy names was *ABC No Rio*—which was inspired by the letters that had either faded out or were missing on a sign spelling "Lawyer And Notary" in Spanish (**AB**ogado **C**on **No**tario).

Dozens of young new artists were producing amazing and exuberant art, often tempering the gritty reality of their lives with Loony Tunes on acid silliness. Among my favourite artists were Mark Kostabi, Dan Friedman, Kenny Scharf, Rodney Alan Greenblat, Rick Prol, Caren Scarpulla, the delightful Rhonda Wall, and Cheryl Laemmle— with her eerie birch bark style applied to any and all subjects. But the greatest of them all was David Wojnarowicz, whose intense corrosive social comment suited me perfectly.

I had arrived smack in the middle of the East Village's pre-gentri-fied golden age! Just walking around the cringy streets of Alphabet City was thrilling—you were exposing yourself to getting mugged or stabbed. With luck, you'd only get assailed by one of Richard Hambleton's boogeymen painted in black, jumping out of a hidden corner.

In addition to the wild stuff in the galleries, there were also kooky anonymous scrap n' junk sculptures fixed to lampposts and walls of buildings. Even in front of the Whitney Museum—then uptown—somebody put up a fake traffic sign on a pole that said NO EXIT, under a mushroom cloud.

The energy and vitality of Punk and Post Punk had moved over to art. Of course, literature being the retarded brother of the arts—as Burroughs once explained—it took a while longer for writing to catch up with Punk. But it did, with the magazine *Between C and D*—more about that later.

The creative explosion in the East Village was matched by us in Montreal, but on a way smaller, more intimate scale. Also with the big difference that *we* didn't have any "uptown" patron money trickling down to us.

There were great art galleries not only in the East Village, but also in Soho. I was lucky not only to catch the Chris Burden exhibit *Some Lucky Subs* at the Holly Solomon Gallery, but the man himself, walking slowly around the gallery like a gentle monk. He was gracious enough to talk to me for at least half an hour. Among other things, I told him I was a structural engineer. That cued him to explain to me his idea of dropping H-beams from a helicopter onto concrete pads, which he in-sisted would punch straight through the concrete. I was incredulous, but he assured me it worked. I later found out he indeed did this in a performance called *Beam Drop* in Artpark, near Niagara Falls—but into *wet* concrete—a far easier task.

I knew about Chris Burden's notorious self-mutilation perform-ances, but I was more fascinated by his sculptures, tinkerings, and in-stallations such as the *Big Wheel*, and his attempt to collapse an art gallery by installing a turnstile that pushed out beams against the walls incrementally each time a patron walked in. You couldn't ask to meet a nicer man, and he allowed me to take a picture of him. Chris Burden remains one of the artists I admire the most.

↗ In May I went down to New York for a last Visage show coordination meeting. Ira invited me to Grace Jones' birthday party that was being held at the Limelight. I never got to see her because she was having a tantrum backstage. The theme of her party was *Jungle*, and there were potted trees and bushes everywhere. For greater authenticity, she also wanted truckloads of earth dumped onto the carpets of the Limelight. Management refused her insane request, so she was throwing one of her notorious diva fits.

At the party I ran into Keith Haring, who was coming down the stairwell to the dancefloor. I told him about the upcoming Visage show, but after a bit we gave up yelling at each other over the pounding music.

During that same trip I also ran into artist Rick Prol, who had an exhibit in an East Village gallery. I told him about the Visage show, and he remarked that it was a smart thing to bring artists from Montreal, because the New York scene had peaked. Not only did Rick Prol look like Sid Vicious, but his paintings looked like the kind of primitive punk stuff Sid would have done were he a painter: skulls, knives, and bony hands spiking a junk needle into a skinny arm ... *La Scuzzy Vita Loisaida*[4].

But Rick was right. By now, everything and *anything* was starting to make it to a gallery wall. One art gallery had dozens of paintings consisting of raw construction materials glued to a canvas: pieces of foam, insulation, electric wiring and junction boxes—as if Jackson Pollock had been a building contractor.

↗ At Monty's suggestion I got in touch with his friend the Serbian-American artist Dragan Ilíc, whose art was made with a contraption that held several markers and drew in parallel lines, like musical staff lines gone bonkers. He brought me to the opening of the new MOMA West Wing and museum expansion designed by Pelli. A gaggle of young artists was holding a kind of *Salon des refusés* on the opposite side of the street. They scribbled and splashed paint on the sidewalk in protest against the lavish elite gala being held there.

---

4. "Loisaida" was the way *Nuyoricans* (resident Puerto Ricans) pronounced "Lower East Side"

They had a point. I remember being struck by the sight of Dean Savard of Civilian Warfare and others of the East Village gallery scene milling around smugly in tuxedoes, holding drinks in their hands. "Punks in Tuxedoes" I mumbled under my breath. Yes, rebels secretly yearning to be accepted into the wide-open arms of rich art collectors. The amazing spontaneous combustion of the Lower East Side art scene, as I and many others had adored it, was already over.

Before leaving, I had time to pop into the Shafrazi gallery to catch an exhibition by French artist Hervé di Rosa. His cartoonish art was even wilder than Kenny Scharf's. Shafrazi was the nut who scribbled "Kill Lies All" onto Picasso's *Guernica* in 1974, when it was still at the MOMA. Now he'd become a respectable art dealer and the owner of the *Tony Shafrazi Gallery* in Soho.

Tony was there. I told him I really dug di Rosa, and bought a poster. He asked me if I wanted to see more of his artwork. I said "sure!" and he let me go down to the basement, where there were tons of other paintings by di Rosa, as well as other artists. I was very impressed by the fact he trusted me to go down there alone. Who knows—I could've defaced one of the paintings, no?

⇆ For some reason I found myself downtown and realized I didn't have enough money for cab fare to La Guardia. This was the pre-ATM era, folks. Credit cards—or even bank cards—weren't prevalent yet, and American Express travellers cheques were still a thing.

So there I was on Wall Street, stopping people at random to explain my predicament: "Sir … m'am … could you please lend me $20 so I can catch my flight home to Montreal? I'll send you a cheque by mail!" Of course the jaded Noo Yawkers smirked and brushed past this inventive scam artist. Eventually I got a hold of Jana on the phone and walked uptown—from Wall Street all the way to East 80th street!—to pick up my emergency loan.

⇆ Preparations for the Visage show were under way. I was making a series of big 4' × 4' acrylic *Machine Paintings* copied off my Commodore 64. I'd let it run randomly, then when I considered a layout particularly interesting, I'd freeze the program and copy the screen onto canvas.

Boris also had his fat bit Apple drawings reproduced on canvas, the gifted Sylvain Grisé had his magnificent paintings in the style of Jacques Monory, and Zilon would be executing *his* paintings live on Joss' fashion models. Sylvain dragged along his brother-in-law Pierre Colpron, who exhibited his photos, and this time Fred Mignault brought paintings instead of neons. To avoid problems at customs, we rolled our paintings up and carried them in our luggage, planning to mount them back up on frames we'd buy in New York.

To save money we took the Amtrack train, which took 14 hours. At times the train was so slow you could have gotten off and walked faster. We were all penniless, so we snuck in and piled into one room at my habitual Washington Square Hotel. How we accomplished this without getting caught I'll never know.

The afternoon of the show, Sylvain and I scrambled around town getting stretchers and stapled our canvases onto the frames. Joss rehearsed her dancers at the empty club—local kids who volunteered.

I invited Ira and Huncke to come see us at the show, and they quite enjoyed themselves. Fred and Huncke were happy to see each other again, and now that I think of it, I'm quite certain Huncke appreciated Fred's good looks.

The graffiti fashion show went very well, with Zilon gracefully drawing his signature androgynous faces on the white living posing canvases, to booming dance music provided by the club DJ. With 3000 people in attendance, the show was a great party, but for me it was a financial flop. No artist I'd brought along managed to sell anything. Sylvain found me outside in the back alley, sobbing out of rage at the abysmal failure of my endeavour.

The following day Zilon and I went to Civilian Warfare with our paintings under the arm, to see if we could interest them in selling them on consignment. We were politely declined. I left one of my paintings there as a gift for David Wojnarowicz. We went on to a few more galleries, where we were met with the same indifference.

We got caught in a pouring rain. Zilon and I started running back to the hotel holding our paintings on top of our heads like umbrellas. The rain totally ruined them, and by then we could care less. Passing by a mound of garbage bags on the sidewalk, we looked at each other and dumped our paintings into the heap and ran off drenched, laughing at the absurdity of it all. And that was the extent of us taking the New York art world by storm.

⤳ Back home, our hangout spot now became Napoléon's place on Dorion street below St. Catherine. It served as a loose art commune, with people coming and going. There were a few keyboards and amplifiers lying around, as well as other instruments, and impromptu music jams were held with whoever happened to be there.

I walked in on Napoléon and others making a film. Bonspiel was up on a ladder waving a big white sheet onto which a scene from Ancient Egypt was being projected: a camel, pyramids, and palm trees. I soon realized it was the blow-up of a pack of Camels.

The soundtrack of choice being played then at the Dorion apartment was *Moments In Love* by The Art of Noise. Zilon, JM and others were lounging around on the sofa. I put on a cassette of my recent noise guitar experiments. Music on the airwaves had really hit bottom with Michael Jackson and Madonna—which inspired *me* to be more radical. The boys were very much impressed, and we soon formed a band. JM was on electronic drums, Zilon on vocals and EMS AKS synth, and I alternated between bass and guitar. I christened us *Débris.*

Our bands came and went like Beverly Hills mom-to-daughter plastic surgery gift coupons: Electro-Luxe, Cleveland Noisegate[5], Débris, Sensitive Organs—all of these bands with wacky names were just like-minded friends getting together to make music. They lasted mere months—we'd do one or two shows and then mutate onto the next phase of our respective artistic evolution. No one bothered to take pictures, and only a few Lo-Fi recordings survive.

I did only two Débris songs on noise guitar[6]. Another was a computer music feedback loop (*Fashion In Kansas*[7]), and the rest were

---

5. Hear them at: https://www.youtube.com/watch?v=RdAdVGi3qhQ
6. Hear *Première* at: https://soundcloud.com/alan-lord-4/premiere
7. Hear it at: https://soundcloud.com/alan-lord-4/fashion-in-kansas

funky grooves I laid down on the bass. The songs sounded as great as their names: *I Like Your Paintings (Do You Like Mine?)*[8], *Baby Wants Flesh, I Feel So Insecure, You Look So Nice*. And with Zilon whining postmodern complaints in his jaded *fin-de-siècle ennui*, our *Clone Café* [9] was as good as anything by The Velvet Underground[10].

We did a first show at Charlie Brown's, on St. Catherine street. The club attracted more of a preppy crowd, used to dancing to Duran Duran and Depeche Mode. And here we were with harsh noise guitar and stabbing synths. They didn't quite know what to make of us at first—they just stood there, perplexed by the noise we were making. When I switched to bass and started laying down some White Funk grooves, they got into it and started dancing again.

➤ Wondering what else to do with myself in this new year of unemployment, I got into exploring neon—with a *lot of* help from Fred. I even landed a commission to do a huge neon sign for *Videozone*—one of those new shops opening up where you could rent movies on VHS tapes. Remember those? If so, you're just as old as I am.

I fixed the neon tubes spelling out *Videozone* in script onto a 4' × 6' slab of see-thru plexiglass one inch thick. The thing was heavy, and I was so conscientious with my work that it ended up costing me more than what I sold it for. There you go—*Lordonomics* at work again.

I also made a painting of the US flag, inspired by Reagan's invasion of the tiny dangerous communist island of Grenada. In the blue star field I put in a McDonalds "M" instead of stars, and parachuting commandos dropped from the red horizontal stripes amid swooping helicopters.

➤ The place for underground Montreal artists and musicians to hang out now was the new club *Les Foufounes Électriques*. It was on St. Catherine Street just east of The Main, and used to be the bar *Les*

---

8. Hear it at: https://soundcloud.com/alan-lord-4/ilike-your-paintings
9. Hear it at: https://soundcloud.com/alan-lord-4/clone-cafe
10. The friendly folks at *Le Backstore* are releasing a vinyl LP of Débris in 2022

Clochards Célestes[11]. Before settling into its definitive name, the place had done a brief stint as the *Zoobar*. Bit by bit, the Foufounes became my headquarters, my home away from home, my arts lab, my Disneyworld. We, the unwashed, louche, music scene and art knock-about habitués, called it the *Foufs*. It was our *Moulin de La Galette*, with plenty of *Tolose Low-drecks* swabbing paintings live during their trademark 3x4 Live Painting nights.

The Foufs quickly became the cool watering hole for rock gods slumming afterhours while in town, such as David Bowie. More than just a bar and a concert space however, the Foufs became a true alternative institution, a bastion and barricade of Montreal's irrepressible fuckyou counterculture, of which I was briefly king. My reign lasted roughly from 1984 to 1987. Amazing how long you can stretch 15 minutes.

The first event I organized there was another graffiti fashion show for Joss, with Débris providing the music. At a certain point Zilon escaped from his EMS AKS synth to draw graffiti paintings on the parading models dressed in white. For the occasion Bonspiel was the emcee, and jumped onstage to launch the show with the greeting "Bienvenue au Carnaval Tragique"[12].

When I first met Dave Sapin, he didn't speak a word of French and used to hang out with other Anglos exclusively. Hanging out now with new artist friend Jacques Boyer, Dave started immersing himself deeper into the underground arts community, and also started participating in the 3x4 live painting shows being held at the Foufs. By then his cultural metamorphosis was complete. He'd gone from being an Anglophone to a 100% genuine Québécois. Our dear Dave now spoke exclusively in French—even more—a *joual* that he savoured like a fine connoisseur of tasty twanged vowels. Whenever I addressed him in English, he answered invariably in French, chewing his savory vowels worse than the most backward of *Beauceron* hillbillies. He instinctively understood that the true nature of Quebec culture was *Ti-Pop*

---

11. Pronounced "Leh Kluh-sharr Seh-lest"; the French translation of Kerouac's *Dharma Bums*
12. Transl: "Welcome to the Tragic Carnival"

(tacky *Théâtre des Variétés* vaudeville-type kitsch). He loved everything that was Québécois, all that was Ti-Pop[13]. His favourite expressions were "C'est Ti-Pop au boutte!"[14] and "It's Ti-Pop and a half!"

ⵣ Without warning, the bottom fell out of my soul again. I'd borrowed my father's car and parked it in front of my place. I was still up at 5:30 AM after the previous night's whatever party wherever with whoever, and in the still dawn I saw and heard my Dad ambling toward the car to pick it up and quietly go to work. At that very instant I felt like the worst piece of shit on this godforsaken earth. He'd toiled and sweat and set aside his whole life for *this?* To walk a whole mile at 67 years of age, to go pick up his car *because his no-good decadent art party "bohemian" son couldn't bother returning it to him?*

Armin must have felt the disturbance in The Force and came to my rescue. Remembering my computer skills from Roche, Armin—now at LGL[15]—hired me in October, along with another guy roughly my age. We only had bachelor's degrees, but unlike most PhD snoots, Armin was smart enough to realize you didn't need a PhD to run Finite Element structural analysis software.

We were to use the *ANSYS* 3D program to model large deep underground silos that served a new wastewater collection network for the island of Montreal. The computer runs were done on a mainframe computer at the downtown firm Control Data. We prepared the input on our IBM PC's and sent them the files via modem.

It was the first time I saw a desktop PC. It had one floppy 5-1/4" disk drive and the screen was green text on a black background. Hard drives and 3-1/2" diskettes were still off in the future. The first task on my new job was to read through a two-inch thick book of operating instructions going by the strange name of "DOS 2.0". It had a weird new language I had to learn: CHKDSK, DIR, BAK, MKDIR, EXE2BIN. It was all Chinese to me.

---

13. Pronounced "tsee pup"
14. Transl: "It's Ti-Pop to the max!"
15. The engineering firm Lalonde Girouard Letendre

The cost just in computing time for the entire project was $100K[16]. Which is laughable now, because once you buy a $3K license, you can run as many analyses as you want on your laptop for free. Naturally, Control Data soon went the way of video stores.

Out of curiosity at LGL one day I opened a door and entered a dark room. I flicked on the light. It was their computer graveyard. There were all kinds of dusty obsolescent devices—like a Tandy/Radio Shack TRS-80 model II, with a huge vertical slot for vinyl LP-sized floppy disks. And in the corner there was a big fridge-sized metal frame holding motherboards and wired circuits. I asked someone what the hell it was. He said "16K of memory". Wow.

"DOS" was just the beginning of Bill's Gates of Hell. He should've stopped at Basic—the language I'd mastered and loved. Instead, he went on to create the computer hell we now live in and can't live without. Those who don't understand what I'm saying never had to use desktop PC's in the oppressive corporate world like I did for 30 years. When PC's came out they claimed computers and technology would free up your time for more leisure. Well *the very opposite* happened. With the advent of desktop PC's, ever tighter deadlines were imposed, everyone wanted things done yesterday, you were on call by e-mail past midnight, and weekends were to catch up with what you hadn't managed to do during the week. Workers died a century ago to give us a 40-hour work week, and now people find it normal to work 70 hour weeks and never take vacations. My engineering job was a charm before the advent of desktop PC's. It progressively became hellish, and I'm damn glad I'm finally out of that dehumanizing racket.

ℤ Now that I had a steady paycheque, I got the idea to invite Huncke to Montreal to do a few readings. I offered Huncke $500 US to come up and do a reading in Montreal on November 11th and 13th, at the Foufs. He and minder pal Jerome Poynton stayed at my place, sleeping on sturdy steel-frame fold-up single beds we'd laid out in the front-room library. Huncke's one request was for orange juice, which he needed to

---

16. $260K today

mix his Methadone. Like Burroughs, Huncke was on a Methadone program, in between the occasional taste of junk.

His other request was for a paper bag, which he placed next to his bed. I'll never forget the sound of him dry-retching and spitting into that bag throughout the night. Even though he wasn't using, he couldn't shake off that old junkie habit of periodically vomiting.

ᐅ He stayed with Joss and I almost a week, regaling us with great stories and anecdotes. Huncke was a master storyteller, and we were like kids around a campfire, listening intently.

He told us Burroughs often used him as a guinea pig, when unsure about some dubious dope he'd just acquired. "Go on, you shoot up first, Herbert (sniff)..." he said, then wait to see Huncke's reaction to the stuff. Scrutinizing Huncke for any signs of discomfort, he asked, "Soooo Herbert, how are you feeling?" Huncke swooned and almost passed out, but grit his teeth, braced himself and moaned, "Oh, Bill ... this is some *GOOD SHIT!* ..." So Burroughs lost no time shooting up. But when the crap he'd just shot in his veins kicked in he glared at Huncke and fumed, "...you bastard!"

Huncke took out and showed us a picture of Burroughs holding a cat upside down by the tail. For Christmas, Burroughs had sent Huncke a red tie and a picture of a cat he'd skinned.

I remarked how beautiful his shirt was. It was midnight blue. "Here, why don't you have it!" he said, giving it to me. So Huncke literally gave me the shirt off his back. I wore it until it fell apart.

He had a special story for us on the occasion of his stay in Canada. It wasn't in any of his books. He called it *Canadian Club*:

In Manhattan one day Huncke was walking along the sidewalk, looking for an easy car to break into. He fell on a car with unlocked doors. He looked around inside. There was a case of Canadian Club whiskey on the back seat, along with bags of money marked with big dollar signs—just like in cartoons. He looked inside the bags—they were full of money! Believing they were props for a publicity stunt, and that the people would soon be back, he lost no time in grabbing the spoils and scrammed the hell out of there.

It turned out it was *Canadian* money. Totally useless. He couldn't show up at a bank and trade it in for American dollars, could he? So he got the idea of rounding up several friends, and they booked a hotel just across the border. They partied and whooped it up in the hotel until the very last of them damned Canadian dollar bills was gone.

At my urging, Huncke typed out the story when he was back in New York, and sent it to me. I kept the sheet of paper folded in my copy of *The Evening Sun Turned Crimson* for years, but I eventually lost it.

⤌ Fred had his paintings on exhibit upstairs at the Foufounes, so Huncke did his first reading during Fred's vernissage on the 11th. Then on the 13th he did a reading on the club stage, with my band Débris backing him for the latter half. The club was packed and the kids were thrilled. Apart from me though, just a handful of people there knew who he was. Sadly, it's still the case today, and it's a crying shame.

Huncke had the soul of an angel—to me he was the very embodiment of Kerouac's "angelheaded hipster". I never heard Huncke either pass judgement or make a disparaging remark about anyone. He was totally incapable of sarcasm. He treated everyone with respect, and his stories were about characters most people would have dismissed as bums, freaks, and winos. Losers? All of Huncke's people were social losers. And Huncke The Junkie was the biggest loser of them all. Because he was too human. He stole from his friends, bummed money off them, spent a good deal of his life behind bars. Surprise: we're all losers. The day we're born. And when we die we lose everything. And that's the bottom line of the human condition.

13

ULTIMATUM

John Giorno was coming to the Foufounes with his band on a promotion tour for the release of his album *Better An Old Demon Than A New God*, which included New York's louche royalty: Burroughs, Jim Carroll, David Johansen, Richard Hell and Lydia Lunch. Psychic TV was also on it, featuring Burroughs acolyte Genesis P. Orridge. The initial pressing of 4000 copies sold in a week, so another 3000 had to be pressed for the tour.

Giorno's show was two nights at the end of November, and I interviewed him ahead of the show by phone for the Foufs' magazine *l'Oeil Rechargeable*[1]. Asked about the state of poetry, Giorno said "a hundred years ago, when people had nothing to do at night, they used to sit in a chair and read a book of poems or a novel. And that's the basis of how those forms and media arose. But now, when I'm home alone at night I'll listen to the stereo, radio or whatnot, so I think when dealing with poetry, one thing that works now in poetry is performance."

That stuck in my mind, and after his shows we talked a bit, and he gave me his contact information.

◆ Furious after the humiliating fiasco of the Visage show, instead of caving and giving up, I doubled down. Montreal's underground art scene was overflowing with talent and intelligence, and I felt it my mission *to do something* about it, promote all the extraordinary poets, artists and musicians I knew. So I came up with the idea of putting together a festival of avant-poetry to be called Ultimatum. I bit the financial

---

1. Pronounced "Luyh Reh-sharr-jhabb"; Transl: *The Rechargeable Eye*

bullet and bought an Apple IIe computer, applied for a Canada Arts Council "Explorations Grant", and got it. I was given $15,000[2] to put on a five-day cutting-edge "Urban Poetry" festival.

For this festival I urged all participants to be creative and spice up their readings using the cutting-edge tools of the day: video, computers, sonic collage tapes, electronically-altered voice, music and performance art. It turned out to be multimedia, before the term even existed. I didn't want just another boring string of meandering poetry readings, so in the contract I stipulated a strict 15 minute time limit. I didn't want anyone enthralled with their own voice to go on doddering interminably, as was usually the case. Make a splash, melt our brains, and scram off the stage.

Why did I call it *Ultimatum?* As I explained in the press release, it was an ultimatum to society to stop for a moment and listen to what its poets had to say. Our venerated poet Paul Chamberland[3] wrote: *"May Ultimatum be to poetry what lightning is to spring: fecundity."*

⊼ The first thing most people do when they get an arts grant is to give themselves a salary. I didn't have to, because I had a good-paying job, so all of the money went into production, advertising, staff and participants' fees. For the festival logo I used Sylvain Grisé's painting of a snarling wolf, and David Sapin took care of the art and printing for the poster, flyers, invitation cards and tickets. *My* job was to contact and gather the talent.

In addition to dozens of Montreal poets, writers, bands and musicians of both languages, I invited people from Quebec City, Vancouver, Toronto, and New York. I got The John Giorno Band to headline the festival, asked Herbert Huncke to come up again, and also invited Sylvère Lotringer of Semiotext(e), whom I really wanted to meet.

My most memorable outing as a talent scout was for the much-revered writer Josée Yvon[4], and Quebec's greatest living poet Denis Vanier, whom you may recall did battle with my old pal Francoeur in a previous festival.

The first time I saw Josée Yvon she was totally fucked up on

---

2. $36,000 today
3. Pronounced "Paul Shuh Bear-luh"
4. Pronounced "Jho-zay Ee-voh"

Mandrax[5], petting a tarantula snoozing on her lap. At the time she and hubby Denis were living on Panet[6] street, where the corner grocer let them run up a beer and grocery bill that their next welfare cheque hardly covered. They were seriously considering opening a pet shop with the Canada Arts Council grant they were getting shortly.

I adored the titles Josée gave her books: *Travesties-kamikaze, Maîtresses-Cherokees, Danseuse-mamelouk, Filles-commando bandées*[7]. She was Quebec's reigning gutter poetess, and with her beads, boas and feathers in her shoulder-length hair, she looked like our answer to Janis Joplin. Her books told the tales of forgotten women at the bottom of the social order—the waitresses, telephone operators, factory girls, lap dancers, whores, the homeless—they were her neglected and marginalized, flayed sisters of this world. She was their champion, their radical fairy godmother, stimulating clits with the tip of her sparkling wand. I desperately wanted Josée and Denis in my festival, and they were all in.

As a timely foretaste of the festival, Bill Vorn put together a *Gizmo Global Show* at Montreal's UQUAM, showcasing the use of computers in video, music, art, poetry, architecture, and photography. Among the participants were Boris, Tristan, Vorn, Bonspiel, and TTP. Vorn also invited me to demonstrate my *Machine Paintings* on the Commodore 64.

↗ The Ultimatum Montreal Urban Poetry Festival was held from May 1st to 5th 1985, at the Foufounes Électriques. There's a CBC TV newscast that shows Bill Bissett, The Toronto Research Group, The Woeurks, Christopher Dewdney, Ken Decker at an Apple computer, poet Anonyme Sanregret[8] being tattooed, and a John Giorno video clip[9].

The festival was a cornucopia of sound poetry, one-act plays, poets wearing wild Dadaist costumes, poets surrounded by dancing boys and girls, poets accompanied by screens flashing videos and computer

---

5. Quaaludes

6. Pronounced "Pan-eh"

7. Transl: Kamikaze Trannies, Cherokee Mistresses, Mameluke Stripper, Commando Chicks w/ Boners

8. Pronounced "Anno-nim Suh-reh-greh"; his name meant "anonymous without regrets"

9. See Appendix B—Video Links—Ultimatum—Video 1

graphics, poets backed by sound-sculpture *musique concrète* mix tapes, poets fronting great bands, a poet getting tattooed live on stage, and yes, even older unplugged poets reading from sheets of paper laconically, as in their good old days.

Concurrently at Articule gallery there was an ongoing exhibit of computer poetry and graphics set up by Alain Bergeron, using a series of Apple IIc computers on loan from sponsor Apple. A conference on Computer Art/Poetry/Music took place with Bergeron, Bill Vorn, Boris, Tristan, Bonspiel and I. There was also another conference on "Oblique Magazine Publishing"—which among others featured editors Eldon Garnet of *Impulse*, Karl Jirgens of *Rampike*, and Sylvère Lotringer of *Semiotext(e)*. Lastly, on the last day of the festival, there was a showing of films and videos with literature as theme, including Ron Mann's *Poetry In Motion*, *Giorno Video Pak 1*, Brookner's *Burroughs*, Lotringer's *Too Sensitive To Touch*, and Napoléon Moffat's *Framed*.

⤳ This time I put up Huncke in a hotel—the Hôtel du Parc[10] on Park Avenue off Pine—where he received many people who were dying to see him. Fred recalls: "The following day after his arrival he called me real early in the morning. He wanted me to find him some coke. Well, finding coke in the morning before lunch isn't the easiest thing. He wanted me to find him a half gram of coke. I finally found a pusher and made it to Huncke's hotel room, and put it on the table. I made two lines—one for him, one for me, and he started telling me a story about a sunrise in Mexico. It lasted three hours."

I didn't get to hang out with Huncke much this time. Hey, *I had a festival to run*. But we sure had a lot of fun yakking backstage. At one point a starry-eyed kid showed up and asked Huncke: "What do you remember best from the Fifties? James Dean? Marilyn Monroe? Tailfins?" Poor Huncke, shaking his head, sorry to have to disappoint the kid, said, "well, I don't remember any of that, I spent most of the Fifties *inside*"—meaning *prison*. We collapsed in howls of laughter.

I asked Bonspiel to organize a party to welcome Sylvère—I wanted him to meet Napoléon, Tristan, Boris, everyone. We assaulted him

---

10. Now the Air Transat headquarters

excitedly talking a mile a second, and Sylvère marveled at how easily we switched from English to French in conversation, even mid-sentence.

Sitting with Giorno during his band's afternoon soundcheck—namely the unavoidable *drum* sound check—I remarked: "Gawd I hate soundchecks." He said, "Oh, I don't even think about it anymore." He'd attained an enviable level of Zen detachment I had not, and probably never could. His bandmates were sweethearts, and intimidatingly accomplished musicians. It must have been a real pleasure for John to have them backing him.

One thing I'm proud of during that festival was getting Giorno and Lotringer to bury the hatchet. They'd been feuding since the 1978 Burroughs Nova Convention in New York—on account of a measly $100 tiff.

Festival highlights:

Confessions d'un ventriloque[11]: in which Sylvère Lotringer interviewed himself using a pre-recorded tape, to which he answered live, alternating between French and English in his soft, timid, squeaky voice[12] ...

French lettrist Jean-Paul Curtay—the inventor of *Body Music* and *Hypergraphic Music*, wrapping his mouth around the microphone to produce his *Sound Super-Writing*—nearly swallowing it like a cock ...

Ken Decker conversing with his computer screen, doing *Backyard Gene Pool* ...

Steve Montambault—dressed as a medieval monk—warbling his text through a voice-altering device, accompanied by sound tapes and a hypnotic video ...

---

11. Transl: Confessions of a Ventriloquist
12. See it at: https://www.youtube.com/watch?v=CfQoG3plySY&t=161s

A one-act play by Endre Farkas re-enacting a right-wing South American dictatorship interrogation, with actors dressed as officers maltreating a leftist suspect tied to a chair ...

Anonyme Sanregret taking a break from singing with his band[13] to sit down and get tattooed ...

Karl Jirgens, editor of Rampike, giving his reading with a pair of guns pointed at his temples, held by a strap over his head ...

Concept Variable, fronted by writer Sylvain Houde, with his adorably cute sister Célina de Romantica, Billy Molécule, and our good old Fred Mignault on bass, giving us cool songs like *The Story Of Billy Manicoti*[14], and *Groënland* ...

Somali poet Mohamud Togane, reading his stunning poem *In Money We Trust*[15]:

> Bushman, you wanna be civilized?
> Go get money!
> It don't matter how
> Get it honestly if you can
> Get it dishonestly if you must
> But by all means get money
>
> Bushman, put money in thy loincloth!
> In God we trust
> In money we must
> Money is the sixth sense
> Without which the other five are useless!

---

13. Hear *Microprocesseur* at: https://soundcloud.com/alan-lord-4/07-anonyme-sanregret

14. Hear it at: https://soundcloud.com/alan-lord-4/11-concept-variable-the-story

15. For the full poem, see Appendix A—Selected Texts

Doomed poet Ian Stephens reading solo, then later fronting his exquisite band Red Shift, doing *This Is The Worst (Of Love)*[16] ...

Mario Campo first appearing with the head of an extraterrestrial, then donning a Bedouin headdress to read his poem *Arabesque*[17], atop an eastern-flavoured instrumental tape by Débris, with Zilon chanting like a muezzin ...

A quite visibly and audibly tipsy Michel Lefebvre[18] dressed as a space alien, knocking over vials of liquid on a table, with a girl in a Hugo Ball costume hovering robotically nearby ...

Writer Colette Tougas singing *a capella* the sultry *Modesty*[19] in her smouldering breathy voice—which *begged* to be included on the festival's documentary LP ...

Tristan Renaud's superb electronic music ensemble Open Mouth, with fellow keyboardist Gaétan Gravel and singer Corrina Viereck, offering us sublime compositions worthy of Philip Glass[20] ...

Boris Wanowitch and Boys du Sévère's production *Misère Plus*, with Boris and the luscious Josée Thibeault wearing those ridiculous shiny black Spanish Guardia Civil hats, sitting at an inquisitorial desk with Bonspiel, taking turns reading an amazing text being printed randomly live on a scritchy dot-matrix printer, using my cut-ups program ...

Boris then sat in a chair reading a newspaper while Josée gave him a haircut, with the loud buzzing electric clipper amplified by contact mics ...

16. Hear it at : https://soundcloud.com/alan-lord-4/02-red-shift-this-is-the-worst
17. Hear it at : https://soundcloud.com/alan-lord-4/10-mario-campo-arabesque
18. Pronounced "Mee-shell Luh-fevv"
19. Hear it at : https://soundcloud.com/alan-lord-4/05-colette-tougas-modesty
20. Hear *Wild Horses* at: https://soundcloud.com/alan-lord-4/06-open-mouth-wild-horses

Then it was on to the musical part of the show, which included their sacrilegious *Jésus* [21]:

> Jesus, he's dead, and Jesus he's alive,
> Jesus, the wives and the daughters and the children's dead
> Jesus the blood, the blood that pours from the children of
>   the dead
> Jesus is quiet, Jesus is sleeping
> Jesus, he's strong, yes Jesus is powerful
> Jesus is for industry and the government
> Jesus, his plan is to make us productive at work
> An eye on us and another on our output

JM Mignault was their digital percussionist, and I joined them on guitar to play the jazz chords of our old Electro-Luxe song *The Wrong Way*, this time with Josée's sexy honeydripping voice …

⇁ Then in no particular order, Canada's top established adventurous poets Bill Bissett, Chris Dewdney, Steve McCaffery, B.P. Nichol, Owen Sound … and I'm still skipping *a lot* of people here …

As for myself, I sang four song-poems—including *Ignoring The Future Today* [22]—and finally, *Too Much Money*—atop electronic music tapes prepared by Bonspiel, with accompanying computer graphics videos done by Boris.

Denis Vanier and Josée Yvon could dispense with all those multimedia bells and whistles—just like a teetering blotto Brian Jones, they were rock stars, no matter how wasted. Josée came on as a surprisingly lightly stoned poet queen, in a lovely pink strap top and jeans, and read a disjointed text too difficult to translate. Then as Vanier was reading, a female fan in the audience started heckling him. He said: "Are you coming up? You coming up or you're scared? (meaning, to read in his place)." The woman came up, Vanier offered her his tome, and she

---

21. Hear it at: https://soundcloud.com/alan-lord-4/12-boys-du-severe-jesus
22. Hear it at: https://soundcloud.com/alan-lord-4/04-alan-lord-ignoring-the

brushed him off with: "I don't need the book." She finished the poem from memory, to great applause. Vanier came back to the microphone and thanked "Marie".

Another surprise was in store. On the last evening an English bloke called Ted Milton walked in off the street and told me he was a poet. So before Lotringer came on after Jirgens, I shoved him onstage. He told us all about "the chauffeur of my limousine waiting for orders to go to Harrods—or to the Duke of Beaufort's estate—to dig his body up again and send his head to Princess Anne as a Christmas present."

乙 Ultimately, it was Jack Five who gave the most memorable perform-ance of the festival. Young Jack had smouldering good looks and never lacked in hot girlfriends. *"Le beau Jack"*[23] the gals used to swoon—*they wanted to have his babies*—and one of them actually *did*. He looked a lot like Welsh actor Ioan Gruffudd in *Horatio Hornblower*. Jack was the black sheep of his family, headed by a top Bank of Montreal execu-tive. He grew up in the wealthy enclave of Mont St. Bruno and was a star football athlete in high school. At age 20 he sailed on the 100-foot-long three-mast French schooner *Le Bel Espoir*[24], retracing explorer Jacques Cartier's voyage of discovery up the Gulf of Saint Lawrence, in what he named *Canada*. Jack then played bass for Roro d'Haïti—the big music star of Montreal's Haitian community—after which he gravi-tated towards Monty Cantsin's orbit, playing bass in his First Aid Brigade.

For his performance—called *Poésie guerrière*[25]—Jack read a few texts, then smashed a mirror, invoking "seven years of bad luck!" He then stripped down to the waist, thus revealing the war paint on his body. He started dancing, prancing and swaying in abandon like a wild man, and soon a regiment of a half-dozen drummers joined him on-stage, one by one—a Post Punk marching band—martially rat-tatting their snares. Jack was feline and menacing, irresistibly magnetic. This was poetry beyond words, like Alex nodding you his glass of *Moloko*

---

23. Transl: Gorgeous Jack
24. Pronounced "Luh Bell Ess-p'wah"; Transl: *The Beautiful Hope*
25. Pronounced "Poh-eh-zee Geh-ree-air"; Transl: *Warrior Poetry*

Plus in *A Clockwork Orange*. When we watch Jack's clip we feel the shock of realizing his performance anticipates by some 35 years that of Joaquin Phoenix dancing down the stairs in *Joker*[26].

↗ The festival climax on the last night was of course our big star John Giorno and his band. He looked real sharp in a white jacket, like a postmodern Tony Bennett. He gave us his classic gems such as *(Last Night) I Gambled With My Anger And Lost*[27], and *Scum and Slime*:

> "Optimism, trust, fearless authority, and disaster ... eating filth and transforming it, with white intentions, into black compassion ... I want to be filthy and anonymous ... scum and slime!" ...

... and *Stretching It Wider*:

> "Some things that work in one decade don't work in the next ... It is so hopeless, you can't begin to imagine ... If there's one thing you can't do is make this world a better place ... I'm spendin' my whole life bein' with people I don't wanna be with ... The only difference between me and a preacher is he's tellin' ya you have a way out, and I'm tellin' ya don't bother, for you there is no way out—besides, they blocked permanently all the exits ... you and I gets to stay here forever, and it gets worse beyond your imagination ..."

Then last on the festival bill—and closing off the proceedings—was our beloved Beat grandpa Herbert Huncke, reading his intimate, poignant stories—not by a cozy fireplace, but to the glow of dulled video screens and the LED lights of the mixing board.

I introduced Huncke, and he led off by saying: "I really want to start off with one particular story here, because I feel that it will fit into

---

26. See it at: https://www.youtube.com/watch?v=dp5RbILEQpc&feature=youtu.be

27. See and hear it here: https://vimeo.com/553330473

the general theme of the festival ... a group of creative people, young people trying to do things, it's very very encouraging for an old man like me[28] ... I want to think that things have progressed a little ..."

Huncke read the heart-rending prison stories *Cuba* and *Alvarez* from his book *The Evening Sun Turned Crimson*, then *Russian Blackie*, which was set in Huncke's eternal 42nd Street—where in the Forties he reigned as unanointed King of Forty Deuce.

And thus the festival ended, in a long outpouring of warm applause—for one of my favourite human beings of all time.

☡ In all, Ultimatum featured 54 poet/writers and 42 musicians, artists and technicians, and the total attendance was about 2000 people. It was covered by local TV and radio, plus Montreal and Vancouver's major dailies, as well as arts magazines. The festival was entirely recorded on audio tape and filmed on 3/4" video—all of the audio is still available, but the only videos to have survived are the readings and performances in French, and a few band clips, including John Giorno[29].

☡ The festival was a glorious snapshot of the overwhelming creativity and vitality that reigned in mid-Eighties Montreal, and I finally succeeded in proving my point. It was a success both artistically and financially—that is, everyone got paid, and we broke even.

I decided to celebrate by taking a trip to New York with Joss. We visited John Giorno, who lived atop the Burroughs Bunker at 222 Bowery. I told him it happened to be Joss' birthday. He got up and went into another room, then came back with a gift for her: a beautiful ring with an inlaid turquoise stone wrapped in gracious art-deco swirls of silver.

Walking around Soho at the end of the afternoon, we managed to squeak into the Leo Castelli gallery at closing time. Joss and I were there all alone, in front of an immense painting that took up a whole wall. It consisted of huge strips of bacon floating in space, with at the

28. He was 70 at the time
29. Concordia University digitized the archives in 2019: https://ultimatum. spokenweb.ca/

tip of a rotating horizontal mechanical shaft, the head of a red-lipped woman that was shredding into shards of electronic … *something*.

We saw Leo Castelli duck into an office at the end of the hall, and then a beaming, ecstatic James Rosenquist came striding toward us across the empty reverberating gallery, waving a bottle of champagne and a couple of glasses. "Here," he said laughing, "have some of this!" And he poured us each a tall flute of the bubbly. We were both stunned and delighted. He was my great Pop Art hero—even more so than Warhol. "We just sold the painting to American Airlines for $100,000[30]," he said. "They're gonna hang it in the lobby of their headquarters."

At the time, *that* was a mind-boggling amount of money for a new painting by a contemporary artist. I later found out the painting was a 46-foot-wide, 17-foot-tall work titled *Star Thief.* In 1997, it sold for $2 million, and now hangs in the Ludwig Museum in Cologne, Germany.

ζ The rest of the year was pretty uneventful, but I'm sure it involved several times of me jumping into a cab at 2 AM to prevent Mario from committing suicide. When not busy saving Mario, I sifted through the festival material in view of doing a documentary book for Guernica Editions. In the end, nothing came of it. I did manage however to put together an *Ultimatum* documentary vinyl LP, featuring Giorno and the best music performances of the festival. It was put out by Randy Boyd and Dan Webster's Psyche Industry Records the following spring, in a numbered, limited, hand-silkscreened jacket done by David Sapin. Giorno called and asked if I could send him footage of his performance. I did, and he synced up the video clip to match a previously recorded track destined for his next Giorno Video Pak.

Joss and I moved into a ground-floor apartment on Papineau street, between Mount Royal and Gilford. Our neighbour was a nice mustached gay dude who was never there. He worked up north in the James Bay hydro dam complex, and left me the keys to his sturdy brown Volvo.

One of the first guests at my new place was a local poet wannabe— we'll call him *Anarprick*—for reasons you'll see later. He dropped in to ask me—quite literally—how to become a poet. I was so embarrassed,

---

30. $250,000 today

I was speechless. I proffered him some perfunctory advice to get him on his way, and out of mine. The earnest "anarchist" wound up following his own fuse, which led him into wince-inducing heavy-handed predictable anti-you-name-it diatribes, entirely shorn of the least redeeming poetic grace. Sadly, this was to become the expected norm among the tedious Anglo Montreal Spoken Turd cabal in the Nineties.

I also had my job at LGL, which kept me fairly busy. The big boss at LGL was this crusty old Italian bastard who'd been a Fascist in Italy, or at least a strong sympathizer. Hearing the name of Mussolini still gave him a hard-on. So let's call that scumbag *Il Duce*. During a company Christmas dinner, one of the draftsmen—a tall, slim, bearded Italian named Carmello—got up, raised a glass of wine, and bellowed the Communist anthem *Avanti Popolo* to his face. Il Duce did his best to appear as delighted as we were.

I finally got to design my first building alone from the foundations up: The *Maison des vins*[31]—now the Roche-Bobois[32] furniture store— in downtown Montreal, corner Aylmer and President Kennedy. It's the glass curtain-walled red and green building with the pointy pyramid at the corner. The architect didn't want any cross-bracing to spoil the view in the bay windows, so I had to design rigid steel "moment" frames north-south and east-west. This is like having a heavy roof on stilts, so it's a bitch to limit the sway during earthquakes. My building was next to an existing one, so I had to beef up my frame column and beam sizes to stiffen it up so as not to batter into it during quakes. This took dozens of computer analysis runs to achieve, and I worked late at night. Il Duce barked: "You're spending too much time on that computer!"— that paleofascist jackass thought I was playing video games! He had no clue computers had become the engineer's main design tool. Il Duce's true fascist leanings were concretely revealed to me when he laid me off for "lack of work"—*twice*. He just couldn't bring himself to tide me over the couple weeks he didn't have clients to bill.

In October, Jack Five invited me to share the bill with him at a performance he'd been invited to—a *Festival of The Arts* thing at the

---

31. Pronounced "Meh-zo deh veh"; Transl: House of Wines
32. Prounounced "Rush Bo-b'wah"

Saw Gallery in Ottawa. As part of his performance, Jack showed his hilarious video *Beat The Clown*—and *Maria Pussy*, in which a sexy nun shaves her legs.

In *Beat The Clown*, a pitiful-looking clown (played by Michel Lefebvre) sits down to enjoy his cup of coffee in a café, when he's assaulted by a tough guy for no reason (played by André Trottier)[33]. He then exits, stumbles around the sidewalk, bumps into a skinhead in white T-shirt and suspenders, and again gets brutally knocked around. Trivia question: In which future blockbuster movie do we get to see a clown get beaten up?

For my performance I raged against the machine with my poem *Hostilities*, wearing a Palestinian Kaffiyeh and leather jacket plus shades, with unshaved stubble. At the time, terrorist freak was still chic, and stubble was for bums. The audience consisted of "bridge and tunnel" shlubs, except there are no bridges or tunnels in Ottawa—only horrible braindead suburbs like Nepean and Kanata. They just stood there looking at me with blank expressions. What was I assaulting these poor folks for? They were just waiting for their *Tulip Festival* each spring. After my performance I didn't explode any vest bomb—I turned to walk away from the sound of crickets.

A twelve-year-old boy came up to me all excited and shook my hand vigorously, thanking me profusely for what I'd just done. Who knows, maybe I inspired a future lil' Burroughs there. But that was the end of my half-hearted attempt at doing Spoken Word. Not my cup of tea.

⇘ That fall, Huncke called me out of the blue, going: "Listen Alan, can you spot me fifty bucks? I'm in a bad way right now and I'd really appreciate it if you could." I said: "Sure Herbert, I'm glad to help you out" and mailed him off a banker's cheque for $50. It happened another time, and again I obliged. When he called a third time I explained, "Listen Herbert, I'm just a working stiff. I'm no moneybags, I can't do this all the time." With the "easy" festival money I was getting, he was probably under the impression I was some rich trustafarian kid—like

33. See the *Beat The Clown* video here: https://www.youtube.com/watch?v=-AY13Fl-ThM

they had plenty of in Manhattan—who slummed around the demi-monde for kicks.

In November, I was asked to read a poem for some radio program and didn't feel like it. So I programmed my Apple IIe to read my poem *Cyclone*, using a software called SAM, which allowed you to build phrases by stringing together vowel and consonant sounds. Quebec countercultural fixture Alain-Arthur Painchaud[34] also invited me to read at his *Plein La Gueule*[35] event at his *L'Attaque* gallery. I read a poem called *Post-Entertainment Blues*. All in all, the year 1985 was a good year for us all. I was finally satisfied, I had pretty much exorcised my demons, and should have left it at that.

---

34. Pronounced "Pay show"; Transl: Hot Bread
35. Transl: Fed up

14
THE WIND FROM MOUNT SCHÄRR

After 1985's Christmas day, Jack and Bonspiel invited me to jam with them and JM on New Year's Day. Uh oh. I suspected it was a trap. They wanted to lure me into forming yet another god-damn band. "Okay," I told myself, "it's just a jam—no harm here. And anyway, what else is there to do on New Year's Day?" So off I went to JM's pad in Old Montreal, where we smoked joints, drank a few beers, and jammed. It was fun, so we continued doing this regularly. It was like our social club, our Bowling Night.

We'd get smashed on hash and beer and listen to Bruno Tanguay's[1] twin *Attaboy* cassettes, issued under the name *Les Biberons Bâtis*[2]. We were hooked on those tapes, and it was all we wanted to hear. To this day those two cassettes are the best thing that was ever done in Quebec. It also egged us on to do songs in French, as Bonspiel had been doing for awhile.

I de-tuned a string on my guitar. Jack started a groove on the bass. I twanged out two dissonant notes. Bonspiel jumped in: "Woke up this morning, my welfare cheque hadn't arrived. So I bought myself some cans of Doggie Dinner at the dépanneur."

We had a first song! It was *Pas d'chance*[3]. Other songs came quick-ly, both in French and English: *Surfin' Suicide, Jump Off A Building,*

---

1. Pronounced "Tunh-gay"
2. Pronounced "leh Bee-bro Bah-tsee"; Transl: *He-man Baby Bottles*
3. Pronounced "Pud shass"; Transl: *No Luck*

Problèmes Sexuels[4], *Béesse*[5] and my all-time favourite *I Need A Rug Cleaner.*[6]

By the time JM, Jack and I had banged out the music of a new song, Bonspiel already had his lyrics wrapped up. The bastard came up with lyrics on the spot! I never saw that ever before or since. Sorry folks, but that's pure genius at work here.

⊰ So I wound up in a band after all. But *this* time it was a *great* one. Coming up with band names was my specialty. I brought a whole list at rehearsal. Of course, my favourite was the most absurd one of all— *Vendu Mon Char*[7]. I didn't say anything. I was banking on them discovering it on their own. As I went down my list rattling off the names, JM nodded with a wry smile at that one, as if to say "that's the winner". The others agreed. Our band now had a name.

A few weeks later during rehearsal I grabbed a piece of paper and said "watch this!"—and wrote out *Vent du Mont Schärr*. Phonetically, it read "sold my car", but the words spelled out *Wind From Mount Schärr*. The boys were delighted. For our first gig we played at the launch of the *Ultimatum* documentary LP at the Foufounes Électriques, on March 21st[8]. We only had four songs played timidly, but already there were a few thrilled hoots from the small but knowing audience.

⊰ I did some of my best writing on the job at LGL, and in the spring came my first serious attempt at writing in French: a book of poetry called *États Limites*[9]. The first section—called *Ultra-Fast Texts*—was composed in a frenetic blur of automatic writing, after reading André Breton and Philippe Soupault's *Les Champs Magnétiques*[10]. It was also

---

4. Transl: Sexual Problems

5. Pronounced "Beh-ess"; Transl: *Welfare Goddess*

6. See Appendix A—Selected Texts for sample song lyrics; search "Vent du Mont Schärr" on Youtube for clips

7. Pronounced "Vuh do mo' sharr" ; Transl: Sold My Car

8. See the record launch videos in Appendix B—Video Links—Ultimatum

9. Pronounced "Eh-tah Lee-meet"; Transl: *Limit States*—an expression found in the engineering profession

10. Pronounced "Lay Shawn Man-yay-teek"

influenced by French cultural theorist, urbanist, and aesthetic philosopher Paul Virilio's tomes *Speed And Politics* and *Pure War*, as translated and published in Lotringer's *Foreign Agents* series. I was told that with its use of techno-military jargon, my book read as a chilling premonition of the Gulf War and 9/11 (a poem called *Toxin Twins* ... as in the toxic cloud of the collapsed Twin Towers).

By now Boris Wanowitch insisted on being called by his original name Pierre Zovilé, and convinced his father to open Montreal's first digital printing shop based on Apple's new MacIntosh computer. They called their shop MacGregor. I thought this MacIntosh system was a brilliant platform to put together my *États Limites* book. So I gave the commission to Zovilé, and he did the digital graphics paste-ups using the new PageMaker software, with scanner. *États Limites* was probably one of the first integrated text/image poetry books done using the cutting-edge Mac desktop publishing technology.

At MacGregor I also made the acquaintance of Jean Dubé[11], who was visibly the only employee the Zovilés had. Along with brainiac software developer Alain Bergeron, Dubé was also member of the SCP—*Société de Conservation du Présent*[12]—a quirky sort of conceptual art trio that fused visual art, technology and "the archiving principle". Among other activities, their habit was to stamp a number on any document or artefact coming their way, thus "archiving" it. Together they made a pilgrimage to the Philadelphia Museum of Art, which houses Marcel Duchamp's main body of work. They had the gall to affix a red COPY stamp on Duchamp's *Large Glass*. Museum officials subsequently scrubbed it off, but Bergeron says a bit of a red smudge can still be seen.

The SCP were often funny, always tongue-in-cheek, and occasionally pretentious. Their theorist was the late Philippe Côté[13]—a walking encyclopedia. When you first met him, in conversation he appeared brilliant, but as he started jumping from one subject to another willy-nilly, you soon realized he was a bit off. He created dazzling works of art: business-card-sized text and image collages, laminated in clear plastic[14].

---

11. Pronounced "Juhn Dew-bay"
12. Transl: Society For The Conservation Of The Present
13. Pronounced "Coh tay"
14. Several of these were reproduced in a book that came out on the SCP in 2013

Dubé was a pioneer of desktop publishing, and also the SCP's digital artist. Jack said Dubé was actually a Neoist wannabe who'd arrived a bit too late. But he had already exhibited his anti-conformist tendencies while still in high school, joining a group of kids with "negative attitudes" that called themselves *Les Électrons*, natch. As if there weren't enough Funny Guys already in our midst, Dubé came along to top them all.

Dubé could have been mistaken for a young John Larroquette. His standard uniform was a black shirt, black pants tucked into pulled-up black socks, shiny black shoes, and a long black overcoat draped over his shoulders, which he swished around like a cape. He was never without his black boxy businessman's briefcase, and would swing it ostentatiously back and forth as he walked with the exaggerated strides of a runway model, as if that extra lurch could propel him with extra momentum. He had this funny little laugh that went *"crik crik crik"*, which in stretches of deep chortling became *"crok crok crok"*, accompanied with big eyes. Some insisted he was pretentious, but I saw him more as an irrepressible eccentric, whether it was an affected pose or not. When wishwilling to reinvent yourself, you become the very person you want to be. One of his pet concepts was *Promess Art*[15]. And in any situation, at the drop of a hat he'd blurt out his mantra *"On veut de l'art!"*[16]

Of course we became fast friends.

⤳ A large part of LGL's engineering staff was moved into a building downtown on Stanley Street, and I didn't have a closed office anymore in which I could write in peace. The building belonged to Monenco, and we were now in the Monenco-LGL consortium to build a sprawling magnesium production complex near the town of Bécancour, just across the St. Lawrence River near the town of Trois-Rivières. The client was Norway's Norsk Hydro, and to entice them to build a plant there and thus create jobs, the Quebec government supplied them with electricity free of charge, whoopee. Now I was just another anonymous

---

15. The Art of The Promise
16. Pronounced "Oh veuh de Larr"; Transl: *We want art!*

microserf in a cubicle, on a whole floor of cubicles. Only the higher-ups had closed offices.

For the rest of the year our job was Phase I of the project: do the preliminary design of the industrial buildings, in order to perform the cost estimate for Phase II, which was to build the whole damn schmeer the following year. I spent many months of my time designing a thousand-foot Chlorination Plant, which was one step in the processing chain to produce magnesium.

We were under the direction of Armin, who was the coolest boss you could ever want. Sometimes for lunch he walked us down the street to Chez Parée, an upscale stripper joint that served a free buffet to the discerning gentleman willing to pay triple price for his beer. The hornier nerds could have themselves a lap dance for dessert.

≥ Anarprick invited me to do a reading at an "Anarchist" soirée he'd organized in a hall on St. Urbain Street. I was amazed to realize it was the same hall I'd done my first paintings as a kid in kindergarten. I brought along my VDMS boys and we sulked drinking beer in an adjoining room, because the acts were so dreadful. As all Anachronists, they were still going on about Sacco and Vanzetti and the Haymarket Massacre of 1886. Unknowingly, we were witnessing the birth of joyless pathetically correct wokism, which was destined to stifle free un-self-censored expression forever.

When it was my turn I hopped onstage and quickly went through my poem. After the show I was asked a lot of questions by a thin middle-aged man wearing a mustache. He definitely didn't fit in the crowd. He asked me about the part in my poem where "American soldiers would get killed." I explained it was only a poetic device, not to be taken literally. It later dawned on me this guy must have been a CSIS[17] agent. He was there to investigate what these scary "anarchists" were up to. So you can be damn sure there's a file on me somewhere in that $1.2 billion CSIS building in Ottawa.

---

17. The Canadian Security Intelligence Service

⋝ Dave Sapin's artist friend Jacques Boyer discovered a complex of wooden barn-like shacks tucked away in a lane in back of the McDonald's at the corner of Papineau and Mount Royal, and Dave moved in, along with his new art partner in crime Christian Dion. Dave christened the place *The Shred*. And now he called his paintings *Shred Art*. Here's an example of his Shred Art: one day Dave told me to come over and see his "computer art". It was a bunch of floppy disks glued to a canvas that he blowtorched into a charred mess, then splattered with paint. Dave loved fire so much, he became a pyromaniac. One night the police picked him up drunk, with packets of matches falling from his pockets—close to a burning building near the Foufs. He spent some time under psychiatric observation. It wasn't the first time.

⋝ That summer, after being together for twelve years, Joss walked out on me. I'll spare you—and myself—the sobs and rancorous details. But as you'll see, in the end she did me a favour. My father consoled me, saying: "You can lose the best woman in the world, you've gained something invaluable—*your freedom*." But I suspect she may have taken advantage of the breakup turmoil to rip up my precious pictures of me with the Ramones and chuck them in the trashcan. In compensation, she *did* leave me a great gift: the first *real* song I wrote in my life. It was called *Shirley*[18]. It was a real song because it was about real things—our breakup—albeit painted in the usual farcical tongue-in-cheek VDMS style. In the song I claimed getting ownership of the stove, whereas in reality *she* was the one who eloped with it.

I showed the song to the boys during a weekend rehearsal at JM's parents' house in Laval, and Bonspiel added a few choice lines to the lyrics. It soon became a fan favourite and a show staple.

⋝ With my freshly minted bachelor's freedom, I started hanging out regularly with Campo at Le Castel Rosalie—his welfare apartment building. We wore the grooves out on his Blue Cheer albums, Cream's *Disraeli Gears*, and he liked to blast the Pistols' *Bodies*, scaring the

---

18. Hear it at: https://www.youtube.com/watch?v=gTFPGkJk484

neighbours at 2 AM. The other "customers" of the Castel Rosalie opened their doors and yelled at us.

One day he picked up the guitar I'd given him and started singing: "She shows off her thighs in clubs … her head's shaved and she lives with her dad … her name is Sophie … *Sophie Stiquée*"[19]. I ran off with that, Bonspiel and I completed the lyrics, adding that our fictional punk socialite was shaving a mohawk on her pussy when she learned Warhol had just died. I came up with an irresistible surf twang for the song, and it quickly became an instant VDMS classic. It's been listed since in the top 150 French-language songs in Canada. Soon after, while we were discussing our deplorable conservative Canadian prime minister, Mario blurted: "Hey Mulroney, ton pays est mal runné"[20]—bang! A *second* Campo-inspired song for us.

↗ I also dropped in on Josée Yvon and Denis Vanier more frequently. They now lived on Ontario street East of Papineau, right across from a tattoo parlor, which explained their ever-decreasing patch of pink skin. Josée always had a stack of library books on the table in front of her, that she'd either borrowed or had to return.

On a sunny Sunday afternoon, I unwittingly walked right into the middle of a marital squabble. Josée had shut herself up in the bedroom, and Denis was hammering at the door with his fist, yelling at her to open the door.

"You fucking bastard," she whimpered through her sobs, "you threw two TV's in my face … not one … *TWO* TV's, you goddamn fucker …"

"Aw, *come on* Josée," the hubby from hell wooed his crazed virgin, spluttering red-faced drunk, brushing back a long lock of greasy hair behind his ear, "gimme twenny bucks for the dépanneur, crisse … *we're outta beer!*"

---

19. Transl: Sophie Stickated; hear it at: https://www.youtube.com/watch?v=6_D_GOD9LRE

20. Transl: "Hey Mulroney, your country's badly run"; see it at: https://www.youtube.com/watch?v=wXdM1gi2ymY

A visit to Josée and Denis' place was often not too relaxing—*this* doomed infernal poet couple were *our* Rimbaud & Verlaine. Once when I was there, Jerry, a lowlife buddy fresh out of prison, dropped by. It was winter, but he was wearing sneakers and gray cotton sweat-pants—the standard uniform of guys who'd done time. He had a big Doberman with him pacing the room nervously, at the end of a jangling chain leash his master kept tugging at with difficulty to rein in the dog.

"Johnny's been looking for you," Denis said to him. "He said he'd fix yer clock once you were outta jail."

"Oh yeah?" Jerry picked up the phone and punched the keys furiously.

"Johnny? Hi, it's Jerry. I'm at Denis' place. Apparently yer lookin' for me? Yeah? Okay then, come on down buddy, I'm not budging from here … don't worry, I ain't carryin'—I only got my lil' Doberman—he won't bite you … c'mon you cocksucker, I'll be waitin' for you …"

I'd been eyeing the door, wondering whether I shouldn't just scram the hell out of there. Finally, "Jerry" left, much to my relief.

Denis rarely left the house, and never dropped in on friends. So it was a very special occasion indeed when he came to my place on Papineau with Josée. I had a few videos I wanted to show them. We'd already started drinking at their place, so I drove carefully all the way over on the short trip. We sat down to watch the videos.

Suddenly I remembered. "Fuck! The two-four!" I'd left the case of beer I'd bought on the sidewalk next to the car. I ran out and of course it was gone. So I went to the corner dep and bought another one. Denis' favourite video was a real hot clip of Lou Reed doing *The Original Wrapper* and *I Love You Suzanne* on SNL, howling solos and all. When it was over he yelled: "Play it again!" We did this at least half a dozen more times until he was satisfied. It must've brought back his old Peace Eye Bookstore days in New York.

Josée, Denis, and I had a cultural exchange program going on. Denis turned me on to the Holy Modal Rounders, Josée gave me a steamy book on Lesbian S&M sex called *Coming To Power*, and I gave them the *Biberon Bâtis* tapes *Attaboy on Souffre* and *Attaboy on Agonise* —our VDMS staple listening.

Josée and Denis spent their summers in a trashy camping site in

Chertsey, blasting the *Biberon Bâtis* tapes out the window of their rented mobile home, 24/7. They terrorized their neighbour Dino Bravo, who used to be a Saturday morning TV wrestling star, along with Gino Brito. Now he was the camping grounds' hash dealer. "Cut it out!" he kept yelling at them, to no avail.

Judging by Vanier's demeanour and behaviour, one would guess his favourite poet to be a transgressive Rimbaud or shambolic Bukowski. But no. I was quite shocked when he confessed it was the thoroughly serene and respectable Saint-John Perse—whose soaring poems featured nature and its elements, and were refreshingly devoid of any embarrassing, quarrelsome humans.

❦ A lot of things happened in July. Louis Côté was part of the triumvirate that owned the Foufounes. Impressed by the turnout for Ultimatum, he asked me to stage poetry and other happenings on Tuesday nights, which was their slow night. I thought about it for a few seconds and said "sure!" And thus were born the *Mardis d'Ultimatum*[21] series that fall.

I also got a call from Ira Silverberg, who meanwhile had become Burroughs' publicist in New York. He asked whether I'd be interested in organizing a reading for Kathy Acker in the fall—Grove Press had set up a book tour to promote her latest novel *Don Quixote*. I agreed immediately, adding that it would fit in perfectly with my planned series of Ultimatum Tuesdays at the Foufs. He sent me her press kit, along with the galleys of *Don Quixote*, and also a copy of her novel *Blood And Guts In High School*.

❦ Then Il Duce sent me on a crappy assignment in Port Cartier, which is on the north-east coast of the Saint Lawrence River—the end of the world as far as I was concerned. My mission was to analyze trusses supporting several conveyor belts carrying iron ore in an industrial building and propose fixes on the spot. The client was Sidbec. On the way there from the tiny airport nearby I stopped the rented car to gawk at a jumble of twisted and frayed steel girders at the bottom of a ravine. A bridge

---

21. Transl: *Ultimatum Tuesdays*

had recently collapsed while being built, under the weight of just one vibrating steamroller—with some poor schmuck behind the wheel. Another grim reminder that if I made a mistake in my profession, people died.

I spent a whole week in Port Cartier, and my revenge for this forced exile was to treat myself to sumptuous surf n' turfs washed down with dry martinis, followed by a bottle of wine. It wasn't allowed on expense accounts, but I made sure Il Duce swallowed my boondock hardship extortion.

I whiled away the evenings in my motel room reading Kathy's *Blood And Guts In High School*, and readily identified with her raw description of feeling devastated by the breakup of a relationship. *I felt exactly like Janey.*

I also played the first rudimentary version of Microsoft's *Flight Simulator* on the tiny 9-inch green screen of the portable Compaq computer I'd brought along for my work. It was bigger than a briefcase—laptops were still years away. In the game I flew over "Manhattan", which was only a flat green expanse, with the World Trade Center's twin towers at the pointy end of the island. I had fun flying the jet between the towers, but when I got bored of the game I decided to go up to Central Park and turn back. I gunned the jet southward at full speed and slammed into the North Tower. Yup, I was unknowingly rehearsing Mohamed Atta's fateful flight fifteen years later.

≥ Canadian artist Tom Sherman of the Canada Arts Council kept calling, pestering me to apply for a grant for another festival. It was the furthest thing in my mind. But at a certain point I caved and did so. Reluctantly. And that fall I was given $30,000 for a follow-up festival[22]. So I got what I wasn't even wishing for: enough rope to hang myself.

My book of poetry *États Limites* was finally launched at the café Place Aux Poètes, at the invitation of poetess Janou Saint-Denis, who ran the place. I read the book in its entirety, accompanied by tapes, and instigated a raucous brouhaha with the help of Bonspiel, Jack Five, Anonyme Sanregret, Michel Lefebvre, Dubé and his SCP boys.

---

22. $70,000 today

While I was reading my texts, Alain Bergeron read off the instructions for one of his programs in Assembly Language, while Philippe Côté and Jean Dubé stamped all the sheets I'd read with an archive number. At the same time Bonspiel shouted "Vente! Vente! Vente!"[23] while Jack gutted a watermelon in an SPCA cardboard box.

At a certain point Janou had enough of the chaos and shut the lights off yelling at us, and as she tried to stop the show, the SCP turned on a slide projector to allow me to finish reading the texts. After that we left, with Bonspiel and Janou insulting each other pretty violently.

Somewhere along the evening's proceedings I also approached a melon placed on a stool and chopped it in half, clean as a head, using my trusty reproduction of El Cid's sword, bought in Spain when I was 13. Yes señor, eet was I, *El Cid Veecioous.*

⇒ By now we were well into the fall with my *Ultimatum Tuesdays* series at the Foufounes. My notes for September 23rd say: "Inauguration (acts unknown)" and I have no bloody clue what happened on that momentous evening. The following week it was the band Severed Heads from Australia, on the last day of September.

October was a busy month, with the *Ultimatum Tuesdays* kicked off by a quadruple bill consisting of Vancouver's reigning underground poetess Judy Radul, and bands Out Out Damned Spot, Psychotic Aries, and The Whooping Cranes from Atlanta. Then the following week it was the bands Sensitive Organs, featuring my old pal Zilon, and Forbidden Fame, featuring artist Joy Lou G, an exile from the Canadian Maritimes, now established as a painter in Montreal. The big headliner of the series was of course Kathy Acker, coming up in early November.

⇒ By now VDMS had a substantial eyebrow-raising repertoire, and we entered Radio Canada's *Rock Envol*[24] battle of the bands contest, which offered the winner money towards making a record.

There were three elimination rounds to the contest, and the jury couldn't fail to notice that for each of our appearances we came up with

---

23. Transl: "Sale! Sale! Sale!"
24. Transl: *Rock In Flight*

brand new songs and stage presentations. We were assisted by our buddies in the SCP—who put up our song lyrics on computer screens, and
Dave Sapin brought in a big fan blowing streamers at us from stage right
(the "wind"—get it?). For our last show we dressed up in suits and ties
and were flanked by candelabras. I played sitting cool on a stool, as if I
were in a jazzy lounge combo in a Hugh Hefner mansion party circa
1967. We even played *The Wrong Way*—an easy-listening toe-tapper
that contrasted with our usual shredding assault.

The jury didn't know what to make of us. This was not your
daddy's run of the mill Rock n' Roll. Needless to say, with our secret
weapon—frontman Bonspiel—stripping down to his skivvies, we demolished the competition, even though the final verdict handed down
was a tie with *Les Taches*[25]—a negligible rockabilly outfit that soon
faded into oblivion. Some in the jury—which included old-time blues
rocker Gerry Boulet of Offenbach—didn't appreciate our distinctly
sarcastic approach to their sacrosanct *Québec Rock*, and refused to hand
us the final victory which was obviously ours alone. Poor Gerry was
reduced to seeking a safe zone with his bloody *Taches*. A fine stain on
your reputation, Mr. Rocker.

≿ The French-language CBC Radio Canada TV network covered
Rock Envol extensively, and the news anchors shook their heads in disbelief, both at our name and stage antics[26]. When my parents saw us
on TV, I was a loser no more. It was the ultimate working-class consecration, the decisive proof of my worthiness. *Being on TV* was a concept
my parents could understand.

We were generating a genuine buzz throughout the media. We
started getting attention in the press, notably Montreal's *Village Voice*
type weekly *The Montreal Mirror*. In a landmark article, rock journo
Martin Siberok said:

"The legend is in the making. That's more than you can say
about a lot of bands kicking around town. Like a strong gust

---

25. Transl: *The Stains*
26. See it at: https://www.youtube.com/watch?v=ga2FJ1HmDJ8&t=67s

of wind, VDMS is having no trouble making its presence
felt. With only six live gigs to its name, this four-piece cannot
be dismissed as flavor of the month. This band is willing to
snarl, bite and even inflict damage with its forceful sound."

No one who ever saw us is likely to forget it. We ridiculed everything
and everyone under the sun, taking special delight in making short
work of self-righteous indignant wokesters, with songs like *Kill The
Whales.*

VDMS were revered locally like the Velvet Underground. We were
an ungodly mix of The Butthole Surfers meet The Sex Pistols meet The
Fugs, yet still incomparable to anything else, either before or since. We
were radically irreverent, pertinent and impertinent, and inspired many
a kid to pick up an instrument and start his own band. We were later
name-checked not only in a song by the band *French Bastards*, but also
in the Québec-dubbed *Simpsons*—the ultimate pop cultural consecration.

We were now the talk of the town, and as I was preparing to greet
Kathy Acker at the airport, I was flying high.

15
KATHY GOES TO MONTREAL

Kathy Acker's reading was set for Tuesday, November 4th at the Foufounes. I did a media blitz in advance and had print and TV interviews lined up. My neighbour was conveniently up north in James Bay again, so his Volvo was all mine.

I picked up Kathy and Ira at the airport on a Saturday afternoon, and brought them to the Hôtel du Parc—the hotel where I'd installed Huncke during Ultimatum. Along the way I explained to Kathy the intricacies of the ongoing English versus French duel in Quebec, as well as a brief history of the province, including the *Quiet Revolution* and the FLQ terrorist *October Crisis*. "It reminds me of Algeria," she said.

The first thing Kathy did in her hotel room was to take out books from her suitcase and line them up reverentially on the dresser. She had about half a dozen books she was currently reading simultaneously— obscure tomes on literary theory and criticism, and others by radical feminists. I was much impressed by that. I later learned from her writer-dominatrix friend Terence Sellers that Kathy was a bookworm—she had literally "read everything". Books lined every wall of her apartment, two rows deep. Terence said she once got a call from Kathy asking her to pack up all of her precious books and ship them off to Seattle— where she lived for six months in 1980[1].

Kathy was wearing the watch Ira bought her, and showed it to me. It was a double watch—two ovals joined together, with two pairs of clock hands. The hands on the left showed the time in New York, while

---

1. "900 boxes for your 72,000 books" (from the literary biography *After Kathy Acker* by Chris Kraus)

the other showed the time in London—her current home. It was a gift to celebrate the contract she'd just signed with Grove Press: $45,000 for three books[2]—which was a fortune at the time—more than my year's salary as an engineer. She explained "I live on a shoestring and have to write blurbs and book reviews all the time, accepting small gigs like that to survive."

I took Kathy and Ira to gay restaurateur Renet-Sens' bistro which was next to the Foufounes. Jack Five was the cook and prepared a steak for me, while Kathy had a seafood dish. While we were eating, Renet-Sens[3] put on Bowie's *Words On a Wing*, pulled up a chair next to our table, climbed on top of it and gave us an impromptu expressionistic mime performance to the music. His contorted face looked like something out of a Fritz Lang horror film. Kathy gazed at him in total silence with an awed expression, while I tried not to crack up. I wasn't sure whether she and Ira genuinely appreciated this, or secretly wanted to strangle me for subjecting them to an embarrassing spectacle.

Since it was Saturday, after dinner I had to take them out on the town. We started off with drinks at Peter's on Peel, and did a few lines from a bag of coke I'd thoughtfully bought in advance to entertain my sophisticated New York friends. Kathy didn't feel like clubbing that night, but Ira did. So I dropped him off at the hottest gay disco pickup spot at the time—KOX—on Montcalm above Viger.

Kathy and I went back to her hotel room, where we continued doing coke and yakked, sitting on the rug next to the bed. I ranted about all her great books and outrageous writing, and fueled by my coked-up enthusiasm I exulted: "You're the successor of William Burroughs!" She acted surprised, but I'm sure she already knew that. She said: "I use *concepts* in my writing." Then she startled me by declaring: "In the future, people will be too busy solving complex everyday problems to be creative."

⇋ I left at about 4 AM, and got home as the sky gave a hint of first light. I slipped into bed, cradling my head in my hands, and wondered

---

2. $110,000 today
3. Pronounced "Ruh-net Saunce"—obviously referring to the Renaissance

at the ceiling. I couldn't sleep. Not only because of the coke, but mainly the buzz of *having just hung out with Kathy Acker.*

The phone rang. I picked it up. It was Kathy. "What are you doing?" she asked.

"Uh… thinking about *you*," I replied timidly, adding " …. *You?*"

Kathy said: "Can you come over?"

I slipped out the door to the Volvo parked in back. My boots crunched on the thin layer of fluorescent blue snow being lit by the waking sky. I drove over in the dawn silence of streets, tiptoed through the hotel lobby, took the elevator, walked gingerly across the hallway and gently knocked on her door.

She greeted me wearing black panties and a sheer black see-thru nightshirt. She tenderly wrapped her arms around my neck, pulled me into the room and we started kissing passionately. We stumbled over to the bed still kissing and I started fucking her madly, every which way.

I yanked her around on top of me like a limp raggedy doll sprouting feverish puckered lips that looked like a raw red hemorrhoidal asshole. "You're a sex maniac!" she gasped. That was like Einstein calling you a genius. "I haven't fucked in four months!" I protested. "Me too!" she whined. I pumped her with my two-hour-long dong till the cows came. Flings go better with coke. I moved her onto the floor. I continued shagging her on the thick white shag carpet. Slooowly.

Dawn was lighting into day through the curtains. I was rocking her slowly back and forth on the rug. I looked at her with a naughty grin and asked: "Is there anything special you'd like me to do?"

She closed her eyes and gave me a wry wicked smile. "Hit me," she said. I froze. I was in a complete panic. I didn't know how to handle this. "Huh?" I stammered. "W-where …?"

"Anywhere …" she slurred.

I looked around and picked up one of her little booties. I whacked her lightly on the ass. "Is that ok?" I asked, not sure about what I was doing. "Harder!" she commanded. I started whacking at her ass repeatedly, harder and harder, making sure it was getting to a blotchy red. She moaned from the delicious pain, her face contorting in ecstasy like a Renaissance pièta. I was getting into it and she was already out of it.

≥ We were woken up late in the morning by Ira knocking at the door. He came in moaning about the equally satisfying night he'd had with a young doctor he'd picked up at KOX.

Kathy did a couple of interviews that Sunday. I remember nothing. That night I took Kathy to a popular gay club downtown called Le Garage, which had a room with the hoods and front grills of old fifties cars, against which you could lean. It was a Hallowe'en party night, and everyone was wearing wild outfits, especially the trannies.

We then hit the dance floor. I was horny. I grabbed Kathy's hand and placed it on my stiff aching cock. She grabbed it through my pants and led me through the crowd and out of the club, clutching it fiercely. We hurried back to the hotel, and once again I banged her pretty severely.

The following morning we were two happy mollusks nuzzling together in a deep armchair in the lobby, moaning eyes closed. It felt good like when I was on heroin. Love is the drug. Aching tired and groggy from too much sex, we cuddled in deep satisfaction, once in a while turning to each other to tongue-kiss. I kissed her head and slowly petted the cute stubble on the shaved sides of her head. Ira passed by and shook his head at the naughty kids. Kathy asked me if I wanted to go to Spain with her for Christmas. "Sure," I said. What's not to like?

That day I went nuts and ran around splurging hundreds of dollars on my hot new girlfriend, buying studded punk belts, wacky jewellery, bracelets and earrings. One was a big pair of rubber bats with wings outspread, ready to dangle off gothic earlobes.

It was the day before her reading, so she shooed me away. The gal was a professional, and she hit the gym and started psyching herself up for her performance the following day. No sex the night before an important gig! There were more interviews that day, and a Radio Canada TV spot filmed at the Foufounes, in which we both appear. She spoke in French. Sort of[4].

Her reading was at 11 PM on Tuesday. It was a great success and was videotaped by Jack[5]. As a dutiful impresario I counted the attendees in the crowd. There were about a hundred people in the audience.

---

4. See it at: https://www.youtube.com/watch?v=fYn8lh86ILg&t=34s
5. See Appendix B—Video Links—Ultimatum Tuesdays

The following day I took the plane back to New York with Kathy and Ira. She was doing her New York reading on Thursday. Ira insisted on hiring a stretch limo for the ride into Manhattan. Of course, as a modest Canadian, I was shocked. Well, when in Rome, try to pass off as a Noo Yawker.

Our destination was the Gramercy Park Hotel on East 21st Street, which was a stately establishment back then, quite comfy and full of passé charm. An old porter recognized Kathy and greeted her with a "welcome back!" She unpacked and freshened herself up, then we went down through the lobby.

As soon as we stepped onto the sidewalk, we were greeted by the howling siren of an FDNY fire truck honking its hoarse horns at us GRONNK! GRONNK! GRONNK!—it swerved sharply around the corner and jumped onto the sidewalk curb, nearly knocking us down. "I love this town!" cackled a delighted Kathy, glad to be back from sleepy London town.

Not two blocks down Third Avenue we ran into none other than her old friend the writer Gary Indiana, whom she hadn't seen in years. They had a lot of catching up to do, and started chatting. Not only did she neglect to introduce me, she now chose to completely ignore my presence. I definitely got the hint my services were no longer required. "Ok Alan," she said unceremoniously, "thanks for everything. I'll be seeing you Thursday."

That was my subtle cue to fuck off. Boy, that was the fastest cold shower I ever got. My torrid four-day affair was over. There was not to be any follow-up "relationship". I'd only been her Montreal Night Stand. Fine. Trouble is you see, *I'd fallen in love* with Kathy. I wouldn't be spending Christmas with her in Spain. Not that I gave a shit about *that*.

I walked the streets randomly, in a hurt daze, a pit of sickness in my punched gut—exactly like one of her jilted characters. At such times, fabulous New York suddenly takes a cruel turn, and you feel real small and alone. Paris and New York can crush you like that. I was thinking, "Shit, it took Joss twelve years to ditch me. Kathy did it in *four days!*" I was heartbroken and forlorn. I'd only been the pirate king of her pussy for a day. Or two. Fucking out of your league is the biggest thrill. But what a brutal comedown.

⤺ I checked into the seedy Carlton Arms Hotel, because that's all I could afford. I inspected the toilet bowl and identified four different species of insects cavorting around the horseshoe lid. When a cockroach is your only friend, it don't get any lonelier.

At that time, when New York was out of social housing, they were parking welfare cases in crappy hotels. Like mine. In the lobby I had to wait until a big Black mama in hair curlers and fuzzy pink slippers was done gossiping on the pay phone. Her cute three-year-old daughter with pink bowed pigtails was playing with a rubber rat, stamping at it with her foot. *"Kiwwit! Kiwwit!"* yelled her mom in encouragement. You could count how many teeth were missing each time she opened her mouth.

After crying a bit and feeling sorry for myself, I sought some solace by downing a few Rolling Rocks and a comforting plate of Chicken Chimichangas, at my old haunt the Life Café, off Tomkins Square Park. Where I sat down to write an 8-page handwritten sob letter to Kathy. It was pathetic, not least of all because it was in bad imitation Kerouac.

Since I was in the neighbourhood, I decided to check out the famed Pyramid club at the other end of the park. As I entered, I was greeted by a chirpy blond dude in a billowy white Fifties chiffon dress, who immediately fell in love with me. He lunged forth welcoming me with arms outstretched, fluttering his heavily mascara'd eyelashes, gulping an excited "Hiiii!!!"

I brushed past and tried to melt in the crowd. What I really wanted was to melt away into a puddle on the floor like the Wicked Witch of The West. But mere wishes doth not make cosmic obliteration come true. A procession of tranny fairies wearing gossamer wings waved their magic fairy wands, as they snaked through the crowd holding hands. This was a fixture in New York clubs at the time.

I then wandered off to the Kit Kat Klub, where I was greeted by oiled musclemen in speedos striking beefcake poses atop pedestals. The place was strewn with beach balls and the cocktail waitresses paraded around in bikinis and high heels. I'd stumbled onto their *Beach Blanket*

Bingo themed nite. I yawned and left. It was high time I crawled back to the *BUGS!* theme night going on at my El Paradiso welfare hotel.

ᴢ Come Thursday I made it to artist Carl Apfelschnitt's loft on Hudson Street for Kathy's intimate reading, to which a select group of friends had been invited. Among other things, Carl was the one whose painting had served for the invitation card to William Burroughs' 70th birthday party at The Limelight.

I arrived early to help Ira with preparations, and as I got there the writer Dennis Cooper was leaving. Ira introduced us, and it was very awkward, because the grinning creep was blatantly *letching* at me. He offered me his limp deadfish hand and I had no choice but to shake it. It felt like someone had poured Jell-O into a medical glove and let it set in the fridge overnight.

The guests slowly shuffled in, and I got to meet a lot of local luminaries such as Darius James, Lynne Tillman, and other women writers I can't remember. The gaggle of gals convened aside in a room, and one of them complained she was sick of them always being the *hors d'oeuvres* garnishing Main Dish Kathy. The others grunted in eye-rolling assent.

Kathy read to the tiny gathering of select invitees in the glow of candles bathing the loft in a warm intimacy. Afterwards I got to have a drink and yak with the potential future recruits for my Ultimatum events. Darius told me he wanted to stage a play based on the work of a writer I just couldn't identify. He kept going on about a "Jhirdge butt-eye! Jhirdge butt-eye"—then it dawned on me—he was talking about *Georges Bataille*. I fear nothing ever came of this project.

In the days following the Acker reading, I pursued my talent scout safari throughout lower Manhattan, meeting up with the people I wanted. Darius gave me the contact for novelists Joel Rose and Catherine Texier, and I showed up at their residence on East 7th street. They ran a literary magazine called *Between C & D* out of their home, and throughout our discussion you could hear the grating *scritch scritch scritch* of the current issue being printed on those annoying old dot matrix printers.

Between C & D referred not only to the street names of the Lower

East Side's Alphabet City, but also meant "between coke and dope". The writings were just as tough as the mean streets the writers lived in. The magazine was printed on fanfold dot matrix computer paper, sold in a plastic bag and featured original artwork slipped inside. The magazine even made it to Montreal newsstands, and it is now seen as a precious icon of Eighties New York. Among the contributors were Kathy Acker, Cookie Mueller, Patrick McGrath, Lynne Tillman, Dennis Cooper and Gary Indiana.

Catherine Texier grew up in France, but wound up living in Montreal's *Plateau* neighbourhood for four years, befriending local musicians and writers such as Denise Boucher[6] and Yolande Villemaire —whose work she particularly loved. During a trip to New York she met Joel Rose, visited him in L.A. where he lived, after which he followed her back to Montreal. They lived on Rachel street from 1979 to 1981, and after the birth of their daughter Céline, decided to move to New York's Lower East Side.

↗ Next I went to visit Victor Bockris—poet and author of my cherished *With William Burroughs* book—who lived on Perry Street in Greenwich Village. He knew Terence Sellers—author of *The Correct Sadist*—the dominatrix writer I desperately wanted to recruit for my festival. Somehow the conversation turned to the French *Beat* collaborator Claude Pélieu—who'd been inundating me with tons of his awful collages mailed to me from France. Victor started pitching me the idea of paying him to do a book on Pélieu. *"Whoah,"* I was thinking, "wait a minute here Victor, I ain't no Saudi prince!"

I guess word was getting around fast that there was this foolish Canadian emissary with tons of government cash, easy to shake down for some arts funding. "Sure, I'm the Canadian Minister of Counterculture, a government-paid arts mogul, follow me down to the bank! What's your account number? I'll dump a load of dough into it. Is $100K enough for ya? Need any more?"

Before meeting Terence Sellers I bought her an expensive jade

---

6. Author of the famous play *Les fées ont soif* (Transl: The Fairies Are Thirsty)

bracelet in the shape of a serpent, with lavish trimmings in silver. What was I, insane? I couldn't afford this! I took her out to dinner, and she agreed to sign on to my *Crazy Boat to Ultimatum.*

I also dropped in on Giorno, and sobbed to him about my aborted tryst with Kathy. He became alarmed. "Careful," he warned, "she likes anal sex and gets gays to fuck her in the ass." Gulp. I hadn't used any condoms—*my specialty.* When broaching the subject of AIDS, I remember Kathy telling me: "My doctor told me to just stay away from the asshole." I didn't get it then, but that would explain why we hadn't *gone there* when I asked her if she wanted "anything special".

I told John I of course wanted to re-invite him to my next festival. He said: "This time I'll be coming up solo. No band. It's cheaper." I asked how much he wanted. He said: "I'll do it for $600"[7]. I balked. I said: "John, that's a lot, just for you alone!" He said: "Alan, this just covers basics—it's like *groceries.*" So I agreed, and it was settled. As I left, John gave me a copy of his book of poetry *Grasping At Emptiness.* He signed it: *"To Alan, more bang for the buck—Love, John."*

Ira suggested we go to a *gay sushi disco bar.* "Only in New York," thought I. We sat in a booth and ordered. As I glanced at the door, in came *Divine*, making a regal entrance as a distinguished portly man in a stylish grey suit and tie, with closely-cropped salt-and-pepper hair teasing a bald spot. He looked like a powerful attorney—like the one played by Glenn Fleshler in the TV series *Billions.*

Before leaving for Montreal I ran around Manhattan's bookstores and bought up Kathy's old books—including her rare TVRT books *The Black Tarantula* and *The Adult Life Of Toulouse Lautrec*—and had her sign them all. *Blood And Guts In High School* is signed: *"All my love and—well, it was wonderful, love again, Kathy."*

On the flight back I drowned my heart out in whiskey after whiskey. By the time I landed I was okay again.

I think.

---

7. $1400 today

16

ULTIMATUM TUESDAYS

Back in Montreal, I still had VDMS and my *Ultimatum Tuesdays* to keep my mind off Kathy Acker. First thing I did was to invite my lifetime musical collaborator and eternal pal the composer Bernard Gagnon to stage his masterwork *Un cycle laurentien*[1]. It was a complex tongue-in-cheek one-hour-plus opus celebrating Quebec's nordic wintry folklore, with an ensemble of acclaimed cutting-edge musicians. It was videotaped, and I'm happy to report it is now safely ensconced in McGill University's *Marvin Duchow Music Library*.

Meanwhile, Alain Bergeron of the SCP was working on a Mac-based software program called *La Calembredaine*[2], which produced poems randomly off any vocabulary that was input, following grammatical rules. He needed a French linguist to accomplish this, and through sound sculptor Philippe Bézy, found one in Myriam Cliche. When it was completed, the Calembredaine created completely astounding poems randomly, and grammatically correct to boot. The Surrealists would've creamed their pants. La Calembredaine was the ultimate tour de force in computer-generated literature, and made a mockery of crude cut-ups programs like mine. It was yet again further proof of the incomparable inventiveness of Montreal artists.

This groundbreaker was launched discreetly in December, to zero fanfare. Par for the course. Myriam called herself "Poutine", and she and Bergeron wound up living together and produced a wonderful son.

---

1. Transl: *A Laurentian Cycle*; see it at: https://vimeo.com/551939471
2. Pronounced "Lah Cah-lum-bread-den"; based on *Calembours*—French for "word play"

⤳ With the great wind that was blowing in its sails, VDMS was asked to host the New Year's Eve party at the Foufounes. It was our custom to spoil our fans, and we were always busting our asses (and meager incomes) to bring our shows a little something extra—a bit of theatrical magic, something out of the ordinary. This was not only meant to keep our *fans'* interest, but also *ours*: costumes, makeup, different themes and quirky gimmicks—to make each show a unique, one-time event you either witnessed or missed. This concern to push our creativity to the limit naturally stemmed from our shared Neoist roots.

So to ring in the *Newe Yeare* of 1987, we choseth a mediaeval theme. Dressed as a knight, I opened the show with an acoustic guitar, playing the melody of a rare song by Leonardo Da Vinci. I was accompanied by JM banging a hand-held drum and Bézy blowing the drone on my father's bagpipes. Dressed as a monk, Bonspiel stepped up and bellowed a pseudo 14th century ditty at the Fouf's urban peasantry. The stunning lyrics of this throwaway song were typical of his effortless gift for spontaneous brilliance[3]:

> "Oh give me sweet futureless days of sun floating medieval
>   melodies,
> borne on winds of flute
> And the inexact rhythms of broken beats from makeshift
>   drums
> Let's invite the peasants, yokels and poor folk
> To a magnificent feast within the castle walls
> And once they're all in we'll lock the doors,
> Set the castle on fire and burn them all"

For all his brilliance, Bonspiel was also quite the character. He soon stripped down to pajamas, then took the top off to end the show bare-chested[4]. He started making it a custom to remove his clothes during

---

3. Jack and Bonspiel insist I'm the one who penned this one. Whatever. My comment still stands for any number of songs penned by Bonspiel—especially *J'va aller m'tuer* (Gonna Kill Myself)

4. See it at: https://www.youtube.com/watch?v=0hmYO_YNUFw&t=505s

a show, and often finished it stark naked. This annoyed us no end. Backstage before going on, we'd warn him "no taking off your clothes tonight, right?" By the end of the show, he was naked.

He was often late for rehearsals, and made up incredible stories. "You'll never believe what just happened to me," he once yelped, entering the room with a limp, "a truck crushed my foot!" He continued to wince in pain for a while at the microphone. By the end of the rehearsal, his foot had miraculously healed.

ϟ In January, an article on my *États Limites* came out in McGill University's French-language edition *Le McGill Daily français*. It was quite satisfying to get some sort of recognition from my old alma mater—even if from the wrong faculty.

Sylvère Lotringer called me out of the blue and asked if he and partner Chris Kraus could come over and spend a few weeks at my place. She wanted to finish up her video *How To Shoot a Crime*, and he'd work on his writing projects. "Fine, no problem," I said, "be my guest!"

I gave them the master bedroom, and I slept on a cot in the living room. They had free use of the place, because I was never home anyway—during the day I worked at my engineering job, and evenings I was busy organizing the next festival and *Ultimatum Tuesdays* at the Foufs, not to mention regular rehearsals and gigs with VDMS.

They sent me copies of their videos in advance, including Chris' *Foolproof Illusion*, which features a clip of the late great David Rattray mouthing off filthy texts by Artaud in English[5], intercut with dominatrix Terence Sellers sneering "come on, wormy!" at one of her clients. Chris couldn't get Terence for a scene, so she dressed up as a dominatrix herself, and is seen out in the winter snow half naked under a giant curly blonde wig, tamping together a horn-shaped snowman. As for Rattray, I found his performance on the tape so gobsmacking, I brought him twice to Montreal.

---

5. See it at: https://www.youtube.com/watch?v=vOlD2oqNde0

⇌ At the time, Chris looked a lot like Pulp Fiction's *Honey Bunny*[6], while soft-spoken Sylvère—as writer Lisa Blaushild says—"was kind of sexy in a literary Yul Brenner kind of way."

My fridge didn't get any fatter with Chris and Sylvère. They seemed to live on nothing, and got by munching on the occasional piece of cheese.

They stayed a month, and of course I slipped them into my *Ultimatum Tuesdays* schedule at the Foufs. They screened *Voyage To Rodez*—a film about Artaud—and Sylvère read his texts off a fanfolded dot matrix computer printout.

Chris edited her *How To Shoot A Crime* at a nearby studio called Vidéographe. In her film, an NYPD cameraman explains what goes into the elements of filming a crime scene, over gritty footage of the actual thing, complete with twisted corpses and spattered blood amid refuse.

One day I walked in on Sylvère and François Peraldi—author of Semiotext(e)'s *Polysexuality* issue—and they were frowning, deeply engaged in a heavy discussion about arcane Marxist dialectics. You could almost see the cloud of deep thought steaming above their heads. When Sylvère saw me his face broke into a wide amiable smile, as if they'd only been trading gardening tips over tea. "Salut mon grand!"[7] he said— that's how he affectionately called me—which can be roughly translated as "hello, my son!"

While Sylvère and Peraldi were heating my house with their brain power, standing listening to them was a thin, handsome sandy-haired young man. He looked like a young Montgomery Clift. His name was Bernard Schütze. He turned out to be not only a respected art critic, but also my future brother-in-law. He said that after the *Rodez* screening at the Foufs, he'd gone over to speak to Sylvère, and wound up being recruited to hold the mic boom while Sylvère interviewed Peraldi.

Before heading back to New York, Chris and Sylvère first wanted to see how close they could get to the North Pole. It was still the dead of winter, their car's heater was busted, and they drove with a plaid

---

6. The character played by Amanda Plummer, opposite Tim Roth in the diner robbery scene

7. Pronounced "Sah-lue moh grah"

green wool blanket tucked over their laps. They must have gotten as far as St Jérôme before turning back—roughly the same distance as Battery Park to White Plains. It was an adorably ridiculous idea, in that endearing way intellectuals often have of being charmingly, enviably naïve.

Before leaving, they gave me a parting gift: a brand new set of bedsheets! I knew it was a sly comment on my homemaking skills, but I appreciated the gift nonetheless. *My* gift to Chris was covering the $600 video editing bill from Vidéographe[8]. In a 2018 e-mail Chris insisted: "You ABSOLUTELY made that film possible, and I remember thinking at various times during that trip, 'I could die now, I'm so happy.' I'd waited so long for someone to believe in that film."

I invited Chris and Sylvère back for the festival in September.

✺ My *Ultimatum Tuesdays* went on, with themes such as *Beatnik Party, Young Blood*, and *Video Night*. In early March it was Lynne Tillman's turn to come to town. She read from her latest novel *Haunted Houses*. I was more interested in her brash classic *Sick Fucks*, but she was trying to get away from the abrasive Lower East Side thing. Poor Lynne, over lunch she had to listen to my sob story about Kathy ditching me after four days. She delicately explained to me that I'd only been her convenient fucksailor in *this* pussyport—and to get over it.

Instead of paying my rent that month, I decided to fly up David Rattray to do a reading. Why did I do that? Because I *personally* wanted to bloody see David Rattray do a reading. My landlord could wait.

David was steeped in French literature, but I explained to him that Quebec's French literature was a whole other fascinating world people knew nothing about. I dragged him around bookstores and showed him our great names—Réjean Ducharme, Jacques Godbout, Gaston Miron, Claude Gauvreau—as well as all the poets I knew personally. In the end, he oddly chose to write about the early 20th Century poet Émile Nelligan[9].

Next up in my Tuesday series was performance artist Karen Finley,

---

8. $1400 today

9. Published in *How I Became One of the Invisible,* a collection of Rattray's work edited by Chris Kraus

and everyone was really looking forward to her infamous *Shoving Yams Up My Ass*. But as she explained to the audience, "I don't *actually* shove yams up my ass. What I do is bend over forward and just *hold* them between my butt cheeks."

She was with her boyfriend manager, and they were the nicest normal Midwest couple you could ever meet. She looked like a school teacher and he looked like an insurance broker. I asked for permission to tape the performance, saying that it was only for personal use, and they graciously obliged. Of course, like the trustworthy idiot I yam, I lent the videotape to Sylvain Forbes' girlfriend Anne-Marie and never got it back. You'll be hearing more about those two later.

≳ What with the videotaping, salary paid to the cameraman, equipment rentals, artist fees, travel expenses, hotel, lavish meal invitations and whatnot, I was going broke with my Ultimatum folies. On a *good* night I'd lose $250[10]. On a *bad* one—like Kathy Acker—I lost up to $1000[11]. Out of my pocket, folks. Yes, *of course* I was sick in the head. It was never my intention to be an art martyr, but I just didn't know how to stop, how to decelerate.

I started inviting some of my friends onstage—like Francoeur. It was way cheaper. The evening it was Mario's turn at the mic, he turned up with nothing to read. Instead, he gave us a long, detailed story of the week he'd spent with a fly in his apartment. Then he proceeded to patiently explain to the kids how he'd failed at a suicide attempt the previous night. He hung a noose from the ceiling lamp and placed the rope around his neck. When he jumped off the chair though, his weight just ripped the lamp right off the ceiling. The lamp fell on his head and he only got a huge headache. The people laughed, they thought it was a real funny story. But I knew better. Once, after an nth 2 AM suicide phone call from Mario, I'd had enough. I told him: "Oh for fuck's sake, why don't you just go ahead and kill yourself?" He never called again.

The most legendary among VDMS shows remains the one where we transformed—in the middle of a snowstorm—the Café Campus

10. $600 today
11. $2400 today

into a basement rec room: the band played sitting on a sofa in front of a coffee table with a portable TV set on it, while Bonspiel sang in a Lazy Boy[12], flanked by a living room lamp on a stand. We all wore multicoloured *gougoune* slippers knitted by my mother—using awful Phentex synthetic yarn. In between songs we watched the TV with feigned boredom, while Bonspiel—wearing pajamas—cooked up some popcorn for us on a hotplate. Amid the hoots and hollers of the crowd, we did our best to remain unperturbed[13]. JM recalls: "That night *Bleu Nuit*[14] was playing, and I had trouble concentrating with those tits in my face." *The Montreal Mirror* declared that night *Show of The Year*.

⇆ In early April I had a Tuesday night scheduled featuring poets Alain Lalumière and Hélène Monette, along with an opera performed by none other than Jean-Luc Bonspiel. And then I got a big surprise from the Foufs. They kicked me out! They didn't want any more of my *Ultimatum Tuesdays*, saying it didn't pull in enough people. True, I wasn't attracting hordes of nose-ringed mohawked Crusty Punks with my "poetry shit". Well, they must've been very happy ever since, because to this day the Foufounes devolved into a cheap beer dive for brainless morons and slumming frat boys. So I scrambled and held the soirée above a bar on St Denis.

For his "opera", Bonspiel screened a film of smiling Ukrainian folk dancers, while hacking at pieces of chicken with a meat cleaver, yelling "le sperme des enfants!"[15]. He then fried the pieces of chicken in the tin lid of a 16mm film canister.

The young frail gifted poetess Hélène Monette followed with her timid poems, and then doomed poet Alain Lalumière—a name that literally meant "the light"—gave us his last verses before shooting himself in the head weeks later. He was one of those young intense gifted people who enjoyed playing *poète maudit*[16]. Along with his friend

---

12. BarcaLounger
13. See an excerpt of the show at: https://vimeo.com/488269050
14. Pronounced "Bleuh Newie"; Transl: *Blue Night*—a soft porn show on cable TV
15. Transl: "The sperm of the children!"
16. Transl: Cursed poet

Sylvain they would strip naked, take drugs, and partake in morbid pagan rituals which involved reciting by candlelight either their own macabre poetry or that of decadent symbolist poets of the 19th century. They built an altar adorned with ceremonial daggers and statuettes, and read passages from the Kabbala while maiming each other with ritual scars. Creepy moans were heard well into the night coming from their apartment, with the walls painted black and blood-red. David Sapin told me it got so crazy during one of their séances that the walls started sweating, they were pinned against the walls by an evil force, they couldn't move at all and started screaming. Or so goes the urban legend.

During the day Alain sat alone with curtains drawn and wrote his *Suicide Chronicles*. He wanted nothing to do with the "real world" out there, and wanted to die of hunger or worse. And soon. Alain gleefully showed his manuscript to everyone, and a girlfriend remembers a passage where he described in minute detail the ritual, setting, and incantations he would employ for an eventual suicide. Of course, everyone just shrugged and expected him to grow out of his silly young goth phase.

They found his body slumped against the arch of a doorway, dead of a self-inflicted shotgun blast, surrounded by candles burnt down to a hardened cake of melted wax and congealed blood. The doorway was elaborately decorated with the same painted symbols and statuettes he'd drawn in his notebook.

~ The next Tuesday, my *Between C & D* guests Joel Rose, Catherine Texier, Darius James and Lisa Blaushild arrived from New York. The material of these tough new writers reflected the harsh street reality of their home turf *Loisaida*.

Still Foufouneless, I was reduced to holding the show at the 259—our VDMS practice hall. First up at the mic was Joel, wearing a black leather jacket. He read the third chapter *Money*, from his novel *Kill The Poor*[17].

Lisa was up next, but we'll get to her last. Catherine read from her

---

17. See Appendix A—Selected Texts

well-received poignant sexy novel *Love Me Tender*, that was published that year. As she explained, "It's about Lulu, a French dancer who works in a strip joint in New York City. She's involved with three men: Julian, a chaotic sexy junkie who occasionally writes poetry—*bad* poetry; Harry, a successful painter who's also an obsessive womanizer; and Mario, a Puerto Rican street boy and sometime drug dealer. Meanwhile, she tries to remember—or imagine—her mother's life, her mother who died when she was born."

Darius read from his hilarious novel *Negrophobia*, which was published in 1992 and reprinted in 2019. A Black kid from Hamden, Connecticut, Darius James was a Basquiat who painted with words, except he had no Warhol to take him under his wing. He was broke as hell, crashed at different places in the East Village, and friends always gave him a little money to survive. He later hooked up with artist Joy Lou G and she followed him to New York.

Lisa Blaushild was the big hit of the soirée[18]. She had everyone cracked up in stitches with her neurotic postmodern urban tableaux. On the videotape the loudest laughter we hear is Dubé's, followed by mine.

I'd discovered her writing in Bomb magazine[19], immediately fell in love with her deadpan wit, and absolutely worshipped her. Lisa was my favourite writer of the Loisaida Contingent, and to this day is still American Literature's best kept secret. She's as if Kafka had lived on the Lower East Side in the Seventies.

I invited her to dinner in a restaurant, and as the evening wore on I was hoping she'd invite me over to her hotel room. Of course I wanted to bang her. But when she told me the date of her birth, I froze. It was August 16th, just like me. That shower was real cold, because in my mind the warped logic figured it as some sort of incest. Cosmically speaking. Or something. What an idiot. I regretted it ever since. Like they say, you never regret what you did, only what you didn't do. Finally she said: "Let's blow this pop stand" and we walked a bit, then went off to our separate bedrooms.

---

18. See the complete *Between C & D* night at: https://vimeo.com/551972168
19. See Appendix A—Selected Texts

My notes for subsequent *Ultimatum Tuesdays* say Gary Indiana, Marie-Claire Blais, and "Last Night" for May 5th. It must have been planned, but scrubbed because of my Foufs eviction. In any case, my *Tuesdays* had to stop, because full attention was now urgently needed for the September festival.

⋝ Finally, our first VDMS album funded by the *Rock Envol* prize money came out—a 12″ EP with six songs. We gave carte blanche to David Sapin to design the album cover, and it instantly became infamous. It showed Dagwood of the *Blondie* funnies sitting in a bath, gleefully handing money to his daughter, who was completely naked, with big round tits and perky pink nipples.

Sapin explains: "The cover art was a wink at The Pop Art movement of the sixties, which was a total fuck-you attitude towards traditional art, but we had the same attitude towards traditional rock music. I just wanted to do something that was as completely outrageous and offensive and silly and blatantly sloppy and derivative and original and as politically incorrect as the music that it was designed to contain. I wanted to design the biggest low-budget belly flop that I could imagine, and offend as many people that I could using limited resources."

That album cover was absolutely brilliant, deliciously shocking, and impossible to do today. It immediately got us howls of protests and a feminist boycott at Concordia University, complete with shrill megaphone chanting and placards waved in front of the campus.

⋝ Napoléon decided to put out a 'zine called *Salut les riche*[20], gathering texts written by local poets and writers. Its "marketing philosophy" was as follows: it was by and for people who made less than $25,000 a year. I had to lobby hard to be included in that 'zine, because by that time I was making $40,000 a year as an engineer. See? All my life I kept getting shot by both sides like that: At work I was considered some kind of weirdo anarchist, and now, via the miracle of gutter snobism, I found myself just as equally snubbed by the work-shy art condescendi. After a bit of lobbying by the others, I was allowed in. As you may recall, the

---

20. Transl: *Hail The Rich*

crowning touch to *Salut les riche* was to have a two-dollar bill glued to the inside back cover, for a publication being sold for *one* dollar.

Dubé's girlfriend at the time was Catherine Perry Meen, a sweet but no-nonsense gal who didn't suffer fools gladly. Especially artistic ones. She had no patience for art shenanigans, so how she wound up with Dubé—*Mr. Art Shenanigan himself*—I have no clue. Opposite bodies must attract, just as in physics. I called her CP Meen, or just CP. She had a doll's face, with a small red-lipped mouth and shoulder-length dark curly hair. She was a feisty, hot-blooded, queen-sized Irish-bred matron—and reminded you that being a Leo, she was also a queen. She became my lifelong confidante.

In turn, CP introduced me to tall, thin Sheila Urbanoski—her friend since teenagehood in their native Saskatchewan. She lived in a hovel on Ontario Street corner of St Lawrence, that opened onto an inner courtyard balcony that communicated with an adjacent hovel. A bunch of student filmmakers squatted there, including Velcrow Ripper —who went on to make award-winning documentaries—and Cynthia Jervis, whom I hired to lead my festival video crew.

On a warmish spring day, the VDMS boys and I took hits of blotter acid and wound up at Sheila's for more—either very late or early in the morning. There was night-time work going on in the street—a truck was spraying paint lines on the asphalt. We ran downstairs and lay down on the pavement in front of the truck, screaming: *"Ils ne passeront pas!"*[21]

Somehow we ended up at my place with Philippe Côté, also on acid. I decided I'd had enough and lay down on my bed to sleep. Of course, you can't sleep on acid, so I stared for hours at my ceiling, now an undulating technicolor sea of throbbing moiré patterns and swirling paisley curlicues.

At dawn I heard someone retching. I got up, and saw my front door was open. I went outside and saw Philippe Côté hunched over the balcony, greeting people on their way to work at 7 AM with his vomit. Feeling a bit peckish, Phil had eaten the slice of moldy green pizza sitting in my fridge.

---

21. Transl: "They shall not pass!"

Bonspiel recalls: "We all warned Côté—DO NOT under any circumstances, eat any leftovers in Alan's fridge!"

For his part, Bonspiel took six or seven showers fully clothed that night.

Normally I didn't invite Philippe Côté to my place, because he stole books from me. He stole books from libraries, bookstores, and every single one of his friends. When by chance I found myself in *his* apartment, I finally had the opportunity for revenge. I scanned his library and found a choice book to swipe—a 1965 Jean-Jacques Pauvert edition of *The Trial of Gilles de Rais*—Georges Bataille's book on the infamous medieval serial killer.

Philippe was a fixture at VDMS shows, and never missed an opportunity to jump onstage and grab the mic during lulls in between songs, and launch into his obsessive theory *du jour*. Yet it was thanks to him that the Surrealist consecration of VDMS became complete: in Lautréamont's *Les Chants de Maldoror*[22]—*the* Surrealists' fetish book—he discovered the phrase "*le souffle de la montagne*"—"the breath of the mountain".[23]

≷ What was I going to call my next festival? I had no idea. In the end I lazily opted for the uninspired Led Zeppelin tradition, and called the second endeavour *Ultimatum II*—not even realizing the supreme irony of issuing a *second* ultimatum. A festival was a fine thing indeed, but I had to keep my job at LGL, so I needed someone competent in charge of organizing the day-to-day operations. May was coming up and the venue for the festival wasn't even booked yet. I began to panic.

There was a multimedia show going on at The Spectrum, ludicrously called *Cabaret Futura*. Out of curiosity, the VDMS boys, Sheila and I went to check it out. It was laughable cheesy crap with bad techno bands and silver-painted "futuristic" cardboard props. The one good part of the show was Carolyn Fe Trinidad, again doing her violent karate-chop dance in a long black slit dress and black opera gloves.

---

22. Transl: *The Songs of Maldoror*

23. Actually, it was jointly discovered independently by my future brother-in-law Bernard Schütze

The event may have been stupid artistically, but I was impressed by the organizational skills of the guy who'd put the show together. It turned out to be Joe Martek, of *Bambi Concerts* fame back in the New Wave era. I hired him on the spot, and he became my festival manager.

I have to confess I often abused my status as a wacko-cultural power dude to schmooze gals with offers of maybe putting them in my festival. One of these was Anne Seymour, whom Sheila introduced me to that night. She was a dirty blonde poetess with black painted finger-nails chewed anxiously. I'd been warned she was "disturbed". She was mentally ill, yet oddly attractive. She was often sexily dishevelled and had that puzzled frown of anguish the demented have, but the night I met her she was calm, radiant, and damn pretty. She wore a tight dress, white patterned stockings and black Mary Jane shoes.

Sheila says: "Yes, dear, troubled Anne … I always liked her. I fell in love with her at this performance art thing where some gal was droning on and shouting and made the mistake of going up to Seymour and shouting at her. Anne went bananas and brought the house down, it was fuckin' hysterical: 'You've got three holes, and your mouth is the one with shit in it'—it still sticks with me."

After the Cabaret show Anne, Sheila, me, and a couple others piled into a cab and went dancing at Poodles on St Lawrence. We sat on these bleachers they had in front of the tiny dance floor, and Anne sat next to me. Suddenly she put her hand on my lap. I turned to her, totally delighted to have an excuse to start smooching. I was horny as hell.

We hopped in a cab and went to my place and lost no time undress-ing. She was a lot of fun in bed, and partook as lustily as I did. "You fuck me like a bull!" she roared. Yeah, it'd been a while and I had to make up for lost time. And I can certainly vouch for the saying: crazy chicks *are* the best in bed.

She kind of moved in. I found her kookiness very liberating, and I didn't feel so lonely anymore. But soon her deep craziness came slowly bubbling to the surface. Out of nowhere she kept reminding me: "I'm going to marry Leonard Cohen, you know." She was obsessed with her goddamn Leonard Cohen, and scribbled a filthy notebook with her thick black pen scrawlings. Poems to her unsuspecting future husband, no doubt.

What a nutjob. What had I gotten myself into? After a couple of weeks I'd had enough and looked for a convenient opportunity to ditch her, but I had trouble getting around to it. The sex was too good. Each time I sat her down to "have a talk", we ended up screwing madly. Eventually I *did* manage to get rid of her. A few fucks later.

ϟ At a salary of $250 a week[24], Joe Martek got things organized in no time. He hired an accountant, balanced the books, booked the wonderful little theatre *Le Milieu*[25] for the festival—on St Laurent below St Viateur—and got us to share offices with the Foufounes Électriques in Old Montreal. We literally shared the same office space and were supposed to split the utilities. Lo and behold, it soon turned out the Foufs weren't paying their half of the bills. Joe suggested we do a "midnight move"—but at six in the morning—a time when every self-respecting Foufouner had just gone to bed. So Joe, Jack, JM and I sped-moved our stuff into a truck, laughing our heads off imagining the look on Louis Côté's face when he'd get to the freshly emptied offices. Joe moved us into the spacious large-windowed sixth floor of the building at 307 Ste. Catherine West, where he was leasing adjacent space to *The Montreal Mirror*.

Joe was best at wheeling and dealing, getting things done one way or another. You could count on him, he delivered, and you can't say that about many people. He had great management and organizational skills, as well as a self-assurance that was contagious. When I was getting antsy about lack of progress on certain matters he'd sit back in his chair, flutter his eyelashes and say, "Look, *it's happening*. Things take time." This was one of his managerial mantras. His others were: "Money talks, bullshit walks" and: "KISS: Keep It Simple Stupid".

Joe was a go-getter, he loved life and gulped it down avidly, moved from one action-packed project to the next. Maybe he stepped on a few toes here and there on the way, but so what—I could identify with that. You can't be friends with everyone, and a man of action will always upset someone, somewhere. You get criticized only if you *do* something.

---

24. $600 today
25. Pronounced "Luh Meal-yeuh"; Transl: The Spot

Joe embodied the notion that people should either "lead, follow, or get out of the way."

Joe Martek was a bit of a Baby Trump. He had the same pout and arrogant self-assurance. He even looked a bit like him, minus the dead blond skunk squatting on the head. Even though our values were totally opposite, I always enjoyed being with Joe, and we often had lunch together, picking up delicious juicy sausage sandwiches at the Slovenia deli on St. Laurent.

I was fond of Joe. But he thought I was a complete nutjob, what with my weird avant-whatever festival stuff. He didn't understand any of it, yet clearly enjoyed the change of business scenery. When I described to him the awesome cutting-edge acts I wanted for the festival he'd stop, take stock of me and blurt out laughing, "What an asshole!" This was his personal term of endearment for me. I was paying him $250 a week to call me an asshole! It was ok, I didn't mind, because he was *such a happening guy.*

Well one day *this* asshole walked into the Canada Arts Council's spanking new $40 million dollar building in downtown Ottawa[26], and sat down in front of a smug bureaucrat. I looked at all the expensive art on the walls and the snazzy furniture all around me, while listening to him politely explain that there just weren't any funds left for art projects. I probably gave him a good piece of my mind. Apparently Joe was much impressed by my fearlessness in dealing with these government-tit-sucking arts apparatchiks with utter contempt. In one of the media articles on the upcoming festival I was called the *Terror Of Ministries.*

Ƨ With Joe at the helm, things were going swimmingly for the festival organization. Thanks to a Quebec make-work program, we hired people on welfare and boosted their income, including friends like Sheila, CP Meen and Jack. For the festival poster I chose an iconic picture from the early, naïvely optimistic days of the Soviet Union: a composer atop the roof of an industrial building, conducting a Constructivist concert of factory whistles. The artwork and printing of the festival paraphernalia was of course handled again by our faithful David Sapin.

---

26. $95 million today

At the Shred one day I decided to thank him by cleaning out his car, which was a mess. It was a beat-up old burgundy 1980 Dodge Aspen station wagon with imitation wood paneling on its sides. It had wide bench seats that could fit six people. The car was a hoarder's paradise, with the cargo space behind the back seats full of junk. You couldn't even sit on the back seat, because the leg space was filled with crap topped up to seat level. At the bottom of my archeological dig I found posters dating back two years, stuck to the floor carpet by the sheer weight of garbage piled on top. I went at it zealously with vacuum cleaner and everything, and left him with a spotless car. I thought I was doing him a huge favour, but instead it threw him into a depressed funk.

↗ Sick of always playing the damned Foufs, VDMS jumped on any opportunity to play outside Montreal. Finally we were offered a good deal—a few days' residency in August at the cheap Île du Repos resort near Alma, which is the northernmost town in Lac Saint-Jean—a big lake roughly 25 miles across, way up the Saguenay fjord. It was a sort of camping site with a beach, and the club hired bands for weekend residencies. We set off with an entourage of about a dozen people in several cars, including David Sapin, Bézy, Poutine, Alain Bergeron, a few VDMS girlfriends, groupies, and hangers-on. It was the first time I saw the Saguenay, and the majestic landscape of mountains and lakes later inspired me the song *Mon Pays*[27].

We had a stopover show in Quebec City, and invited the legendary Bruno Tanguay to come and see us. After the show, a tall, slender, six-foot-tall guy came over to talk to me—it was Spike—the former punk show promoter of the Nelson Hotel back in 1979. I hadn't seen him since. He said, "Hey Alan, can you change a welfare cheque for me?" I said, "Spike, your cheque will be honored at any bank." He confided: "Er … it's not in my name." I told him, "Sorry Spike, but I can't help you here."

---

27. Transl: *My Country*; hear it at: https://soundcloud.com/alan-lord-4/mon-pays-les-frogs

☇ It was around August 16th—which is not only my date of birth, but also the date Elvis chose to die. Which means that every year on my birthday it's also goddamn *Elvis Day*. Might as well laugh about it instead of cry. So on my birthday I fooled around writing what would become our song *Aloha From Heaven*. I sang it that night, mimicking The King crooning mawkish lines from the hereafter.

While I was scribbling away at the lyrics, David had given himself as mission to erect a *Temple of The Elvis Cult* on the beach, around which we were later to party, culminating in an immense Saint-Jean bonfire at dawn.

Dave found a big tree trunk washed up on the beach about 300 feet away—perfect to serve as the central totem pole of our Elvis Worship Temple. With its jagged stumps of snapped branches, the four-foot-wide trunk was very hard to maneuver. It had to weigh at least 300 pounds. You couldn't drag it over the sand, so Dave and Bonspiel pushed it into the water and managed to float it over, which was easier, but still a struggle to handle. Afterwards, others assisted to hoist it up in the center of the Temple of The Elvis Cult, grunting "Hoo! Hoo! Hoo!" like a buncha Neolithic idiots.

The boys continued dragging *pitoune*[28] out of the lake and made a ring of logs to sit on. It was *a lot* of work. Apparently, I was lounging on a lawn chair sipping cocktails while all this was going on.

That night was one of our best shows, and has been the source of a few live releases since. Afterwards, our hosts forbade us to set fire to the magnificent log Elvis temple, for fear of setting fire to the forest—even though it was pouring rain. We did, however, manage to build a decent camp fire on the beach in front of our lodgings, and continued to party with joints, beer and bongos, singing songs on acoustic guitars.

☇ My big birthday present was getting to gently boink our faithful groupie Catriona on the beach until dawn. *Sex On The Beach* works better as a drink than the actual thing. When you screw on a beach,

---

28. The colloquial québécois term for floating logs of wood destined for the paper mill

the sand gets in everywhere, and it hurts like hell. I saw her a couple more times (well, *fucked*) and one day I came home to find she'd left me a bottle of *Kwellada* shampoo. I didn't know what that was, so I called her up. She asked if I'd seen any "little friends" on me. Then I discovered the crabs on my belly. I'd never seen that before. Totally disgusting. I freaked out and started ripping them out, then shampooed my infected zones like crazy.

If the Île du Repos wasn't enough of a bash, my parents then organized a birthday party for me in the ridiculously small backyard of their dinky little house on Cartier Street in the Plateau[29]. Over 30 Ultimatum staff and VDMS friends were crammed in the 15' × 15' space. My dad manned the BBQ grill and the food and wine flowed, accompanied by drunk jamming and dancing. The following morning my parents woke up to see Jack fast asleep on the rocking chair in the middle of the backyard lane, the sun beating on his face. He hadn't been run over by a speeding car overnight by sheer luck.

That summer I turned 33—the perfect age to get crucified.

---

29. A popular Montreal neighbourhood

17

ULTIMATUM II

A t Monenco-LGL, we were now onto Phase II of the Norsk Hydro project—designing the magnesium plant for real. To my surprise, the whole 1000-foot-long Chlorination Building I'd spent a good part of the previous year on was gone from the project—it had been eliminated from the process line. So Armin put me in charge of designing the foundations for the 1000-foot-long Electrolysis building. There were many load combinations possible, so to simplify my task I wrote a *Footings* design program in Basic.

My neighbour in the cubicle next to mine was a Vietnamese guy in his forties. Instead of working on the project he was quite openly working on an accounting software he was developing for his brother-in-law's business. Well, he wasn't the only one shirking his duties—half the time I was on the phone, taking care of Ultimatum business. My office was at my office.

First thing was to choose the guests. For sure, I definitely wanted Burroughs on the bill. I called up James Grauerholz and asked him if Burroughs could come and do a reading. He told me the trip from Lawrence, Kansas would be too much for him. For a while, we looked into the possibility of having him broadcast live from a satellite feed. That also came to naught, as he warned me Burroughs liked to start drinking at dinnertime and would be plastered by showtime.

I also tried to invite the Korean-American video artist Nam June Paik. I got him on the phone and introduced myself. He said: "You Canada? You CBC? One million dollah!" I tried explaining to him what my festival was all about. He cut me short and kept repeating: "You Canada? You CBC? One million dollah!" I gave up.

For some reason Kathy Acker didn't wind up in the festival either. Maybe the plane trip from London and accommodations were too costly. Or maybe because I'd been jilted by the bitch. Still, Burroughs and Acker appeared in the promo videoclip we put together for the festival—there was no budget to re-edit. It played in an information booth at the exhibition *Images du futur* in the *Old Port* of Montreal during the summer. The tape alternated English and French versions of the trailer, with clips of various artists from the first festival shown in between. The videotape was an hour and a half long and had to be rewound by a staffer when it got to the end. Tristan composed the epic breathless *Ultimatum II theme*[1] of the festival, and for the promo clip I dubbed on top the voices of Burroughs, David Rattray, Terence Sellers[2], Acker, Huncke, Giorno and Lotringer[3]. In her seductive voice, Josée Thibault announced:

"Ultimatum II: New Literatures—an event that will take place from September 11th to the 19th at *Le Théâtre Le Milieu* in Montreal. *Ultimatum II* bill bring together over 100 writers, poets, performance artists and musicians from across Canada, The United States, England and France. As was the case for *Ultimatum: The Urban Poetry Festival* held in May '85, *Ultimatum II* will showcase writers and artists who use the latest technologies and methods to present their texts. In addition to live shows on stage, *Ultimatum II* will also hold conferences on computer literature and the publication of parallel magazines, book launchings, and an online real-time transmission of texts through an international database …"

Again, a bit of false advertising. We never held a conference on computer literature, or put together an online text database. But with the live performances and other stuff, the public was more than well served.

1. Hear it at: https://soundcloud.com/alan-lord-4/ultimatum-ii-theme
2. *"You're a disgrace to Humanity!"*
3. Hear it at: https://soundcloud.com/alan-lord-4/ultimatum-ii-theme-with-voice-track

After working at my day job, I'd pass by the offices of my *real* job—the one that didn't pay—and catch up with the day's doings. I held a weekly staff meeting on Fridays, and handed out task lists to everyone for the week ahead. I prepared spreadsheets, schedules, and calendars with deadlines that maybe Eisenhower could've used for D-Day.

⇆ Among the Ultimatum staff, CP Meen and Sheila were my double power towers of female sanity keeping it all together—my twin secret weapons, my dynamic duo, my no-nonsense right-hand gals from the prairies of Saskatchewan.

To any creative ideas or art schemes I dared propose, CP invariably retorted "Such foolishness!" or "What a thrill!"—and Sheila was super effective. She intimidated Joe Martek, and shocked him with how she could pull stuff together—all the while served with attitude and plenty of snark. I later learned CP and Sheila called Ultimatum "El Tomato" behind my back. Had I known this, I would've changed the name instantly. *El Tomato Too*. Now *that's* cool.

Cynthia Jervis was a short-haired, high-energy scrappy gal who would've been drop-dead gorgeous if she only had a nose. Picture Angelina Jolie without a nose if you can. It was a birth defect. She had plastic surgery to put in artificial cartilage, but her body rejected the implant. After that, she just decided to live with it. She'd made a short documentary video called *No Means No* and had this huge feminist chip on her shoulder. Which spread to her face. She was adamant about preserving her distracting, unsettling concave face—it was a badge of defiance against everything she was supposed to be. Yes, it was a brave statement against the "women's body image" thing—but still, it was an odd anti-vanity form of vanity.

Cynthia was hardcore *MeToo* decades before #metoo. To the point that when I gave her the job of filming the festival, she reverse-discriminated by insisting on manning her crew exclusively with women—with token male friend Alan Quinn thrown in. But her video amazons did a great job, editing the three cameras on the fly, and quickly mixing the day's footage down to a one-hour show that was broadcast each night on the Vidéotron cable channel.

⇆ Our Ultimatum offices became a hip locus and we began attracting attention from all quarters—both high and low. Like the time a distraught cute blonde Edie Sedgwick type waif from L.A. stumbled into our offices, moaning she couldn't find any party going on. "What kind of a place is this? They told me there was always a party going on in Montreal!" whined the poor little bored darling. CP and Sheila rolled their eyes and shoved her in my direction, figuring maybe I could "have some use" for her. I got up from my desk, placed my arm around her, and escorted the disappointed snivelling thing to the door, consoling her: "Listen sweetie, we got *work* to do here. I'm sure you'll find a party around here *somewhere*!"

Word was getting around about Ultimatum. In fact, it even got to the famous Anne Waldman, because one day I received a nice handwritten letter on beautiful Naropa Institute stationary, asking to be invited to the festival. I sent her a polite rejection letter. I was put off by her attempt to recycle herself into a Laurie Anderson type pop star, as seen in her *Uh Oh Plutonium* video[4]—it was like putting postmodern lipstick on a beatnik pig.

I didn't feel like re-inviting people from the first festival. I wanted new faces. I made a few exceptions of course, and re-invited Giorno, Lotringer, Eldon Garnet, Karl Jirgens, Jack Five and Ian Stephens. Among the exciting new names were David Rattray, Chris Kraus, Lisa Blaushild, Darius James and his Lower East Side crew, the SCP, VDMS, Violence & The Sacred, Nick Toczek, and tENTATIVELY, a cONVENIENCE.

⇆ One day at the Ultimatum office I was busy working at my desk, and a dozen people barged in. They were all dressed in black—black trench coats, fedoras and sunglasses—like the black spy in Mad magazine's Spy vs. Spy.

They suddenly broke into a song and choreographed dance. I sat back with my feet on the desk, enjoying the impromptu show. When they finished, they froze with pleading outstretched hands, and looked at me with big smiling expectant faces. Yanking an imaginary Broadway

---

4. See it at: https://www.youtube.com/watch?v=FHX-PU9SN8A

producer's cigar out of my mouth, I threw a finger at them and bellowed: "Okay kids, *you're IN!*"

They were called *Les Sanscoeurs*[5]—a play on words on many levels: literally, it meant "heartless", but in French, the word for "heart" (coeur) resembles "choir" (choeur), and also phonetically, it can either mean a hundred choirs, or hearts. Crafty little devils.

ᔭ As previously explained, the nine-day festival was completely audio and videotaped, filmed on 3/4" video by Cynthia's team and broadcast on Vidéotron. In the end I managed to raise a total of $60K[6] in cultural grants and corporate sponsorship for the event. I would've needed at least *double* that. But never mind. They say you go to war with what you have, not what you want. One thing I didn't need though was that, two weeks before the start of the festival, Joe Martek quit. It was a shock. Did he know something I didn't? Did he see the iceberg coming at the ship? I didn't have time to dwell on it and ponder the implications. Because *my* September 11th was … *SHOWTIME!*

DAY ONE: *Salut Les Riches!*—the French Montreal night

After the official launch of *Salut Les Riches* at *Le Set*—a bar across the street from the venue—I kicked off the festival wearing a snazzy suit and shades, and cut the ribbon being held by Sheila and her *Pantry Partner* Patrice Fortier. Then *Official Festival Emcee* Jean-Luc Bonspiel made his entrance jogging in T-shirt and sweatpants, and stripped down to his skivvies while welcoming everyone to the festival. He picked up a just-bought blue shirt, unwrapped it from the cellophane and put it on, while telling people that: "Ultimatum registers itself in the annals of the struggle for freedom, and the relentless search for Love." By the time he finished his wonderful monologue, he'd completed his emcee outfit, pulling on a pair of black pants and knotting his striped tie.

---

5. Pronounced "Leh Saw-kirr"
6. $140K today

The SCP followed, putting the theatre's giant screen to good use, plastering it with their digital graphics. After that, the magnificent Myriam "Poutine" Cliche, resplendent in a yellow cardboard tent dress, read extracts from her excellent *Seven Poutine Manifestos*. She was accompanied by a drummer wearing a vertical snare he banged with his hands, and a guitarist punctuating her text with noise guitar squelches.

Then we had a fresh young face in the shape of Claude-Michel Prévost[7], reading from his *Karma Archipelago*, followed by Bézy, Napoléon Moffat, and a *very* nervous Jack Five in whiteface, dressed as some Pagliaccio, strumming an electric ... hey Jack, is that *my* guitar you happen to be playing?

Next up was *Allée Oups!*—artists David Sapin and Christian Dion working on a *Shred Art* mural, while Nitroglycérine—an all-female band dressed as cavewomen—grunted out poetry and noise. Their handbill promised us "20 thousand years of pagan mythology meets 6 months of household garbage, set to atonal experimental music with strong industrial tendencies."

David explains: "Christian Dion and I built a 8' × 12' wall on stage and then proceeded to demolish it, starting with sticks and stones, then proceeding up through farming tools to electrical appliances. We ended the event by stuffing the wall with large quantities of low-end explosives of the type that are typically used by Hollywood FX to simulate a machine-gun barrage."

As David is seen picking up his stuff at the end of *Allée Oups!*, Bonspiel steps up to the mic and starts reciting the Baudelaire poem *Evening Harmony* from memory, asking "was that ok?" to cheering howls. "You haven't stopped eating misery," he bellows, taking off his jacket. "Let me explain to you a bit the political situation ... it's beautiful sheep who await either the butcher's sharpened knife, or the shepherd's turgid cock"—he then introduces VDMS, and we cut to a sweating shirtless Bonspiel singing our songs *Welfare Babies, Shirley, Loto Vedettes*[8], and my favourite VDMS song of all time—*I Need a Rug*

---

7. Pronounced "Clode Mee-shell Preh-voh"
8. Transl: Lotto Stars

Cleaner[9]. A definite highlight is Poutine and Sheila dancing together during our "love" ballad *Shirley*, with both coming over to exaggeratedly "flirt" with me while I'm playing the guitar. Poutine provided me the best offhanded compliment ever. Jack told me she told him: "Alan does just what's needed on the guitar—no more, no less."

⇆ So that was the wrap for Day One, and the festival credits rolled on the giant screen, as they would every night, to the magnificent Ultimatum II theme composed by Tristan Renaud.

That first night had been a logistical mess: the stage hands took too long switching sets between performances, and we'd ended two hours later than planned. After the theatre emptied I sat down with the staff in the audience seats and we had a pow wow, planning how to do better than that.

DAY TWO: *Cold City Fiction*—the Toronto night

Stepping up to the mic wearing pajamas, Bonspiel intoned—in a dry, authoritative, baritone that could have been mistaken for a BBC arts program on the English painter Constable ...

> "Good evening, and welcome to this tumultuous and ecstatically impacted evening of delirium, which we call the *second* evening of *Ultimatum II*—you've seen the paradox— *New Literatures*. This evening our guests are from Toronto. Which is nothing to hold against them (laughter in the audience). And this evening as well we herald the Montreal launching of Rampike magazine and its theme *Terra Incognita*. But as we're setting up for Eldon Garnet, let me tell you a couple of things about what I think of Toronto (more laughter, claps). I spent six months of service in the service of the servant of Vishnu[10]. And it was not unlike

---

9. See it at all at: https://www.youtube.com/watch?v=-4DnOTZ119A

10. He was speaking of his stint as Gordon W's chapati cart assistant

being reborn as a worm in the impacted intestine of a meat-eater, doing great service to millions of other worms. For we are the Proletariat, *n'est-ce pas*—the people who like to say "no" (more laughter). I'm so glad that you are in a giggly mood, because we are in for some serious culture."

Spoiler Alert: To anyone who sees the Ultimatum II videos[11], it quickly becomes evident that with his brilliant monologues and spontaneous quips, whether they be in English or French, the *real* star of the festival was Bonspiel. Not only that, but he also made the food to feed the staff. So hats off, Jean-Luc!

↯ Eldon Garnet introduced his computer-generated event *I Shot Mussolini* as "basically, a re-enactment of a crime never committed, or never completed." Projected onto the large screen was the screen of a MacIntosh showing text filing by, along with pictures of John Hinckley and brain scan slices labelled "Hinckley's Brain." The music accompanying the presentation was a majestic funereal dirge, with bowed cello notes and deep vocoder "ohs" and "ahs", composed by none other than … yes, *Bonspiel*.

Violence And The Sacred's performance was astounding—a dramatic industrial sound collage, against a backdrop wall of amazing expressionist videos.

Bonspiel introduced Karl Jirgens with a jocular: "And with us now, the editor of Rampike magazine, karate practitioner, and a man whom I thought was a nerd until he published me …" Karl read a piece called *Anachronic In White*, specially written for the festival.

Bonspiel introduced writer and *Globe And Mail* architecture critic John Bentley Mays—with his *Project For An Opera of The 20th Century* —thus: "In a few moments, we will be greeting the Nibelungenbüro, but as we wait for them, we do so."

Wearing suit and tie, John Bentley Mays read a text explaining the genesis of the opera—or rather, the project for one. It was played by an

11. Broadcast tapes of five days of the festival survived—see Appendix B—Video Links—Ultimatum II

ensemble consisting of three keyboardists, a bassist, and a percussionist wearing a tuxedo with bow tie.

Thankfully, this pretentious interlude was offset by the irrepressible mad monk and faithful Neoist Gordon W. Zealot, who kept rushing up and down the aisles banging his tabla, whirling like a dervish, whooping and heckling his fellow citizens on stage. Someone turned to me and said: "You couldn't get these people on the same stage in Toronto."

"I'm gonna dedicate this to Gordon W," announced Susan Parker, telling us she'd be reading from her *Sankirtan Stories*. The piece was published in Rampike's *Propaganda* issue—and now that the whole collection is available online[12], I invite you to read it for yourself[13].

DAY THREE: *Borderlines*—Vancouver and Baltimore

That night, Bonspiel appears in a wifebeater, atop a gray sarong skirt: "We are very very pleased, and more than a little bit enthusiastic to be receiving our friends, acolytes, colleagues and partners in crime from both Vancouver and Baltimore. It made sense to *me* (wry side glance). So first up, allow me to introduce a man who introduced himself to me as Monty Cantsin on at least one occasion, and who has lent his anus in kind complacence to just about everyone else's eyeball … John Berndt …"

Berndt read from his *Dialectical Materialism*, that references capitalism and metaphysics, in front of a keyboard emitting a spooky drone punctuated by aggressive stabs of harsh electronics. Accompanying him were throbbing images and text stroboscoped onto the giant screen. It should be noted that Baltimore scion John Berndt was a long-time associate of Tentatively's, and thus very familiar to us.

Before introducing the anarchist band Mecca Normal, Bonspiel first paused to read a striking passage from an arcane biography of King Michael I of Rumania. The songs done by the fearless waif-woman-voice and guitar-antihero duo Mecca Normal were the frantic *Richard The*

---

12. https://scholar.uwindsor.ca/rampike/about.html

13. It's on page 77. Bonspiel's text is in the same issue, page 61—strangely enough, opposite Francoeur's.

Spineless, One Woman, and the slightly more delightful mid-tempo *I Know A Little Bit*. During *Will He Change?*, a string broke on the guitar. Thanks to the miracle of frantic Noise Guitar Strumming, no one noticed.

↗ Bonspiel: "This concludes the politically correct portion of our program. And now I would like to introduce to you the artist herself. You have seen her on the cover of *The Mirror*. You have seen her in your wildest nightmares. And perhaps your most lubricious dreams. I speak of none other than the already very famous and soon to be great open pop star of tomorrow ... *Judy Radul* ..."

A few good lines from her rant: "Reality is its own best terrorist, taking itself hostage again and again, until the drama becomes unbelievable—a coverup ... if you seek inspiration like other people seek a bulletproof vest, then maybe you should wipe the ejaculate from your eyes, and cease to seek understanding, standing under beneath a structure bequeathed by a dead relative unseen by me ... we are babies and must behave accordingly, down on our knees ..." Whereupon Judy lays out flat on the floor, spreading arms and legs as if to make a snow angel, but face down. Her voice is repeated by a long phased echo device, then she gets back up and says something quite prescient: "The virus is transmitted by the ventilation system—it was obvious that we were all infected ..."

I, Braineater came on all dressed in black leather, including a *Wild Ones* motorbike cap and leather fringe hanging off the arms of his jacket. He looked like a baby-skinned young Marlon Brando, but proceeded to croon like a punk Elvis, accompanying himself on a hiccup-strummed electric guitar.

Lastly, trading his wifebeater for an *I, Braineater* T-shirt, Bonspiel introduces Tentatively, a Convenience thus: "The first person I saw one morning was Tentatively, a Convenience. He hadn't bathed for three months. He had spent his entire time sticking little plastic cowboy hats to the backs of crabs in shopping centers. The man was ecstatic. The man was way out. And in fact this evening he will *wig* out. Let me tell you, wigging out *is* the term. In a few moments, a man full of *Usefulofshitlessness* himself ... *Tentatively, a Convenience*. Cue the tape ..."

↗ Quite simply, tENTATIVELY, a cONVENIENCE's performance *Generic As-Beenism* was the high point of the festival, hands-down. The short extract we see on the Videotron mixdown doesn't do it justice, but luckily Tent provided me with some of the original video that accompanied his performance[14]—which had three separate screens going simultaneously. The performance began with Tent sitting on a throne, with next to him an assistant wearing huge mechanical angel wings strapped to her back that were beating slowly. Projected onto the giant screens were astounding films flickering a collage of sound and images at a dizzying speed—literally at hundreds of frames per second.

Tent's assistant angel proceeded to shave his head, revealing a brain tattooed onto his skull in 3D. Tent then got up and walked into the audience, approaching each spectator one by one, and let them inspect his brain carefully with 3D glasses, while his assistant held a flashlight. Tent was Cirque du Soleil as imagined by Throbbing Gristle.

DAY FOUR: *Anglomaniacs!*—English Montreal

↗ Bonspiel greeted us wearing a crisp new pyjama. He threw a box on the floor and stood on it: "I have a chip under my feet. Some people have a chip on their shoulder. I find this more convenient. However, yes, this *is* the fourth day. And we *are* receiving a number of people worthy of note. Among these, an olive-skinned woman. A woman who has a black ass—or so she says—a poet, painter, *and* multidisciplinarian—don't you wanna know where *she* gets her lingerie—and a good friend of mine—presenting an ode to Arthur Lipsett[15], entitled *Lipsett And Infinity*, with her friends ... Joy Lou G ...

Lipsett films are projected on the giant screen. Onstage, an artist paints black lines on a naked woman, while the woman holds a can of spray paint with an outstretched arm. She's spraying in red a framed painting behind which Joy is crouching, wearing a mask. Joy lifts the painting, sways slowly back and forth, then after the reel ends she disappears into the shadows.

---

14. See it at: https://vimeo.com/552128815
15. A Canadian director of short avant-garde collage films

Brought back from the first Ultimatum festival, Mohamud Togane followed, this time reading his poem *The Black Tin God*[16]. He also re-read his powerful—*and funny*—poem *In Money We Trust*, from the first festival.

⯾ Bonspiel: "And now, rich with the experience of his master's degree in English (howls of laughter), rich with the experience of his having laboured in the depths of the underground music scene with such luminary essences as the participants in *Red Shift*, and most recently in *Disappointed A Few Monty Cantsins*—or *People*, as you may wish to choose—I give you, with great personal relish, a man whom I have appeared with side by side in print, or at least somewhere along the book … my friend—or at least he was until a minute ago—*Ian Stephens* …

Bathed in a red light, and under a backdrop of black and white slides on the screen, Ian gave us his poems while manipulating his voice on a synthesizer—with a tad too much echo—while a bass player throbbed out a mesmerizing groove. His stage demeanour was striking, very reminiscent of Jim Morrison.

After his performance, Bonspiel joshed him: "Do you have any communicable diseases, Ian?[17] … He's not gonna tell me. So, while we're all collecting money and keeping Ian like, sort of strapped down in order that we can get him a blood test …"

Then a radiant Anne Seymour, wearing a large floppy red beret came on, angrily thumping a book, shouting: "This is the book that's gonna come out in 1988, and it's going to be titled *Black Roses* … and it's going to be dedicated to the grandaddy of poetry Lenny Cohen."[18]

She read from her sneak preview: "It's called *The Hall Of The Dead* … There is a secret place where evil creeps like a snake, and encoiled in visions of dark mastery, priests play and women lie veiled to greet their laughter … Sex. This is my gun, baby. Sex is like a bullet. But I never use it as a weapon …"

When Anne is done and picking up her things, Bonspiel says:

---

16. See Appendix A—Selected Texts
17. Ian Stephens was gay. He died of AIDS in 1996
18. … groan …

"There is often great wisdom in madness, and I would like to thank a woman of mythological sexual prowess ... Anne Seymour" and leads the audience in applause. On her way off stage, Anne passes behind Bonspiel and attempts to lower his pajama pants. While he's struggling to keep them on, he announces a short intermission, to much laughter.

⇄ Designed to give us a breather midway through the festival, DAY FIVE was *Films & Videos Night*. We screened the videos of the best performances from the 1985 Ultimatum festival, *The Manhattan Video Project*—featuring Allen Ginsberg's excellent poem *Father Death Blues*. Also screened were Chris Kraus' *How To Shoot A Crime*—which you'll remember I helped underwrite—and lastly, Giorno Videopak 3—called *It's Clean (It Just Looks Dirty)*—featuring such luminaries as Burroughs, Hüsker Dü, Einsturzende Neubaten, Cabaret Voltaire, Psychic TV, Robert Frank, Diamanda Galas, and of course The John Giorno Band.

DAY SIX: *Ultimatum Talkshow*

After screening a video of the 1985 Ultimatum festival's conference on alternative magazine publishing, we held *Samizdat Canada*—our follow-up conference on alternative magazine publishing.

Next up was *La Désertification culturelle*—a conference on what I called the "cultural desertification" in Quebec, North America and elsewhere, with Sylvère Lotringer and François Peraldi of Semiotext(e), Italian communist activist Francesco Piperno, and iconic Quebec poet Paul Chamberland among others.

The *Ultimatum Talkshow* followed, but first there was *Cooking With Gordon W,* with hosts Jean-Luc Bonspiel, Jean Dubé, and of course our maître chapati-making chef Gordon W.

Then we moved over to the fake "talkshow" itself, following the classic TV format: Bonspiel sat at a desk stage left, with a row of seats for the guests to his right. Some of the guests were Terence Sellers, Tentatively, Judy Radul and Sylvère Lotringer. Throughout the ersatz talkshow, Bonspiel was the consummate witty host, in top shape, ad-libbing brilliant asides—his specialty. We even had a "house band" off to the side—the rest of VDMS—that is me, Jack and JM. In between interviews we played brief snippets of our songs, just like it was done on TV.

The weird thing is that our talkshow was being seen by only a few thousand people over local cable TV, yet our guests acted as if it were being seen by millions. Terence Sellers opened up about her profession as a dominatrix. She said after therapy she once tried quitting and took up a secretarial job, but she couldn't even afford dry cleaning for her raincoat. When asked about the creepiest client she'd ever had, she told us this guy had once brought her a paper bag, in which there was a dead bird. And she had to stomp on it with her high heels.

Ostensibly irked by Judy Radul, who asked him to switch seats with her so that she could "sit next to someone famous"—namely, Lotringer—Tent theatrically dropped his handheld mic onto the floor and walked off the set in pointed disgust. Knowing Tent, he'd probably planned to do this all along, and was only waiting for the slightest excuse to do so. Feigned outrage for a fake show.

After our phony talkshow, the public was invited to sample something *very* real indeed—Gordon W's yummy delicacies.

DAY SEVEN: *Au délà de Là Modernité* [19]—Quebec poetry, in French

Day Seven started with a fistfight in the lobby. I'd set up a book launching of Denis Vanier and Josée Yvon's *Travaux Pratiques*[20] in the lobby, before opening the doors to the night's events inside the theatre.

Among the patrons present was a six-foot-two, slim and graceful Black dude called Errol Wood.

We heard a loud crash coming from the bathroom. When Denis saw Errol enter the bathroom, he began shouting: "Nigger Black! Nigger Black!" Errol, very sturdy and now absolutely out of himself, was pounding Denis' face into minced meat, with huge punches to the head. But Vanier didn't give up so soon. After every heavy punch in the

---

19. Transl: *Beyond Modernity*
20. Transl: *Practical Exercises*

face—to a stomach-turning thwack, I should add—he kept walking towards Errol unrelentingly—"NIGGER BLACK! NIGGER BLACK!"—they tumbled into the lobby, where Errol picked up one of those big heavy movie theater lobby standing ashtrays, lifted it over his head, and threw it at Denis, who crumpled to the floor ... "Come on nigger, fucking nigger!" Vanier continued, bleeding like a pig. I went over and blocked off Errol, begging him: "Stop it, man! Can't you see he's just a crazy guy? Leave him alone, he's mental!"

�< Inside the relative safety of the theatre, L'ATTACQ Orchestra kicked off the night's performances, with lifelong countercultural warrior Alain-Arthur Painchaud animatedly spewing his poetry to the accompaniment of jerky guitar noodlings by Quebec's professional jerky guitar noodling nerd René Lussier—who wore his eternal red & black squared lumberjack shirt and black horn-rimmed glasses. Lussier was playing sitting in front of a lectern, diligently reading off a sheaf of sheet music. Gee, I wonder what the notation looks like for jerky guitar noodling.

∠ Visibly struggling with some form of intoxication—as was par for the course for her—Josée Yvon came on and read her great texts teetering fairly controllably, to occasional hoots of affection from the audience. Now *there's* a Quebec poet in desperate need of translation—any scholar out there sick of *Finnegan's Wake*? Her Wikipedia entry in English states:

> "Josée Yvon was a Quebec poet, playwright and screenwriter. Her work relates largely to marginalised groups in society ... Her work was highly influenced by the American lesbian and revolutionary literature. The description of marginality has a major role in it: homosexuals, drug addicts, prostitutes, transsexuals, or transvestites are recurrent characters ..."

Newcomers Irène Mayer and Hélène Monette followed, accompanied by piano and aggressive guitars respectively, followed by a big Off-Broadway stage production by *Les Sanscoeurs*. Another doomed poetess,

Hélène Monette died in 2015 at the age of 55, of cancer. Which begs the question: why are poets *always doomed?*

Last on the bill that night was the noble-miened Paul Chamberland —arguably Quebec's most important living poet and essayist. That is, before pedophilic accusations relegated him to a literary purgatory that will surely last beyond his lifetime. He read from his *Multiple événement terrestre*[21], assisted by SCP-produced computer graphics projected onto the screen.

Denis Vanier was slated to wind up the evening, but as we've seen, he was otherwise incapacitated.

➤ Crisis du jour, DAY EIGHT: Darius James had insisted on curating a whole evening titled *Montreal's First Annual Mutant Junkie Corporate Dinner*. To accomplish this, he brought up several of his less respectable associates, in order to reproduce for us a genuine evening of spoken word and mayhem as typically found on the Lower East Side. Fine.

Problem is, now they were refusing to go on until they were paid upfront. *In heroin.* Well they didn't call themselves junkies for nothing, did they? But Montreal wasn't a smack town. It was a pot town. And even if there was some smack somewhere, I was clueless how to find it. It would have to be coke. But I was out of the loop—I didn't do coke. The Kathy Acker night had been a one-off exception.

I called Louis Côté of the Foufounes in a panic. "Louis, where can I get some heroin?" He hadn't a clue. "Then how about some coke?" Luckily, *this* was doable. So I ran to the bank—with Tent in tow—withdrew $150 and gave him his fee, then another $250 for my twitching pals starting to feel the breath of cold turkey running down their necks.

I ran around, got the pile of coke, and that tided over the Mutant Junkies. The show must go on. And it did. On coke. They put on a great in-your-face *Loisaida*-style show—just as Darius had promised me—climbing over the seats and literally assaulting anxious faces in the audience. A living Theatre of Cruelty. The *real* cruelty was that this story became the source of the rumour that I'd snorted all of the festival money up my nostrils.

---

21. Transl: *The Multiple Terrestrial Event*

The following day all of those junkies got up early and disappeared, scrambling back by train to the Big Rotten for a proper fix.

ↄ DAY NINE was the last day of the festival, and arguably the best. It featured mainly guests from Manhattan, and was named ominously enough *In The Shadow Of The Twin Towers*. Unfortunately, just like the towers themselves, no video of it survived.

After the book launch of Terence Sellers' *The Obsession* at the bar Le Set, the evening started off with Montreal's Ken Decker doing *Stop For Gas*—a computer text performance. Chris Kraus' name appears nowhere on the festival program, but she too was in the festival. She came onstage wearing a gorilla suit for her pal Suzan Cooper's performance.

Another name not on the program was the anarchist poet and English gentleman Attila The Stockbroker. He was in town, so I recruited him on the spot, pushed him onstage, and he delivered a rant my wife Caroline still remembers fondly. Yes, she was in the audience but we hadn't met yet. It would take another nine months.

First though, Attila seriously pissed me off before going on. He insisted on being paid upfront, so I went around and borrowed cash from everyone and shoved it at him. Attila planted his feet widely apart, bracing himself to speed-count the bills faster than any backroom casino money-counting machine. It was a disgusting crass spectacle from yet another self-righteous "anarchist".

ↄ But now came the great man himself—and once again the biggest attraction of the festival—John Giorno. I was with him while he was warming up in the wings. He always lit up a joint to relax before going on, and shared it with me. This time he was without a backing band and did his rant poetry alone with a mic in hand, animatedly yelping out his greatest hits, including *Life Is a Killer...*

> "I wanna be filthy and anonymous... SCUM AND SLIME!..."
> "We got here yesterday, we're here now, and we can't wait to leave ta-morrah"...
> "I'm spendin' my whole life bein' with people I don't wanna *be* with!..."

Then David Rattray came on and ranted his astounding diatribe *Yoga of Anger*, which tore apart all of the hypocrisy of the Beat Generation and its oppressive pious Naropa Buddhist bullshit. Here are a few excerpts[22] ...

> "I didn't come in here tonight to talk about love and sex. God doesn't love a single person in this place. Who cares for the love of God anyhow. I don't. I'd rather deal with something more tangible like a pair of breasts for instance; and I don't believe God has breasts...
>
> What we are dealing with at this point is anger. It's universal. Anger is all over the place and rightly so. Did you know there was a yoga of anger? Right. All these swamis coming over here with a message of sweetness and light. What we haven't yet seen is the yoga of anger ...
>
> You don't need ups, downs, goofers, speed. alcohol, psychedelics, or any of that shit. Just go for the pure nerve, adrenaline. Anger. Anger is the name of the game. Fuck peace. Fuck quiet. Go for anger. Be like the headlight of an oncoming freight train. Climb down the world's throat like a locomotive ...
>
> Go for the jugular if it's within reach ... This is what we need more of. Anger. That's my message. Dare to dream like a volcano dreams. Blow your stack. Kill. Smash 'em through the floor."

And if that wasn't enough, Lisa Blaushild brought the house down with her *Love Letter To My Rapist*[23]. In her review of the festival in New York's *Cover* magazine, Chris Kraus said: "She had the all-woman video crew in hysterics." To this day Lisa Blaushild still remains America's greatest unknown writer. And this, my friends, is absolutely criminal.

---

22. See Appendix A—Selected Texts for the complete text
23. See Appendix A—Selected Texts for excerpts

Sylvère read from his *Desert Notebooks*—in French—and Terence Sellers read from her novel in progress *The Degenerate*.

And lucky him, Monty Cantsin wound up getting top billing by default, closing the festival with his *Born Again In Flames* performance—which typically consisted of an unrelenting barrage of his heavy-handed slogans screamed hysterically. He waved and flailed his arms, going: "I am the self-proclaimed leader of The Lower East Side!" Darius James asked me, "Who *is* this guy? He *Polish* or sumpin'?"

As Caroline told me years later, after all the noise and flash of Monty's "performance" was over and the lights went up, people just sat there stunned, wondering—and not in a *good* way—"what the fuck was *that*?"

⇆ So the credits rolled for a last time, and the lights went up for good. It was finally all over. I went down front and slumped into one of the seats, next to my VDMS VIP invitee Anne Powell, as well as a few remaining staff still hanging around. I was relieved, exhausted, and yes—even contented.

Monty came up to me and complained "your festival was not subversive enough." I immediately spat back: "Excuse me ... what do *YOU* do that's so subversive? All you do is sit around all day writing arts grant applications—it's not 'Total Subversion'—it's 'Total Subvention!'"

At that Monty lunged at me, and people had to keep us apart.

⇆ There was an after-party at The Shred. So I corralled Giorno, Terence Sellers, other festival guests and staff, and we all piled into cars. I led the procession, snaking slowly through the night streets of Montreal, to David Sapin's Shred in the back alley of McDonald's at the corner of Mount Royal and Papineau.

Earlier that day, I'd spotted Dave in the street, passing by in his station wagon. I flagged him down and rushed over. He rolled down his window to see what I wanted. I shoved a pile of money at him—250 bucks[24]—and said: "Dave, I want you to go over to the SAQ and buy

---

24. $600 today

as much alcohol as you can for tonight's party." He grinned and cackled "ALRIGHT!" and sped off.

Everyone piled into The Shred and rubbed elbows, mainly due to the lack of space. Glasses were clinked and the celebratory alcohol flowed.

"A barn! I LOVE it!" Giorno exulted, looking around at the digs. Terence also squealed "a barn in the middle of the city ... wow!"

Well, now ... *John Giorno in The Shred, lighting a joint*—now *there* was a high friend in a low place. In fact, the lowest in Montreal.

Downing my drink, I turned to Sapin and said: "Now the shit hits the fan." He countered: "Ah, forget it ... it was worth it."

ζ And he was damn right. The financial disaster shit hadn't caught up with the fan yet, so I enjoyed cruising on the post-festival buzz for a while longer.

18

MY DOLCE VITA BEFORE THE STORM

I'd been wooing Anne Powell throughout the festival and it worked. She was a good-looking, sexy lawyerette in leather miniskirt, black stockings and high heels, and with her banged jet black hairdo she looked exactly like Uma in *Pulp Fiction*.

Earlier in the year, when VDMS had an unplugged show plus interview at Radio Centre-ville[1], she was on the road listening to the live broadcast, slammed the brakes on her MG Spider and jumped into a phone booth to request a song. She was our top VDMS superfan, and we treat those with kid gloves. And mine made it all the way up her skirt.

She was definitely out of my league, thus the more delectable the lawyered-up lay. I zoomed around riding shotgun in her MG Spider and we had a ball. And balled some more. We didn't have a Trevi Fountain to splash around in, but our Dolce Vita kept my mind off things, the wind whipping my hair in her convertible, yelling to talk over the noise of the engine and the road.

We drove up to Morin Heights for cocktails at some art professor's Swiss-chalet type house. He was an expert on German artist Kurt Schwitters and there were paintings, *Merz* collages and sculptures by him everywhere. This invitation was an offshoot of the *Littérature et Métropole*[2] symposium at the University of Montreal, to which I'd been invited by literature professor Hans Herbert Räkel. I talked about Ultimatum II and read a few selections from my *États Limites* in French, pausing after each line to hear his simultaneous translation

1. Transl: Downtown Radio
2. Transl: *Literature And The City*

into German. The famous writer Marie-Claire Blais[3] was in the audience. After the reading she came up to me and said: "Tu dis ce que les autres n'osent que penser"[4].

⇄ The day after the festival—the 20th—we'd held a party for the Ultimatum staff at the offices. Nothing memorable to report. However, another party—on the 30th—*is* memorable. Through Hans Herbert Räkel I invited a cultural delegation from West Germany to show them what we were doing at Ultimatum. I asked the staff to spend some of our precious little kitty money on hors d'oeuvres and cheap Henkell Troken bubbly to welcome the delegation. We laid out the comestibles on a buffet table around 5 PM. The staff was tired and wanted to go home, but I begged them to stick around a bit longer. The party was late, our people were getting hungry and wound up eating and drinking everything, leaving scraps for the *Kulturati*. Who decided to show up sometime past 7 PM. The well-fed, well-financed Art Eurocrats were miffed and shocked at being treated so shoddily, and stormed out muttering angrily in German. Sorry volks, we were more Baader Meinhof art terrorists than Karl Lagerfeld art poodles with lavish budgets. Fucking kunsts.

⇄ In October I was invited to participate in the *Rencontre internationale Jack Kerouac*[5] in Quebec City, where I had the privilege of sharing the stage with Allen Ginsberg, Lawrence Ferlinghetti, Jack Micheline, and also Josée Yvon, Denis Vanier, and Francoeur. Anne Powell drove her brand new boyfriend to Quebec City in record time.

I got the chance to talk with Ginsberg, who was now hobbling around with a cane. Francoeur quickly butted in, and started chatting up ole' Ginsy in a storm, and to my surprise they began reciting in tandem *A Season in Hell* ... in *French*. Well *that* was something.

The high point of the evening was of course Ginsberg, who gave us

3. Author of *A Season in the Life of Emmanuel*
4. Transl: "You say what others only dare think."
5. Transl: The International Jack Kerouac Symposium

his bucket-kicking anthem *Father Death Blues*[6]—proof again that he had not lost any relevance. When my turn came, I read selections from my *États Limites*. A sampling of the works read that night came out in the book *Québec Kerouac Blues*.

I hadn't seen Francoeur since his *Ultimatum Tuesdays* gig, and after the Kerouac soirée we decided to go grab a bite—he, Anne and me. We stopped at a nondescript Arab fast food joint and swallowed a quick kebab.

It was around midnight and we still had to make the 250 km[7] return trip to Montreal. Francoeur had a hotel room. We walked together on the sidewalk a bit, but our directions were opposite, so we had to leave each other. After taking a few steps toward his hotel, Francoeur stopped, stared at the sidewalk, then barked authoritatively, "So, you comin'?"

Huh? What? Francoeur was trying to *steal my girlfriend?* Just like that, right under my nose? Anne and I stared at each other slack-jawed, unable to believe it.

"C'mon, let's go" he insisted, as if she were just another one of those dimbulbs he loved to humiliate in his songs. Anne hooked her arm around mine and pulled me away to the parking lot. All the way back to Montreal Anne and I laughed to tears at the irresistible animal magnetism of my old buddy.

⇝ Anne thought the world of me and encouraged my music-making. She let me languish afternoons strumming my guitar at her place. Then after hours, she let me strum *her* place languidly.

She brought me to a dinner that was held regularly by her friends and law colleagues, to show off her new boyfriend. Throughout the dinner they made snide remarks, rolled their eyes, looked at each other and snickered openly as if I wasn't there. They knew I was only Anne's bad boy toy of the month, and would have a replacement by their next dinner appointment.

Anne's beautiful tanned skin was the softest I'd ever touched. One

---

6. Hear it at: https://www.youtube.com/watch?v=hrM41x_Db1c
7. 155 miles

day I was on top, shagging her tenderly, rocking back and forth gently inside of her. She started sobbing softly. Well *that* wilted my chamberlain. I asked her what was wrong. She never said anything.

Once during our pillow talk I asked what her specialty was in Law. She explained she'd had a hand in writing up Canada's immigration laws, knew all the loopholes, and was now making a killing going down to Haïti and flying up Haïtians through the very loopholes she'd drafted. God bless her cute smart head.

Another time her pillow talk turned to her out-of-body-experiences. "I feel myself going," she said, gesticulating with her arm, her hand pulling something invisible out the top of her head, "and then I see myself floating down the hall, and I'm freaking out because I'm fed up and want to get back inside my body, but I just don't know how."

We lasted together a couple of months, then I just sort of wandered off. We could've made a go at it, stayed together, it could have worked. She was a great gal, very supportive. What went wrong? I dunno. I was used to moving on without thinking.

⇌ Back at my Monenco-LGL job, I was in a cubicle on a whole floor of engineers and draftsmen, still working on the Norsk Hydro project's huge Electrolysis Hall. Sitting nearby was this jovial portly Italian in his sixties. Every so often he'd blurt out "Culo la balena! Culo la balena!"[8]. It was his highly original way of saying "fuck it", or "piss on it". It was a great mantra, very liberating.

The construction site was now screaming for the design drawings of the Electrolysis Hall's concrete floor beams. These were the design responsibility of my Viet cubicle neighbour—the dude who'd been too busy working on his bro-in-law's accounting software, remember?

Armin turned to me and said: "Alan, I need rebar steel in those drawings. *Today.*" I protested: "What the hell has *Tran* been doing all this time? Armin, we're talking about the design of a hundred concrete beams here!" Armin was adamant: "Throw me some rebar steel into those beams. RIGHT NOW."

In school, you'd get a week or more to design a concrete beam. Now

---

8. Transl: "Whale's ass!"

I had to churn out *a hundred* beams in a couple of hours. Welcome to the real world, kids. So what did I do? I slapped rebars covering the maximum likely bending moments for continuous beams, top *and* bottom. Which—for all you people itching to be civil engineers—meant $WL^2/9$. Fast track, fast slap. And *Culo la balena.*

ζ One day Armin called me over to his office and asked: "Do you know anyone who's good with computers?" Thinking of all the engineers I knew, I replied "no". Then I thought of Gagnon and said: "Hey wait a minute, I have a friend who's a wiz with computers ... but he's not an engineer. He programs computers to compose music." Armin's eyes lit up. "Fine, bring him in," he said. "We'll give him a try!"

And that's how Gagnon was hired. No resumé, no going through interviews, none of that *"where do you see yourself in five years"* HR crap. He was hired on the strength of my word alone, just like that. Try this today. Impossible. He did fine, and even wound up designing concrete slabs for engineers using Lotus 1-2-3 spreadsheets. It was his first I.T. job, from which he made a decent living the rest of his life. I felt real good about getting Gagnon a job, after he'd dropped his job for Francoeur. Thirty-two years later, Gagnon's son (and my godson) gave *my* son a summer job. Karma can be such a hoot sometimes.

Gagnon thought engineers were the weirdest bunch. We witnessed this guy fighting over inches of territory with his next cubicle neighbour. He kept pushing the partition that separated them for more space, then the other guy would push back—just like the two dweebs tugging at that shared desk in the movie *Brazil*. One day we heard shouting, everyone looked up, and we saw two engineers duking it out ferociously. A white guy and an Asian. We suspect the white guy brushed by calling him a "chink" or something. They were both fired on the spot.

Engineering is an odd profession that attracts a lot of peculiar people—lots of socially awkward, borderline quasi-autists who relate better to numbers and machines than people. Lots of psychopaths were also engineers: Ahmadinejad, Arafat, Osama Bin Laden. Scary.

ζ With VDMS, despite our occasional triumphs, disenchantment gradually began to settle in, for lack of any real success. The new songs barely arrived, and were not as high caliber as in the beginning. The Schärr cart began turning in circles. Plus, I was getting sidelined in the band, when I was the one providing the best songs. It was Jack's habit to rush out and register the copyright for *my* songs four-ways. Thank God there was no money to be made, or I would've been seriously ripped off. I was at the height of my song-writing powers and needed a new vehicle with which to do so. *My own.*

I convinced Gagnon that French-language rock was a thing now in Montreal, and we put a band together with our old friend Angel, plus Denis Duran on bass—both from the freshly defunct Rational Youth. Thus *Les Frogs* were born. Our songs were a mix of power pop, some country, but mainly hard R&B smokers propelled by Gagnon's phenomenal lead guitar playing[9].

Gagnon also composed the songs, and with the Frogs I experienced for the first time the joy of being in a tight song-writing partnership—much like Lennon-McCartney's must have felt. We completed each others' songs, mostly howling with laughter—and often on the job.

Denis grew up in a large Franco-Vietnamese family in France, and had a bewildering amount of siblings, cousins and in-laws, whose names I couldn't remember. He had a brother and a cute sister who worked in vintage garment stores on St Denis. In addition to their superb musicianship, both Denis and Gagnon were a laudable rarity: junkies who'd succeeded in kicking their heroin habit. Cold turkey. So hats off, fellas.

⤨ Meanwhile, the VDMS circus continued, and we gave a raucous show at l'Usine[10]. We had another show coming up at the Foufs, and I wrote a new song for the occasion: *Le Rap à Raël*[11]. Raël was the French leader of The Raëlians—a ridiculous UFO cult that had many adherents in Quebec. Their symbol was—I kid you not—a swastika in the middle of the Star of David.

I made 6-inch diameter silver-sprayed medallions of the Raëlian logo for us to wear onstage. Dubé accompanied me wearing the

---

9. Hear it at: https://soundcloud.com/alan-lord-4/2-babel-baby
10. Transl: The Factory
11. Transl: *Raël's Rap*

medallions, and on the way to the Foufs we danced through the subway like loons, singing "Le Rap à Raël, le Rap à Raël, y'a plein d'ovnis qui descendent du ciel!"[12]

We opened our show with that song, and wearing the medallions around our necks. Jack remembers: "This crazy chick jumped onstage and ripped the props off our chests."

↗ Burroughs' novel *The Western Lands* came out on December 14th. It was to be the last in a trilogy with *Cities Of The Red Night* and *The Place Of Dead Roads*. Of course I was excited and called up editor Eyal Kattan of *The Montreal Mirror*, and got the commission to review the book. For the occasion I interviewed Burroughs by phone, which I taped. It was around the time of the Palestinian Intifada in Israel, and I asked him what he thought about that. "Nothing new," he drawled, "they'll be fighting each other forever."

My review appeared in February 1988, and I got them to put Burroughs on the front page. It was my media scoop number one. My second one would come a year later.

↗ Of course, it was that time of year again, and the Foufounes asked VDMS to do the New Year's Eve show. This time the theme chosen was Japan: kimonos and Kabuki makeup, and a backdrop of Kamikaze planes painted by David Sapin. The gorgeous Foufs barmaid Audrey applied my Samurai's eye makeup delicately, bending over me. Her crotch was in my face. I lost it, and grabbed her pussy. She didn't say anything. We had to go onstage in a few minutes.

---

12. Transl: "Raël's rap, Raël's rap, lotsa UFO's droppin' from the sky!"

19

GUTTERDÄMMERUNG

A s our crestfallen hero Alex says in *A Clockwork Orange* ... "This is the real weepy and like tragic part of the story beginning, O my brothers and only friends ..."

The Ultimatum II Postmortem

Ok, fine, the festival had been a great artistic success—no doubt about *that*. It featured a total of 158 artists, poets, writers, musicians, dancers, and audio-video technicians from seven cities, with roughly half the performances split between English and French. A total of 35 hours of shows had been taped audio and video, and the team of 30 techs had used three Sony cameras to mix on the spot broadcast-quality videos that were aired nightly on the Vidéotron cable channel. TV, radio, newspaper and magazine coverage had been extensive, exposing over 2 million people to the event.

Chris Kraus wrote up a glowing article about the festival in *New York Cover* magazine, saying Montreal was "a lyrically romantic city" set between New York and Paris. Yet although the festival was brilliant artistically and technically and everyone was pleased as punch to having been part of such an amazing event, it turned out to be a financial disaster.

↗ When did things start unravelling? Well, for starters, two weeks before the start of the festival, my super indispensable manager Joe Martek quit. *Not* a good omen. He obviously knew something I didn't.

Had he stayed, things would have definitely turned out differently. Until he suddenly left, Martek and I were already planning next year's event: *The Art Olympics*, to be held in Montreal's Olympic Stadium. Luckily, my future mega-delirious plans were soundly dashed by impending Reality.

If my manager quitting wasn't enough, our bookkeeper Susie got sick a week later, and remained sick at home throughout the festival. By then I was too busy running around getting last minute shit done to start worrying about balancing the goddamn books.

Anarprick had been busting my balls to invite his goddamn Mecca Normal to the festival. I caved and did so, just to get him off my back. That cost me $600[1] in plane fare alone from Vancouver, when all acts were supposed to be getting a $100 per diem[2] to cover *reasonable* transportation—i.e., *bus*.

Once we were well into the festival, Cynthia suddenly needed this and that video tech doohickie. I had to rush out and rent it. Then soundman Guy Bou[3] was missing this or that sound doohickie. I told him to just get it and I'd pay later. You'd think I'd learned something from my *Ultimatum Tuesdays*. Well, I had a fucking *festival* to run here, and keep the show oiled.

Then HRH Eldon Garnet flew into Montreal from Toronto and presented me his Air Canada ticket: $250[4]. No bus either for *this* regal Can-Art star. I handed him the full amount. *Why?*

Mid-festival, Anarprick presented me Attila The Stockbroker, a professional anarchist rant star, who happened to be in town. He wanted me to squeeze him into the programming. "Sure" I said, out of my spontaneous good-natured enthusiastic Ex-Neoist zeal. The guy asked for $200 or so[5], and wouldn't go on until he had the cash in his hands. I got it and gave it to him, as previously explained. *Why?*

---

1. $1400 today
2. $230 today
3. Pronounced "Ghee Boo"
4. $575 today
5. $460 today

 Regardless of the many snowballing causes, a few weeks after the festival was over, the shit *did* start hitting the fan. John Giorno's $250 cheque bounced. Terence Sellers wanted to know when I'd be sending her back her unsold books that were on consignment. John Bentley Mays howled at me, sending letters left and right, promising to blacklist me to the moon.

Standing on the sidewalk in front of the Ultimatum offices I broke the news to Bonspiel I couldn't pay him back the $600[6] he'd fronted for the food to feed the staff, plus his emcee fee. He began beating a parking meter Thwack! Thwack! Thwack! with his big meaty fist. I felt very lucky it wasn't my face.

Soundman Guy Bou held the audiotapes for ransom[7]. I handed over *second* soundman Bézy my collection of Burroughs books as collateral. I eventually paid *him* up and got the books back later. That evil Anarprick started telling everyone I'd taken off with the money. *What* money? The *real* problem was, the coffers were *bare*! He was painting me as some kind of Bernie Madoff of the underground scene—when all along *he* had been one of the many causes of my out-of-control festival cost overruns.

Anarprick was one of the people I *did* manage to pay back, and still the douche kept on slagging me. Publicly. To this day. Were I to run into him, it would take a herculean effort on my part not to stab that weasel in the face. He was one of those pathetically correct judgmental wokeflake cunts—a strident moralizing self-righteous professional finger-pointer, who never did anything of value or built anything for anyone.

The only one who instead of criticizing actually helped me out was Karl Jirgens. He got sick of hearing one of those career arts-council titsuckers going on and on about me, and gave him $250 to shut him up. What a mensch, that Karl. He was the only one who understood.

 In a downtown bar I spotted Ivan of the Hats. He asked me how I was. I told him I owed $10,000[8] after my Ultimatum fiasco. He said,

---

6. $1400 today
7. That cultural criminal eventually erased the precious festival audio archives out of pure spite
8. $23,000 today

"Well I just finished a tour, and I owe $100,000!" It didn't exactly cheer *me* up. He told me *he* was in town shopping for a video production company he wanted to buy.

While I was doing my festivals, I kept wondering why no one else was doing this. If you stopped to think about it, it was totally nuts. Good thing I didn't stop to think about it, or else there would have *been* no Ultimatums, and nothing for me to tell you. I should give seminars, like Ted Talks:

> "Do *you* have what it takes to be a glorious failure? No?
> Well stick with me, I'll show you how! First you get a crazy
> idea. Like putting together a $100,000 nine-day avant-lit
> festival with only $30,000 in grant money."

Why did I do all this shit? *I wanted things to happen.* And if I learned something in life, it's that if you want things to happen, you have to *make* them happen. And then serendipity fills in the rest. If you're lucky. But a Giorno song had a line for me: "Bankrupting yourself with generosity."

So I owe you, huh? Did you factor in *my generosity of spirit?* What's my discount for *that?* It's worth *millions.* People being people, they don't think of that. It's easier to be an outrage junkie than balance the yin against the ka-ching. Well, fuck 'em. I stopped kicking myself after a few years.

Ultimately (ha), my generosity of spirit was abused. Like that idiot "without regrets" who was in my first festival and wanted to sue me because I hadn't put him in the *second* one.

First of all I was not well in the head to put on these festivals. And then by a miracle you expect me to be well in the head with money? Were I sane enough to avoid financial problems, I would have been sane enough *not* to put on these festivals in the first place. Is it reasonable to expect an artist to be reasonable? With like, money? Give an artist money, it'll disappear. Because he wipes his ass with it.

⇄ That my friends, is the story of Ultimatum II. And now, 35 years later, it's being hailed as the era-defining countercultural milestone it indeed was. But in the meantime, it took years for me to recover from my nervous breakdown. Like Giorno said, "you gotta burn to shine."

During my Ultimatum frenzy I was always wondering how I could decelerate. Well, hitting a wall works. Ultimatum wound up ruining me both financially and mentally, and it took me decades to build back my self-esteem and confidence.

"You're infamous!" exulted Karl Jirgens. Yeah, to this day I get bad-mouthed by people. You see, *they* didn't fail. *Because they did nothing.* And all the little lambies who played it safe all their life *hate* it when a tiger shows up in their midst.

Being a glorious failure is both depressing and liberating. People who used to kiss my ass now left me alone.

For a while I tried to fix the mess. I tried getting a bank loan, and wrote nice letters to government arts councils for emergency money to bail me out. My efforts went nowhere, and I no longer had any staff to help. Every evening after work I went to the offices and sat down at my desk, trying to be diligent and figure out what to do, where to start. By October the days were starting to get shorter and the sun was setting earlier and earlier. I wound up sitting staring off into space through the windows in the dark, all alone, in silence. My prospects were getting equally dim. I had to face the fact I was doomed. Normally energetic and decisive, forever grabbing the bull by the horns, I now felt over-whelmed and paralyzed, and alone. Because I was. Now that my big parade was over, no one wanted to stick around to sweep the elephant shit with me.

When I got home, the only thing waiting for me was a stack of bills I could do nothing about. After a while I stopped opening the envelopes and just frisbeed them into a growing pile in the corner. My answering machine was full and always blinking, overloaded with messages. I ig-nored it.

⇒ I started not going home after work. I had no one waiting for me at home anyway. I wound up being the first one at the Foufs, at 6 PM, and chatted up the barmaids until someone walked in I could drink with. Usually it was Sapin.

The barmaids at the Foufs alone were worth the detour. They were a wild sexy bunch. There was Ava Rave, Valkyria, Audrey, and Sandra the raven-haired Vampirella beauty. You wanted to bang them all. But I got to paradise only with Audrey. Valkyria was a fierce gal, and a Viking would have thought twice about messing with *her*. I had a crush on her, but she was too intimidating. As for Ava Rave, she wound up living in Wales with none other than Jet Black of The Stranglers.

If Dave Sapin wasn't there, whoever else was would do as a drinking buddy. With what was left of my paycheque after making the minimum payments agreed upon with all my suppliers, I drank and paid everyone drinks. And started doing coke. Boy do you make a lot of friends when word gets around that you have a small packet of the magic white powder. Sapin became my main single-malt Scotch and coke pal. I'll never forget the way he grinded his teeth sideways yakking a mile a minute. Everyone I gabbed with on coke had these fantastic projects, all kinds of cool things they wanted to hatch with me. The following day those plans evaporated. *Coke Talk.*

Sapin's Shred buddy Christian Dion was another regular patron of the Foufs. As soon as he saw me walk in, he'd sidle up to me and go: "Hey, Lord, un pichet? Un p'tit pichet, Lord?"[9]—meaning that I should buy myself a pitcher of beer, so's I could pour him a glass. Soon he didn't even bother asking and just helped himself to my pitcher while I was busy talking to someone.

Another regular was Joe Bébel, who later became an artist, but for now was still only a lowly sewer worker and erstwhile plumber. There was always this whiff of sewer smell accompanying him. He was a small guy, almost dwarfish, and had a cleft palate and a funny nasal voice I can still imitate. One day I got to the Foufs and found him sobbing unconsolably. I said, "Joe, what's wrong?" He said: "In the year 2000 I'll be out of a job!" He explained that people would be whizzing around in shiny saucers and there would be no need for plumbers like him anymore. I wrapped my arm around his shoulders and calmly explained to him: "Joe, even in the 21st century, we'll still have to pump drinking water to the top of skyscrapers, and toilets will still get flushed!" He wiped his tears and runny nose and beamed at the

---

9. Transl: "Hey, Lord, a pitcher? A lil' pitcher, Lord?"

revelation. "Really? Oh wow … thanks, Lord!" And he left, bouncing along cheerfully now, with a big grin. Yes, "Le Lord" *does* work the occasional miracle. Not long after, I found him again in a corner all alone, sulking over his beer in silence. Then suddenly, for no apparent reason, he yelled out loud: "Chu pas une tapette!"[10] Well Joe, this time I can't do anything for you, man.

↗ By winter and then springtime 1988, I was spiral crashing my way down into the gutter. For the first time in my life I paid for sex. I went to see a hooker in her crappy apartment in east end Ville d'Anjou. The whole experience was as depressing as Ville d'Anjou. Sometimes, instead of spending my nights at the Foufs I spent them at Campo's apartment in The Losers Palace, drinking. You could always count on him for that.

By then Sapin had become a starving artist quite literally, and slept on the floor of his unheated Shred. He clued me in on all the perfectly good food and produce you could find in the dumpsters behind restaurants and food marts along Mt. Royal street. Here Dave, have another toot on me. Want another Scotch? It's only 3 AM at the Foufs, the night is still young, and our lives are going nowhere.

↗ Luckily, there was music to take my mind off things. Barely. In March VDMS did another show at Café Campus. This time, in between songs Bonspiel placed the needle on an album of the world's national anthems on a turntable, as we stood in strict attention with stiff military salutes.

After the show we were hanging out in the kitchen having a beer, when a slick Frenchman from Bordeaux named Luc Natali came in and started chatting us up. He wanted to be our manager and promised us a ton of stuff. I looked at his feet. He was wearing a ratty pair of cowboy boots, with the heels practically worn off. What the hell could *this* guy do for *us*?

He said he knew people in France who could put out our records. We sorely needed a manager, so he would have to do.

In April, my Frogs played at Poodle's. I felt hollow, but I soldiered

10. Transl: "I'm not a fag!"

on for the troops. Gagnon recalls: "We played our new epic *Appel au Clan Panneton*[11], and Mario danced in a state of trance, totally fucked up, but really immersed in our music. He seemed to be the only one, by the way—lol."

Trying to replicate the success of VDMS, I entered the Frogs into that year's *Rock Envol* battle of the bands contest in early May. We made it to the final round, but lost out to *Possession Simple*, who disappeared even faster into obscurity than we did. We managed to turn a few heads, however. We started the show with Gagnon wailing a wrenching blues harp atop an ominous droning Velvets-ish dirge. We had our backs to the audience, and our backdrop was a wall-sized painting by David Sapin, which featured his logo of a grinning frog wearing a white cowboy hat and sunglasses. Laurent Saulnier[12] of *Voir* magazine admitted to future radio personality Benoît Dutrizac[13] that the Frogs were the best band ever to come out of Quebec. Our drunken Mario heartily concurred, again abandoning himself in a spastic trance dance in front of the packed hall of The Spectrum.

⇁ Even though I was a wreck psychologically, I still managed to show up for work, sober and on the dot. As always. My day was now split between two major industrial projects. Mornings and early afternoons I worked on the Norsk Hydro project downtown, then around 4 PM I took the subway all the way up to Sauvé, then a bus, and worked at LGL until 7 or 8, on the expansion of a 5-storey phosphorus plant for Albright & Wilson in Varennes. Yes, it was my dorkest hour. And again, Il Duce thought I was wasting my time on the computer. I was now modeling the whole building using the crude software S-Frame, doing 3D modeling several years before it became standard practice using more sophisticated software.

The LGL office was above a crappy strip mall at the corner of Sauvé

---

11. Transl: *Calling The Panneton Clan*—a tongue-in-cheek paean to a family that owned a fleet of moving trucks; Hear the song at: https://www.youtube.com/watch?v=DP8QdD7AAos

12. Pronounced "Low-ruh So-knee-yay"

13. Pronounced "Buh-n'wah Dew-tree-zack"

and l'Acadie, and I hated it. It's been torn down since. When I passed by the Sauvé office one day, a draftsman took me aside and said, "Listen Alan, when you were breaking up with Joss, I didn't want to tell you, but I saw Joss nuzzling with a guy in the subway." Great, that really made my day.

I got a call from a mid-level manager at my bank. He wanted to see me. So I went to their stately building in Old Montreal. The fiftyish guy with a salt and pepper mustache started grilling me. "What's your *problem*, Mr. Lord? You're an engineer, you have a good job … we make about the same salary, I would say … but I have a wife and kids, I have a car, a house, and in addition I have money set aside for an RRSP[14] … yet you, with the salary you make, have no RRSP's set aside and have all these debts. Do you have a *gambling* problem? Or a *drug* problem? What's your *problem*, Mr. Lord?"

What could I tell him? That I had an *Art* problem? That I once was a *Neoist*? That I could only shit on his normaloid values and wipe my ass with his sacrosanct "money"? That instead of paying my rent I preferred forking out $600 for David Rattray to fly up so I could listen to him do a reading at The Foufounes Électriques? How could a bank manager make any sense of *that*? He frowned and consolidated my debts—I now had just one payment to make every paycheque, but I had to follow this schedule strictly.

With this "minimum payment" arrangement, I often had only $100 left to carry me through two weeks until the next paycheque. One day at LGL I went downstairs to the mall, to see what I could buy for lunch. All I had was 49 cents in my hand. So I bought a packet of grape-flavoured Kool Aid—appropriately purple. I went back upstairs to the office, spooned it into a glass of water and watched it fizz as I sat forlornly at my desk. *That* was my lunch for the day. This moment was *definitely* the lowest point of my life up till then. Pretty hard to beat.

This was a level of insanity even beyond *my* limits. I couldn't continue living like that. Fuck *that* bullshit. I wasn't gonna be no Art Martyr being self-flagellated by everyone else. Then one morning I walked into the LGL office and there was a goddamn punch clock on

14. Retirement savings plan registered with the Canadian government

the wall. For *engineers? Come on!* It was time for me to go. So I gave my notice to Il Duce, glad to finally have the opportunity to leave *him* in the lurch, and gleefully dove off the social cliff with the surprising energy that being utterly doomed gives you. I had now joined the ranks of those who really have nothing to lose.

The evening I quit—after four solid years of service—I celebrated by getting blind drunk. As I staggered home I paused to yank my sacrosanct Engineering Ring off my pinkie, and shoved it through the nearest manhole grating.

≥ I started eyeing my bookshelves suspiciously. I decided maybe *that* was the cause of my problems: Rimbaud, Burroughs, Baudelaire—my worship of all that sinister, decadent literature—and where it had ultimately led me. So I got rid of them in one fell tabula rasa swoop. Bézy already had my Burroughs collection as collateral. I sold off the rest of my precious books I'd so painstakingly accumulated—including rare edition Surrealist art books—with one that even included an original André Masson print. I gave Mario all of my record collection—including the good stuff: rare original Clash and Pistols sleeved singles. Of course, he sold it off bit by bit for beer money.

I borrowed the VDMS Econoline van from Jack, parked in front of the Foufs, and ran up to get Louis Côté. I opened the van doors and showed him my two 3/4" videotape U-Matics and various sound equipment. "How much can you give me?" I asked. I left a few hundred dollars richer. Anything else I could sell? Sure, my fridge and any other appliances and furniture I had left.

I skipped out of my now-bare Papineau apartment owing three months' rent, $600 to Hydro, $350 to Bell, and $15,000[15] to my bank. Yeah, fuck you, Mister wife-kids-car-house-RRSP's!

By now I was totally paranoid and imagined all the debt collectors swarming after me waving court orders and pitchforks. I found an apartment building I deemed anonymous enough and paid the first month's rent on a basement apartment. I split to get my stuff and move in.

No. I changed my mind. It was too depressing there, and maybe

---

15. $35,000 today

too tempting a place to end my misery. Eureka! I'd move into *Mario's* building. Yes! I'd be neighbours with my bosom buddy in *this*, my darkest hour. *That* would tide me over till my next lifetime.

I knocked on Rosalie's door. She was the concierge of the Losers Palace—or *Castel Rosalie*[16], as he called it. Even though she was plain ugly, Mario entertained sexual fantasies about her. He said: "I want to get her pussy wet atop the clothes dryer in the basement laundry room."

I was in luck. There was a vacancy! She gave me a room which had a view on the fire escape and windows of the rest of the apartment block. It was literally "a room"—with a small bathroom. It came with an ugly orange Naugahyde couch that folded out into a bed. It was sticky and stank of the old dried piss crust of bygone drunkards and losers. I moved the few possessions I had left into my choice new suite. Curiously, it was the same apartment Mario had started out in, back in the 6th Apartment Festival—No. 23—also Burroughs' eternally recurring fetish number.

∠ It was a small suicide. *A social* one. But the no-nonsense peasants' survival genes I inherited saw to it that matters wouldn't progress any further. Although the idea often *did* cross my mind.

With Mario as my damaged guardian angel, I was saved. For now.

---

16. Transl: Château Rosalie

20

DOWN AND OUT IN MONTREAL

I can't count the days, evenings and sleepless nights I spent with Mario in his dingy apartment, drinking and talking about music, art, literature, politics and metaphysics. Even at 3 o'clock in the morning we blasted the Sex Pistols, Ramones, Damned, Vibrators, old Stones records, Cream's *Disraeli Gears*, and Blue Cheer's insane albums so appreciated by San Fran bikers on acid.

Campo would recite to me Baudelaire and Rimbaud from memory, and I showed him our latest VDMS songs on the cheap guitar I'd bought him. Sometimes he sang. His favourite song was Dylan's *Knocking On Heaven's Door*—but as done by Guns n' Roses. Mario wanted to be a guitarist, I wanted to be a poet. We both failed.

A typical day at the Losers Palace? I usually woke up just in time to catch the CBC news on TV at noon. Then I looked at how much I had. I could either afford a sandwich and a beer, or a sandwich and a newspaper. I had to choose. I brought in empty bottles and cans for the refund money, but I often had to steal cans of *Paris Pâté* deviled ham from poor old *Monsieur Minh*, my local Viet dépanneur. He was right across the street from famed Quebec songster Plume Latraverse's[1] place.

I didn't have a phone, which made things interesting. To call someone I had to go to the phonebooth around the corner. If people wanted to see me, they had to come and knock on my door, or slip me a note under it. I loved it. Sometimes I was there and saw a note being slid in, and giggled silently.

---

1. Pronounced "Pleuhm Lah-trah-vairss"

As you entered my 10' × 12' apartment, to the left was my 6' Ikea bookshelf, filled with the few precious books I'd kept. Then against the left wall was the lovely fluorescent orange Naugahyde couch, which took up half the room when opened into a bed. Next to it was my dresser, on top of which was a boxy old TV with rabbit ears and five channels: the English-language CBC and CTV, and French language Radio Canada, TVA and TVQ. Being a not-quite-yet-on-welfare bum now—and too lazy to bother getting up and turn the bulky rotary dial to change channels—I jury-rigged a "redneck remote" out of an unbent wire coat hanger, which I taped to the rotary dial with duct tape. That way I could stretch out on the couch and twist the hooky end to change the channels. Final proof that laziness is the *real* motherfucker of invention.

On the right side of the apartment was a narrow closet which also housed my tall dark green four-drawer metal filing cabinet—that held my precious archives. Next to the window on the right side was "my office"—a Phillips PC on a flimsy white board sitting on inverted-V frame legs, and my ugly brown checkered fabric office chair—which was ratty by now. This was my father's gift when I graduated from McGill—no doubt he expected it to be the first piece of furniture for the engineering firm I was to found. Then at the far end of the room— about 10 feet away—was the "kitchen"—cupboards, counter and sink, with the fridge to the left. The tiny bathroom—with the occasional stray cockroach skating in the tub—was to the right. A cockroach would amble idly across the kitchen counter once in a while, but I'd splatter it quick with my fist.

It was the best of slimes, it was the worst of slimes.

On the first day of the month, the mailman opened the entire panel of mailboxes to insert the welfare cheques. Everyone in the building was on welfare. They were weird. At midday one guy opened the door of his apartment and grilled himself some hash meat. Like clockwork, every noon I was subjected to the sound of his hash sizzling in the pan, as well as the smell. Through the window of Mario's apartment, we saw that one of the building's windows was blocked out with yellowed newspapers. We tried to guess the secret of this mysterious occupant.

ᔕ Every emotion I'd compartmentalized since my big breakup with Joss caught up with me in a huge wave. I was never the depressive type. But now I cried in bed, and had a hard time finding a reason to get up in the morning. Sometimes events swallow you whole. I lurched around in the streets under the hot sun like a zombie. I ran into an old Ultimatum staffer, who asked me about some document she needed. "Sorry," I brushed her off, "I can't even put a stamp on an envelope and put it in the mail." It seems ridiculous now, but when you have a nervous breakdown you can't function. Doing the simplest chore becomes an insurmountable task. It's like when you've broken a leg and can't stand on it anymore—you can't understand how it feels until it happens to you. That's why I never pass a panhandler without giving him something. And don't you ever dare make a snarky remark—you'd only be adding to their misery.

ᔕ Every day during that oppressively hot summer I swore I wouldn't go to my mom's for lunch. And wound up walking the 2.5 km there every damn day. She was great, she never asked me any questions—like, "why aren't you working?" My father was off to Spain again, and she was just happy to see me. It was the best time we ever had together.

I passed by the Café Cléopâtre[2] and complained about my poverty to the DJ—who was Dédé, before he became Traké. He said, "Hey Lord, why don't you go on welfare?" Folks, I have the great honour of introducing you to my financial advisor—*Dédé Traké*[3].

The first of the month now, Welfare Day found me in the long snaking line at the bank amid all the other losers waiting to cash their welfare cheques. Ah, the erstwhile socialite conversations I overheard in the welfare line … "Oh hi Justine, what have *you* been up to? *I'm* rehearsing in a new play!" … "Oh really? Well, that's absolutely *marvelous*, dahling!"—Christ, they were chatting as if at a Vanity Fair Oscars after-party. I felt like turning around and yelling: "Hey people, get real: *YOU'RE ON FUCKING WELFARE!*"

---

2. A seedy stripper joint on St Laurent below Ste Catherine—within walking distance from the Foufounes Électriques

3. He became a local rap star in 1992: https://www.youtube.com/watch?v=PsYb8Ea989M

乙 I didn't know what to do with myself, so I started hanging out at the small shop *Mot Clé*[4] on Cherrier street, right around the corner from the Losers Palace. Dubé worked there now, doing desktop publishing. While Dubé pasted up stuff on *Pagemaker*, I played the few games available on the Macintosh, including one that involved piloting a helicopter through city skyscraper canyons. *"SDC sighted!"* the game kept saying. And when I was about to crash, it warned: *"Pull up! Pull up!"*—yes Lord, why don't you heed that advice, and *indeed* pull up? I took it as a personal insult.

The French have a beautiful word to describe what I'd become—*désoeuvré*[5]—which is a conflation of *idle, listless, defeated, drifting.* It was also one of Philippe Côté's pet concepts in the SCP.

I'd come in and slack around, doing stupid shit on the Macs while Dubé was busy working. At a certain point Doob got fed up with me and yelled, "Lord! Make some Art!" So I took up the flung gauntlet and speedily composed ten fanciful automatic poems in one sitting—a collection aptly called *Éloigné des spectacles*[6]. I also made naïve etch-a-sketch drawings on the Mac to accompany each poem.

乙 Whether with me or anyone else or all alone, Dubé's art project ideas were always flying a mile a minute. He was a night owl and his brain kicked in precisely at that moment when ours tired and shut down. Dubé loved to create fake corporate logos and subvert existing ones. But his greatest talent—which he was casual and nonchalant about—was photographing people. He employed a unique method which went like this: he'd walk around the person aimlessly a few times, dangling the camera limply at the end of his arm. Then he'd stop, swing up the camera quickly, and click at the flick of a wrist. And that was it. Without even looking through the viewfinder. Dubé had a rare gift: he could photograph *someone's soul*. His snap of Caroline taken a year later during a Burroughs cocktail reception shows a distressed and conflicted being, while a picture he took of me captured the sad young man inside.

---

4. Pronounced "Moh Clay"; Transl: Key Word
5. Pronounced "Dih-zuh-vray"
6. Transl: *Removed From Showbiz*

⋝ Dubé's idea of cheering me up was to drag me to Montreal's seediest strip clubs: l'Axe on St. Denis, the lousy Café Cléopâtre, and even sometimes the more "upscale" Chez Parée and Super Sexe clubs downtown. Tristan was also a devotee of strip clubs. He had a bizarre relationship with his girlfriend. No sex was involved. She liked to take long baths, and he just sat there next to her, propping his chin like *The Thinker*, marveling at her beauty. Of course, he was a horny bugger as hell, and both he and Dubé spent many an hour in strip joints. They kept bugging me to come along and join them, but I found it pointless.

⋝ Lucky me, one day Audrey showed up at my roach-infested penthouse suite. She sat on the ugly orange Naugahyde couch. "Wanna fool around?" I asked her. "Sure," she shrugged. I started petting her. She let me play with her all I wanted, without budging or batting an eyelash. I had my very own live fuck doll to fool around with as I pleased!

Wow, what a body. She had perfect ski-slope tits, that ended in perfect perky pink nipples. Too bad she had the intelligence of a toaster. She didn't move or say anything, just let me cavort in her garden of fleshly delights. But an inflatable doll had way more personality. Rubbing plastic gets really boring, and I was relieved when my Blowup Bimbo Barbie finally left.

I banged her using a condom. It was my first time using that thing. I didn't like ejaculating into a balloon. What am I, a fucking clown?

I used to run into The Bimbo's boyfriend at the Foufs. He'd been in the army and had a black belt in karate. He could've made a pretzel outta me in a sec, but I protested: "Hey, *she's* the one running after *me*." Luckily, my being in VDMS conferred me the status of *Piece Of Dogshit Sprayed In Gold*.

⋝ VDMS launched a limited edition four-song 7" vinyl EP called *Joie de vivre*[7] at the Foufs. This time the sleeve was done by the musician-artist Henriette Valium. Again, the artist was provided total freedom, and this iconoclast came up with something unthinkable today: an assemblage of dismembered women's body parts held together by

---

7. Transl: *Joy of Living*

bondage ropes. Valium went on to enjoy R. Crumb-level recognition as "the pope of underground comix"—notably through his skewed scatological parodies of Tintin—called *Nitnit*. Unfortunately, Valium died in 2021, just as his work started to be more diversified, richer and complex, displaying a maniacal attention to intricate detail. He had moved on to making paintings that were exhibited in art galleries, including a show planned for Serbia. His death, at the age of 62, was a brutally shocking reminder to family and friends alike that life indeed can be unfair[8].

⚡ At the Foufs one day, Louis Côté comes up to me and goes: "Hey Lord, you're an engineer, right?" I said: "Yeah, why?" He said: "We want to build an outdoor terrace off the second floor. Can you do it?" I said "sure," and in a few days I handed him a sketch of the concrete deck, steel support beams, posts and foundations. I forgot all about it and one day I passed by and it was already built. And I hadn't gotten paid! Stupid me, I'd considerately included the steel beam weights needed on my sketch—you're supposed to provide those only *after* closing the deal. So the next time you pass by the Foufounes and see that terrace—now covered—you can think of me. I designed that bloody terrace and never saw a dime. Vintage Louis Côté. He and his two co-owner buddies later sold the business for over a million.

⚡ In June, VDMS gave a show at the University of Montreal. As we were packing up our gear afterwards, I was surprised to see my old pal Ivan of the Hats show up. He said he'd heard about us and took the plane from Toronto to come and see for himself what the buzz was all about.

This swami of electro-pop music inspected us carefully, narrowed his eyes and murmured "guitar…bass…drums, huh?"—as if he'd just stumbled upon the Coca Cola recipe at Los Alamos. Yes Ivan, you just discovered the *secret formula of garage bands*—what *I've* been doing since age 11!

---

8. Strangely enough, his last work was doing the cover for an eventual edition *of this* book in French.

Later that June VDMS was also part of a four-day French Rock Festival going on at The Spectrum: the *crème de la crème* of punk bands France had to offer—such as *Pigalle, Parabellum, OTH*. I wasn't too interested, but of course Luc Natali insisted I go every night. Being a musician, I took it as the kind of obligatory business convention I had to attend, professionally speaking.

VDMS played on the second day. Guess what. Bonspiel got naked. And so did I. Only later at "home", after picking up an olive-skinned Corsican girl called Marie Noelle[9]. She had a monumental hooked nose, but in my febrile state of terminal horniness I glossed over *her* horn, and—oh well, the rest isn't history.

Of course, being the guitarist in VDMS attracted me the girl-friends. My habit was up to juggling a sixpack simultaneously. Among the delightful coos I heard from my VDMS harem were: "How come you're so cool?" and "You play me like a guitar! ..."

Let me count the pathetic lays: One was a girl I talked and talked into coming over to my loser's pad. I never saw nipples like hers. Huge brown fire hydrants. Like the erasers at the end of a giant novelty shop pencil. Plenty to chew at, if that's what you liked. She was cheating on her boyfriend with *me*. She enjoyed my expert clitology, but those nipples were too much of a distraction—like Austin Powers with that *mole*. She came back for more until she made up with her boyfriend.

Then there was the occasional E.F.F.—my desperate 3 AM last call Emergency Fouf Fuck (break glass).

ζ On the last evening of the festival I got there early, bought a beer and walked over to the mixing desk in the middle of the floor seats. There was no one else around yet. Then I spotted this cute diminutive chick in a white miniskirt and a great pair of legs, restlessly striding up and down the aisles. She looked like the Talking Heads' Tina Weymouth, and her blonde page boy haircut bobbed up and down with every step.

As the show began I forgot about her, and several excruciatingly bad French punk bands later, the awful *Souris Déglinguée*[10] was playing. As

---

9. Transl: Mary Christmas!
10. Pronounced "Soo-ree Deh-gleh-gheh"; Transl: Fucked-Up Mouse

I winced, the blonde girl with the gams came up to me. "Are you Alan Lord?" she asked. "Yeah," I said, adding, "let's get outta here" and we went out into the lobby, relieved to be at least one sonic firewall away from the agonizing racket.

She told me her brother Bernard had dragged her to this terrible fest, that he knew me, and that they were working on translating Jean Baudrillard's book *The Ecstasy of Communication* into English for Sylvère. Bernard pointed me out and she came over to talk to me, even though she was painfully shy. We hit it off immediately and started yakking nonstop. I was grateful to finally find someone to share an oasis of intelligent conversation with, amid the strident neanderthal pus of French punk.

Her name was Caroline, and we decided to escape to the Foufs. Her brother was already there and she introduced me. After a few drinks we took a long walk over to the corner of Amherst and Sherbrooke, and I hailed her a taxi. We'd barely met, but as she ducked into the cab and I bid her goodnight, I knew instantly we'd be together for a long time, at least 25 years. *Sometimes you just know.* This time I was determined to be an irreproachable gentleman with this very special lady, instead of the usual gutterman. I waited a whole 24 hours before jumping on her. The following day I brought her to a Mexican restaurant on Rachel—west of the fire station, corner Préfontaine. Being the consummate bottom-feeding musician, I graciously let her pay the bill. After that I walked her over to her place on Bordeaux, and stopped at the bottom of the staircase in awkward silence.

"Would you like to come up for some tea?" she asked. "Sure," I said, and followed her up the stairs to her apartment. Her boyfriend was away. He'd gone off to the Magdalen Islands to see his mom. Just like that, without inviting Caroline.

I sat on the couch as she was making tea. Her two cats Ludwig and Jujube leaped on me and I petted those two pussies with my magic hands. I have quite a technique with cats: scratch the head, scratch the left chin, then the right, then both at the same time, then pet the back towards the tail, and finish by patting lightly while they arch their back. I got them purring madly and they kept pushing their heads against my hand, begging for more.

Unknowingly, I'd passed Caroline's *Cat Test*. With flying colours. She later told me I wouldn't have stood a chance with her had her cats not liked me. I need say no more. Decades later she confessed I'd also passed a *second* test: she asked her girl friends about me, and the verdict came back: "He's alright. *If* you can keep up with him." And here we are, still together after 34-plus years. I'd finally met someone who challenged me, a sane woman who could more than match my sardonic wit. We were total opposites at the mercy of the laws of attraction, the only hardcore realists in town, washing ashore together amid a sea of delusional, rudderless flakes.

⤳ A few days after we met, I was at Caroline's apartment, and she sensed something was wrong. Caroline was naturally psychic, and this included cats. She began worrying about Ludwig, went down the backyard stairs and immediately found him hiding under the balcony. Cats that are seriously injured hide like that. Ludwig had apparently fallen from the apartment's third floor balcony railing. We brought him to the vet and had to have him put down. Caroline was in tears, and so was I. Not knowing what to do, I got the crazy idea to bring her over to meet my mom.

My mom greeted her yammering a mile a minute like a crackhead, but it was only the natural high she was always on. She showed Caroline the pile of wonderfully tacky multicoloured Phentex slippers she was always knitting, the 300 cassettes of Lawrence Welk polkas and schmaltzy pop music she taped off the stereo, and her library of astrology books and the binder of astrology charts she made. She asked Caroline excitedly: "What's your date and hour of birth, latitude and longitude?"

Caroline found her a riot and soon forgot about Ludwig. She was too busy laughing doubled-over at this unwittingly funny and ridiculous mom of mine, who was now maniacally shoving at her a piece of the Angel Food Cake she'd just made. She never tired of making that cake. *Ever.*

⤳ When her boyfriend returned from the Magdalen Islands, Caroline and I had to shift our athletic encounters over to my Losers Palace suite.

In my less-than-deluxe bachelor pad I greeted Caroline with a bottle of white wine and nothing else in the fridge, dressed in a dirty red satin bathrobe, like a Salvation Army Hugh Hefner.

What *is* it that attracted her to me? The *Bad Boy* thing, which many women find so irresistible. When she met me I was a bum in a band and a starving everything else. But she knew that inside me lurked a nerd engineer who would be a dependable and dutiful provider. And in time I *did* deliver, from the twilight of the Eighties onwards. As for me, it was very simple. Had I not met my six-winged angel Caroline, I would've died before the decade was out.

⇄ I paraded Caroline around, proudly showing her off to my friends. Of course, I had to introduce her to Mario, so on a Saturday evening I invited him over to have drinks with us in my apartment. We talked a lot and they hit it off. After he left, we were watching *Bleu Nuit* on the TQS channel, as was our habit. It was a great show that screened soft porn movies like *Emmanuelle*, or the excellent erotic French television series *Série Rose*[11].

We heard a loud "POK!"—there was Mario again, exploding a beer bottle against the wall outside his window, this time in girlfriendless frustration.

⇄ Comparing our social notes, it turned out Caroline and I had crossed paths many times without knowing it. She went to the same parties and bumped into the same people: Velcrow Ripper, Sheila, Debra, and a thorough nutjob gal called *Moonbeam*.

She was also in the audience at Ultimatum II, sitting behind me and Anne Powell. She felt sorry for her—I kept getting up and leaving every five minutes. Well I had a *festival* to run, sweetie.

Caroline even saw VDMS at our *Usine* loft show. "There I was," she said, "merrily dancing to one of your bouncy songs, and I stopped in my tracks in shock when I realized what *Jump Off a Building* was all about."

When I met Caroline I had six girlfriends. "And six venereal

---

11. Transl: *Pink Series*

diseases," she never fails to add. So one by one I had to patiently explain to them that it was over, since I had a serious thing going on now with Caroline.

Then there was the showdown with the boyfriend at the Foufounes. Both he and Caroline happened to be there one evening. Awkward. I dragged them into a corner and said: "Listen Caroline, it's up to you to choose—either me or him. I don't care one way or the other, you guys figure it out." And I left to drink a beer at the bar, while minds were being made up. I could afford to play the magnanimous honest broker only because I knew I'd already won.

Back then Caroline was as much an *habituée* of the Foufs as I was, and we wound up hanging out there a lot. At 4 AM closing time, she even fought with the Fouf's huge bouncer *Le Gros Michel*[12], going: *"Whaddaya mean, we have to leave?"*—and he'd just slowly shove us down the stairs and out the door with his humongous beer belly. Caroline protested in vain. With her five-foot-nothing height she only made him chuckle, but others had less luck. He was known to pick up Last-Call-challenged crusty punks by the seat of the pants and scruff of the neck, and toss them down the flight of stairs into the steel door, head first.

⇀ Since she and brother Bernard were translating books by Baudrillard and Heiner Müller for Lotringer, he was always at her place. Her Bordeaux street apartment was quite a Grand Central Station, what with her two brothers practically squatting there, and an endless assortment of droppers-by. They were quite the coke fiends too back then, which always attracts interested partakers. On a frantic quest for the enchanting white powder one evening, Bernard and I wound up in a Peruvian coke den on Colonial street. They told us to wait on the couch. On the wall behind us was a huge poster of Scarface, with Al Pacino scowling at us, gun in hand. Here we were, two pathetic scrawny white boys swaggering and looking as tough as we could for our fine hosts. They offered us a Heineken, and popped in a VHS cassette of *Scarface*, with the sound off. These businessmen were *focused*.

---

12. Transl: Big Mike

⇐ VDMS was opening for the great Nina Hagen at the Metropolis on July 19th, and I was proud to have the chance to impress Caroline by putting her and brother Bernard on the guestlist. I plied them with drinks and got them good seats in the mezzanine balcony.

The theatre was jam-packed and our opening act was such a success, we even had an encore. When we were done, I fetched Caroline and brought her down to the dressing room to expose her to a bit of the backstage glamor. When we got there, Nina was yelling and throwing things, having a royal diva fit, swearing at her guitar player in German. Caroline translated.

JM recalls: "The guitarist had long hair, but it was a wig. He tore it off and slammed it to the ground. We were shaken—what had we done? Nina Hagen and everyone was pissed off at us. Because *opening acts are not supposed to have encores*—you just don't *do* that. So she took it out on her guitarist and they had a big fight."

⇐ On July 28th 1988, Dubé and I decided to call up Nam June Paik. We dialed up his number in the morning and when he answered we yelled: "Wake up Nam June Paik, today is Marcel Duchamp's birthday!" He yelled back at us excitedly "Duchamp! Duchamp! Duchamp!"

On the same date the previous year—Duchamp's centenary—Dubé and the SCP had set up a computer installation at the Philadelphia Museum of Art, which houses Duchamp's main body of work.

That August, Caroline left for a two-week vacation in the Magdalene Islands with her cousin Danielle. I didn't want to be alone on my birthday, so I took Sapin and Bernard to a bar on Mount Royal and did a bit of coke with them. While Caroline was gone I hung out more at my parents' place. Often during summers my father's lifelong friend Francisco Ríus[13] came from Barcelona and stayed with them for a month. This time my father was still away in Spain, but Ríus came anyway, and it was good company for my mother.

Ríus and my father became buddies as expats in France in the early Fifties. On a whim they decided to go together to Canada—you know, that land-o'-plenty where you didn't have to work because money grew

---

13. Pronounced "Rhee Oooss"

on trees. Their boat landed in Montreal. My dad stayed, but Ríus wound up in New York, where he drove subway trains in Manhattan. When his wife got cancer, he was holding three jobs to pay for her cancer treatment. He spent $250K[14], and she still died. Ríus—who was Catalán—now lived with his current wife in a small town on the outskirts of Barcelona.

Passing by to visit my mom, I saw he was in the living room watching the news on TV. As Reagan appeared on the screen, Ríus growled "Fockin' Reagan sonnovabeech" in his thick *Vicente-Fox*-like accent.

---

14. Over a million today

21

VDMS IN EUROPE

—————————————

In an uncharacteristic burst of enterprising zeal, Jack contacted the Wallonie-Québec agency, and through their cultural exchange program wangled a month's residency in Brussels for VDMS.

My preparations included asking Mario to fill out my UIC[1] cards bi-weekly in my absence, and mail them off, so as not to interrupt my crucial unemployment cheques. I also had to get a passport. Fast.

My Brussels notebook says: "Sept. 1. Made passport photos. Drinking beer at Le Blues Clair waiting for Mario. He showed up, says he blew his paycheque fucking two whores. He fucked a Jamaican and an Asian chick after ten dances at the Cléopâtre. He whipped the Jamaican while the Asian sucked him. Blew his paycheque. He has $5 left to live on for two weeks. He wants to save $5000 for plastic surgery. He was hinting at a sex change operation."

That day I passed Poutine on the street. "Don't forget your *Art Test*!" I said. Dubé and I had founded the SPDP—*La Société pour le dépaysement[2] perpétuel*—or *The Society for the Perpetual Disorientation of People*. The SPDP was typical of our overnight disposable art movements—abandoned mainly due to our ever-evolving attention spans. Tired of our friends' posturing as *Great Arteests*, we'd decided to find out who really knew their shit, and who was just a know-nothing poseur. So we put together the *SPDP Art Test*: a nifty 100-question

—————————————

1. Unemployment insurance
2. A conflation of "refreshing change of scenery, and unsettling disorientation"

quiz that tested one's general knowledge in art, literature, music and architecture[3].

That evening at the 259, Dubé and I set up chairs and desks like in a classroom. A dozen of our friends filed in and sat down for the test. Dubé and I greeted them, handed them the test, and slowly walked around like schoolteachers, with our hands clasped behind our backs, ready to assist if need be. It was a great sight to see everyone sitting still in all seriousness, diligently completing their *SPDP Art Test*. They all took it quite seriously! When you find out how much you don't know, that's when you really start learning. I was so elated I had to get drunk that night.

Not to our surprise, Philippe Côté was the only one who got an "A" on the *Art Test*. He even corrected a few of our questions, which garnished him a few extra bonus points. The prize was a custom one-copy-only print of a booklet of texts I'd written. The title came to me in a dream: *Failure Against The Tallest Skyscraper*. Dubé pasted up the graphics, and chose the image of Manhattan's World Trade Center to grace the cover. There you go—another disturbing premonition of 9/11.

Monty, the one among us who had the biggest recognized "career" in the arts, turned out to be our Art Test's big dummy. He flunked it, and stayed to protest his grade, arguing with us. We went through his answers again one by one, and wound up giving him a pass, just to get him out of our face.

≥ My notebook entry for September 2nd says: "Got my UIC cheque. Had lunch with Gagnon. Told me a funny story about shit on paper toilet bowl." Explanation: I received my unemployment insurance cheque, and Gagnon—who was still working at Monenco-LGL—had the following story: Some engineer had placed toilet paper on top of the toilet seat cover in a bathroom stall, and carefully laid out his turds all around. What the hell is *wrong* with these engineers? Shows you the kind of sick fucks the profession attracts.

On the 7th we went to Mirabel airport and boarded our Nationair

---

3. See Appendix—Selected Texts for sample questions

plane to Brussels. Nationair had an open bar policy. You could drink to your liver's content throughout your flight. Music to a rock band's ears. We were grounded for over an hour on the tarmac in our jet—one of the last DC-8's in service—due to some "logistical problem". So they placated us with booze. No surprise, Nationair was another of these short-lived airlines.

Once we were at cruising altitude and enjoying the uninterrupted flow of free drinks for the next six hours, Bonspiel looked up from the newspaper he was reading and sighed: "Ah ... they finally made a condom size that can fit me."

Our Wallonie-Quebec host Patrick Sels picked us up at the airport. After we got to Brussels and deposited our bags, Bonspiel and I took a walk to enjoy the fresh enchantment of Old Europe.

"I love *le dépaysement perpétuel*!" I exclaimed. "Not I," Bonspiel countered, motioning to the sidewalk below our feet. "I wish to know the story behind of each one of these paving stones *intimately ...*"

We sat down at a curb table of the first brasserie we found—which in Brussels was practically at every street corner. You couldn't walk half a block without being tempted by a Belgian beer. Sitting back in relief, our normally brooding Bonspiel broke out in a wide grin and let out a sonorous guttural guffaw of deep contentment. I brought to my lips the first taste of a *Blanche de Hoegarden* on tap, served in a tall glass. It looked like cream. It tasted like heaven.

In *this* sacred Valhalla of inebriating suds, you were provided not with 72 virgins, but *hundreds* of marvelous beers to sample. You were confronted with a dizzyingly poetic holy litany of beer names: Chimay, La Chouffe, and Duvel (all at 8% alcohol)—then Carolus (12%), Mort Subite, Gueuze, Kriek, Vieux Temps, Radieuse, Fruit Défendu, Primus, Bush (12%), L'Arc (28%), Rodenbach, Orval, Loburg, de Konninck ...

Just as exotic were the names of Brussels' countless bars and clubs: Le Moeder Lambic, Le DNA, Le Mukalo, Le Travers, Le Montmartre, La Vague, Le Vol de Nuit, Le Pantin, Le Mal De Mer, Le Maltais, L'Amour Fou, Planète, Le Bièreodrôme, Le Grain d'Orge, Le Dernier Jugement, Le Flaubert ...

I sorely regret never making it to Brussels' famed *Moeder Lambic*— the Mecca of Belgian beer: 1100 different brands, with 110 available on tap, all in line along the counter[4]. I can hold my liquor better than most folks, but after three *McEwan's Scotch Ales* at the Mukalo, I was on the floor.

Beer wasn't the end-all, however. During the day we also slinked into an arab café in a Flemish neighbourhood, and sat down to sip a sickly-sweet mint tea. Bonspiel shushed us when we started speaking in French—most unwelcome in these parts—we shrugged and switched to English.

ᴢ VDMS spent the month of September 1988 at Fred Blanc's place on the *Rue Gray* in Ixelles, Brussels' immigrant neighbourhood. It was a large one-room apartment with separate kitchen, above a car body shop run by Turks. In between swallowing fumes seeping through the floorboards whenever they spray-painted a car, we got ripped smoking Amsterdam hash or smack, puffed off small pieces of aluminum foil with a straw. It was called *chasing the dragon*. We also went often to the Delhaize—the Belgian supermarket chain—to get crates of Maas Pils and Jupiler beer.

These Belgians—in fact, all Europeans—never heat their places, they just huddle in the damp cold in misery. There was a small coal stove, but they didn't use it. So we bought the coal. Canadians don't freeze in the cold—we *heat*. I never saw anything like the weather in Brussels. It switched from sunny sky to overcast drizzle half a dozen times in the same day.

People came and went in Fred's place, some lounging around all day. And what a cast of characters. There was Éric—a vaguely sinister James Dean look-alike, AWOL from his Belgian military service. He went to Spain, fell off a dike and broke his leg. And here he was on the couch, wearing a cast, and playing with his silver butterfly knife, repeatedly opening and closing it *slik slik slik* with a flick of his wrist. You felt like ambling over and slapping the thing out of his hand, like Bogart wearing a fedora askew, hands a-pocket in his trenchcoat: "I've had enough of your punk mug … now scram … gawwan, *beat it*."

And then there was squat, sausage-fingered junkie Bébert. He sold

---

4. See it here: https://www.youtube.com/watch?v=Hp1dalUT354

smack and "took care of" the hookers in the red light district of the Gare du Nord[5] district. Only recently did Jack tell me "he often had a gun on him." One night Bébert snuck in to prank us while we were all sound asleep drunk. In the morning we woke up to big black marker doodles he'd scrawled on our faces: thickened eyebrows, Keystone Cop moustaches, and psychotic spirals drawn on our cheeks. JM recalls: "Bébert drew a cock on Fred Blanc's face—which got him real pissed off. He gathered gallons of house paint, found Bébert's motorcycle and splashed paint all over it."

Most of our time was spent lazing around like criminals in a safe house, waiting for one of these morons to come back from Amsterdam with some heroin to chase on a crumpled tin foil. Or going to the Delhaize yet again for another case of those ridiculous tiny beer bottles of Maas Pils that couldn't get us properly drunk. Yes, we were high and definitely in a low place, but these losers sure weren't any friends of ours.

To escape from this ship of fools I'd dart off to visit the Magritte Museum and the Royal Museum of Fine Arts, which featured lip-smacking works by Brueghel, Paul Delvaux, de Chirico, and a shockingly hilarious painting by Francis Picabia called *L'Éclipse*: it represents the Virgin Mary in a classic pose, standing on the terrestrial globe and crushing a fat green snake underfoot. Her face is hidden, because Picabia plastered over it a cartoon Black Sambo face, complete with bug eyes, curly afro and huge lips—definitely BLM-incorrect today.

Another diversion offered by Brussels was its unique gastronomical delicacies. At Place Flagey down our street you could buy a huge paper cone of *frites mayonnaise*[6] from a street vendor's wheeled cart, or little plastic containers of fat snails bobbing in their broth, eaten with a toothpick. Gawking at the majestic centuries-old buildings of the Grand-Place one day, a Black dude came up to me and curtly demanded: "Where's the Pizza Hut?" Taken by surprise, I immediately pointed and motioned "over there". As he left I kicked myself, thinking I should've asked him: "*One*: why did you presume I could understand English?

5. Brussels' train station—also known as *Noordstation*
6. Transl: Fries with mayo

And *Two*: why don't you sample a local specialty instead, such as a *Moules-Frites*?"[7]

So this was our famous "European Tour" promised for so long—languishing broke in Ixelles, dreaming of *Moules-Frites* washed down with Gueuze.

Finally we were invited to play in a festival at the legendary Plan K hall in Molenbeek, where Joy Division, Bauhaus, Cabaret Voltaire, Human League, and The Psychedelic Furs had played. It was a lugubrious industrial music festival—a Brussels specialty at the time—and a dozen mournful Gothic synth bands, with darkened eyes and gloomy music, were waiting to take turns playing. Unfortunately for them, with our cheerful bouncy songs the audience started dancing and having fun—obviously against the wishes of the festival promoters. After our show, everyone left. The hall was empty, and their Dying Undertakers Fest gave its last sigh. We'd managed to destroy a festival!

⤵ Chasing the dragon, trying to get drunk on Maas Pils, trying to get to lay the ONE chick that was hanging around to tease our cocks, and trying to win at *Le Nain Jaune*[8] was all fine and dandy, but the new songs we were churning out in Ixelles were pretty substandard. I was out of sorts, and Bonspiel was uninspired. His Songwriting Well had finally dried up. All he could deliver now were songs either involving suicide, or his favourite part of the human anatomy—the anus. *While Buggering King Baudoin*[9], anyone? Or how about the one about a Flemish ice cream vendor "who liked small children a bit too much"? Henceforth, we were running on our past glory. The sacred fire of VDMS had gone out.

Luckily, a young Swiss named Speedy came to our rescue, and booked us a few shows in Switzerland. We piled into a rented van and drove the ten hours from Brussels to Lausanne, cutting through Belgium, Luxembourg, France, and Germany, before arriving in Switzerland.

7. Transl: Mussels with fries
8. Transl: *The Yellow Dwarf*—a Belgian board game
9. The Belgian King

Around 5 AM I was the relay driver in Germany. We were doing about 110 kmh on the highway, right lane. There was an exit coming up. All of a sudden a blonde Nazi bitch in a Mercedes zoomed by my left at 200 kmh, and cut me off to catch the exit at the last second. I slammed the brakes and we came to a teetering, screeching halt, toppling the piles of cases of cheap beer brought from Brussels on top of us. Bonspiel says: "I woke up against the windshield."

We finally made it to Fribourg, where we opened for the legendary anarchist band *Bérurier Noir*[10] in front of a thousand people, at a hall called *Le Fri Son*[11]. It was a chaotic monster show that was repeated a month later at the Spectrum in Montreal.

Except that for us, it was a disaster. The kids were there to see their venerated *Bérus*, and had no use for us. Plus, for these restless ruckus-awaiting crusty punks, we made the mistake of opening with our pleasant dinky *Shirley*. After sweating through a seemingly interminably long set to zero crowd feedback, we trundled off back to the dressing room dejectedly. Bonspiel collapsed histrionically on the sofa, bringing a hand to his feverish forehead palm-up, croaking: *"They didn't like me ..."*

I had no patience for his little Norma Desmond moment. "Stop acting like a goddamn *Castafiore*[12]," I lashed out, "Shut up or I'll fucking *hit* you." Come to think of it, I'm the only one in the band who never came to blows. They all had a go at each other. The reason for such unwelcome friction? The knavish noodling of each other's girlfriends, mostly.

To top off our horrible evening, a balding middle-aged mustachioed sales rep for Swiss beer Cardinale barged in and started schmoozing us. He cracked bad jokes and tried being one of the guys by loosening up his tie. But in his clownish brown and yellow checkered jacket, with broad yellow and brown striped tie, it didn't work out too well.

---

10. Pronounced "Bih rue-yay N'wah"; Transl: a dirty black obese drunk shameless grumpy handyman

11. Pronounced "Luh Free-soh"; Transl: *The Shiver*—and also, phonetically—"The Free Sound"

12. The opera singer in the Tintin volume *The Castafiore Emerald*

Eventually he got the message and left us with a case of his awful Cardinale beer, which gave you a headache by the third bottle.

⇘ Next stop was Lausanne, where we were to participate in one of their famed *Concerts Sauvages*[13]: at the last minute the location was spread through word of mouth, and the kids thronged into a designated abandoned building for a free show. Bands shlepped in their gear in a hurry, power was siphoned off a nearby electric pole, and the shows went on until the cops arrived with sirens blaring.

We never got to play, because in fact it was a whole *riot squad* that showed up. They piled out of their vans with submachine guns and German Shepherds tugging at their leashes. They managed to nab a few of the scattering kids and checked their ID's. We just stood there, smugly expecting our respected Canadian citizenship to protect us. They asked for our passports. After verifying them to their satisfaction, they handed them back, informing us we were banned from ever entering Switzerland again. For life. Only JM lucked out, finding a good hiding spot.

After that we went over to the bar La Dolce Vita and sat in for an impromptu set after two bands played. We gave an excellent show, warmly appreciated by the locals. As we exited into the warm night, I noticed a poster announcing John Giorno the following evening. Good thing I wasn't gonna be around and have to explain his bounced cheque.

I caught up with Speedy's young sister Ludivine, and steered her to a quieter area of town. She was 16, I was 34. And we started necking passionately. For the rest of the night all I did with her was stumble around and stop occasionally to resume our very chaste, heavy necking. I didn't even feel her up. I was reliving my teen years as an awkward sex retard.

We wound up at the train station, and squeezed in a last few desperate sessions of deep kissing, as we waited at dawn for the first train to whisk her back to her parents. I made it to Najkine's place at 16 Tivoli Street totally exhausted, and plopped down on the couch. Before going to sleep though, I had to jerk off thirty times in a row to relieve

---

13. Pronounced "Coh-sehr Soh-vajh"; Transl: Wild Concerts

the pressure Ludivine had built up in my severe case of *Blue Balls*. Everyone was fast asleep and no one noticed.

After what seemed like only a couple hours of sleep, the phone rang. I lifted a groggy eyelid, and Bérus manager Marsu answered. It was CBS Records offering yet again a million dollars to sign the very anarchist Bérus. Marsu told them to go fuck themselves and slammed down the receiver.

⇜ On the way to the German-speaking town of Bern, we stopped to visit a Roman amphitheater. Our destination was the Reithaller—a real anarchist commune. Wow. I was excited, and really looking forward to seeing an actual anarchist community in action.

The reality of it was a complete shock. The so-called "anarchists" were emaciated zombies constantly bumming cigarettes off us. The kitchen was filthy. With the shabbiness and state of disrepair of the Reithaller, plus the mountain of dishes in the sink no one wanted to wash, we were far from the exemplary selflessness and dedication of Durrutti, Ascaso and Oliver.

After a nondescript "meal", Bonspiel quietly went over and washed their goddamn dishes. Coming on the heels of my nasty experiences with Anarprick, the Reithaller killed off any romantic notions of anarchism I had left. This Anarchyland was no utopia. It was a squalid shit hole.

Regardless, the show we gave there was one of the most memorable. Many in the audience spoke neither French nor English—such as their house soundman, who went by the name of Goofy. Even though they couldn't understand a word of the lyrics, we were a hit and they had a hell of a ball. Proof yet again of the universality of music. Or was it our VDMS magic?

⇜ Jack decided to stay and catch up with us later in Brussels. On the road back we passed by a dispiriting makeshift sign that said: *"No Sex No Drugs No Rock n' Roll"*. It was made by some hardcore austere anarchist puritan wackos, who'd obviously inherited their elders' stifling Swiss Calvinism. "Anarchists" are always quick to condemn, point fingers and self-righteously moralize people. They have a cop mentality, with an endless list of Do's and Don'ts. What would my life have been without Ian Dury's liberating, fun mantra? Fucking "Anarchists". Fucking Neo-Calvinist killjoys, intolerant Woke Talibans. I'd rather go out for a drink with a banker. At least *he'd* buy me one.

We stopped for lunch at a trucker's canteen on the border between Germany and Luxembourg, and when we arrived at Ixelles, we dropped fast asleep. Jack arrived a few days later, and we even managed to squeeze in a last band rehearsal before returning to The New World.

ᴢ Back in Montreal, the first thing I did was run to the Foufounes. Because I knew Caroline would be there. I ran into a gaggle of her girl friends at the bar. "Where is she?" I asked, "I missed her! I love her so much *it hurts*." The girls were stunned. "Hold my drink," one of them said, "I'm gonna go barf." Caroline showed up, and we quickly exited to more pressing matters at her place.

Mario had bad news for me. The Unemployment people had called and wanted to talk to me. Seeing as no reply was forthcoming, they cut me off, and so here I was, again penniless.

Then hell froze over. *Mario got a job.* A childhood friend of his had a travel agency called *Nouvelles Frontières*[14], and hired him. Mario quickly learned how to book flights with confidence. He worked late, often on Saturdays, and replaced sick employees. He knew his job well, and became the champion of flight transfers, when a flight was canceled at the last minute. He regaled Caroline and I with great stories. Like hicks calling him and asking: "DC-10? Is that a plane with motors?" And the time an Air Khartoum plane landed in Europe from Nigeria— the passengers had huge bites and welts all over them and had to be hospitalized. While scouring the plane they found the problem: a blanket infested with fingernail-sized fleas.

Mario was still an alcoholic, but a model employee. At noon, his "lunch" consisted of two tall Molson beers at the corner tavern. He never ate. One evening at his apartment in the Losers Palace he was hungry, and decided to make himself some food. He fumbled in the cupboard and pulled out a box of Kraft Dinner Mac n' Cheese—*the*

---

14. Transl: New Frontiers

welfare meal of preference. I said, "Mario, what are you doing, still eating Kraft Dinner? You *work* now—you can eat *a steak* if you want!" Mario stopped in his tracks and took stock of this awesome revelation. "Ah! *Of course,*" he looked at me flabbergasted, "it's true—*I'm working* now! I can buy as many steaks as I want!"

There was only one problem with Mario's job. He stopped writing. The only time I can recall Mario ever being boring, is when he held that job. But it allowed him to travel for free to Europe anytime he wanted. And he could now also afford hookers. He went for lap dances at the Cléopâtre, and confessed he had a thing for the oldest, ugliest broad he could find. The ones still with a beehive hairdo, in scuffed white thigh-high boots and small white leather fringed purses dangling off their shoulder. He asked one: "Would you like to come to Paris with me?" She looked at him puzzled. "Where's Paris?" she said.

Thanks to his salary and free flights, that fall he flew to Paris, then on to Brussels by train, and finally Amsterdam. He made a quick beeline to the Red Light zones and hired hookers in every capital. As a precaution against diseases of any kind, Mario explained: "I always carry a bar of soap in the back pocket of my jeans, and carefully wash my cock in the train's bathroom." His only regret during his trip to Paris? He couldn't find Baudelaire's tomb in the Montparnasse Cemetery.

⇝ VDMS were lined up to go to Paris and do shows there in January. On an Art Dare, Dubé and I resolved to write a letter saying we were respectively quitting the SCP and VDMS. I called Natali and gave him the news. He ran over immediately and slumped down in my chair dejectedly. He brought a bottle of whiskey. It took a few drinks to get me to change my mind.

And thus my year of great misery (me) and hope (Caroline), had come to an end. And where else to wrap up dismal 1988 but at the Foufounes yet again—where VDMS was summoned to provide the New Year's Eve entertainment, for the third time in a row. Bonspiel baptised the show *Souffrance ou Misère*[15], and this time decided to have a huge game show wheel built, with each spin of the wheel giving either

---

15. Transl: Wheel of Misfortune

a booby prize like "Try Again", "A Kick In The Ass", or naming a song we had to play.

↗ It should be to Quebec's everlasting shame that it took a Parisian record label to put out our VDMS album—both vinyl *and* CD—which was a brand new medium then. We were now on the *Boucherie Productions*[16] roster, along with the cream of French punk—which was finally having *its* heyday, at the tail end of the Eighties.

When we received our "import" album we went to the Café Cléopâtre to celebrate. Dédé Traké was the DJ that night. He put on the album and made the strippers pole dance to our charmingly sick songs. The manager told him to stop it. Dédé shrugged him off and cranked up the volume. He refused to take it off and was fired, right in front of us. Poor Dédé. Lost his job because of *Vent du Mont Schärr*. You can see now to what extent we could electrify our fans.

JM's brother Alain was there with us, and was getting a lap dance when his angry girlfriend barged in. JM told me: "You bastard, you made things even worse—you kept sending girls and paying lap dance after lap dance for poor Alain, laughing your head off."

↗ In January of 1989, Boucherie invited us to share the stage at the *Printemps de Bourges*[17] festival in France, with Manu Chao's Mano Negra, Stellla, Les BB Doc, Les Garçons Bouchers, Los Carayos and Pigalle.

After landing at CDG[18], we piled into a small car and drove off to a Boucherie staffer's place in Paris. Bonspiel was riding shotgun in front and kept hammering his right thigh with his fist, moaning and complaining the cramped space was killing him. We rolled our eyes.

For all of us it was our first time in Paris. We didn't have much time, but I dragged JM with me to at least visit Notre Dame de Paris and Les Invalides. I knew the tomb of Napoleon wouldn't fail to impress him.

---

16. Pronounced "Boo-shree"
17. Pronounced "Pray-tuh de Boorj"; Transl: Bourges Spring
18. Paris' Charles de Gaulle airport

Passing by the Élysée Montmartre theatre, the marquee said *SUICIDE* tonight. Wow! What luck to be able to catch this legendary band—and in Paris, yet.

I went with Jack. Once inside I couldn't believe my eyes. Martin Rev stood impassive behind a folding-leg cafeteria table loaded with crappy-looking stomp boxes all patched up with tattered duct tape. Yet this pile of junk was blasting an ear-splitting pounding noise at you. Alan Vega kept pacing nervously sideways back and forth across the stage, whooping like a demented Elvis, while furiously wrapping and uncoiling the microphone cord around his arm like a junkie prepping a fix.

After the show we went to the café l'Oiseau Bleu[19], where we got seriously plastered with Jean-Luc Fonck of the Belgian duo Stellla, plus a few guys from Boucherie. In France you had to pay to pee, so I was taking a pee in a men's room raised urinal, when two chicks barged in and jostled me aside, climbed up and squatted to pee free of charge. I love French chicks. They're the wildest. Any trouble from males, they just yell in their face and threaten to kill them.

On the way to Bourges, we gave a quick show in Poitiers—the site of the famous Hundred Years' War battle. For a history buff, I was well served. After the show we kept dancing in the club. I tried to pick up a cute Frenchette reveller, without any luck.

JM recalls: "As we arrived in Bourges at dawn, Jack reached into a recess in the back of the van, found a can and pulled it out. It was a can of mace. He pushed the button and everyone screamed as a jet of tear gas flooded the cramped space."

"Guy Bou started bleeding profusely from the nose," Jack recalls, "and we had to stop on the side of the road because we were gasping for air."

Z The legendary François Hadji-Lazaro greeted us in Bourges. His reputation preceded him. He was painted as the Commie's Commie. On the occasion of his band's first gig at the Foufs, he walked into the downstairs dépanneur and "liberated" a two-four, carrying it under his arm right out the door in front of the owner, stopping to stare at him

---

19. Transl: The Blue Bird

daringly. Hadji-Lazaro was a squat, no-neck 300 pounder, and looked like a surly *luchador* you wouldn't think of messing with. He'd once been a teacher, but now he was running *Les productions Boucherie*[20], churning out albums by several bands. He was a songwriter, sang, played guitar, banjo and accordion, and had three bands going simultaneously: *Les Garçons Bouchers, Pigalle,* and *Les Carayos*[21]—with Manu Chao and his brother Tony—who were also in *La Mano Negra.*

So we got to share the stage with our old friends Stellla, plus Les Carayos, Pigalle, Les Garçons Bouchers and Mano Negra—future international superstar Manu Chao's excellent band at the time. They had a crack horn section and delivered rockin', smokin' anthems effortlessly, one after the other. Theirs was a level of professionalism that we just couldn't match. JM later confessed to feeling as dejected as I did. Sure, VDMS was a lot of fun, but we were very limited musically. The fact I was the most pro of the lot alarmed me no end.

After the show, we milled at the back of the hall with all the other musicians, bottle of beer in hand, and watched with bemused curiosity our tireless force of nature Hadji-Lazaro take down the stage equipment, huffing and sweating as he lugged off the huge speaker cabinets and rolled up the cables, all by himself. What a bunch of shameless, selfish, lazy motherfuckers we were! Regardless, we wound up on the compilation *Concert à la Boucherie*, released by Island Records.

My best memory from that event is when I got to jam until 3 o'clock in the morning—bottle of Jack Daniels in hand—with Manu Chao's brother Tony, and Shultz of Parabellum and the Carayos. For the occasion, Shultz withdrew from his shirt pocket a small black and white photo of Chuck Berry, which he placed reverentially beside him as he played. It was a very touching moment. I played them my Frogs song *Mon Pays* on an acoustic guitar, singing it in the puzzling Québécois twang that amuses the French so much. My new friends were visibly thrilled by this authentic slice of Canada—which in their mind was still a mythical untamed expanse of endless forests and dangerous animals. Well, they weren't entirely mistaken.

---

20. Transl: Butchershop Productions
21. Spanish slang for "cock"

In retrospect, I clearly realize I was indeed privileged to have landed smack in the middle of France's golden age of Alt Rock and Punk.

Before leaving, I wanted to see the Bourges Cathedral—a jewel of Gothic architecture. JM and Jack preferred to stay in the van smoking cigarettes. I took my time to inspect the cathedral, storing in my head all the details I could. Bonspiel followed behind, walking softly, his hands clasped behind his back, like a medieval monk sworn to secrecy.

⤳ Back in Paris, Luc Natali summoned us to a great feast, washed down with endless bottles of wine at *Le Baratin*—a wine bar in Belleville. He'd invited several of his friends, including staff from Boucherie. We were about twenty around the table. It must have cost an arm and a leg. It later dawned on us that he'd paid for this sumptuous repast with *our* money.

A last surprise shock: Salvador Dali—one of my top five artists of all time—died while we were still in Paris. I rushed out and bought up all the newspapers I could, without exception. Dali was on the front page everywhere: *Le Monde, Le Figaro, Libération, France Soir*—even the soccer weekly *l'Équipe*. The huge titles said *Au revoir Dali*. Farewell indeed. I was glad to have made my Dali pilgrimage long ago.

Before leaving for Montreal, I made a quick trip to the Montparnasse Cemetery, found Baudelaire's grave, and brought Mario a Polaroid snap—which he proudly taped to the wall of his apartment.

22

BURROUGHS' SHOTGUN PAINTINGS

arly in 1989 I learned that Montreal artist and gallery owner Daniel Dion was putting together a show of Burroughs' *Shotgun Paintings* at his Oboro Gallery on Saint-Laurent, and also at the Atelier[1] Roger Bellemare. *Of course* I had to be in on this! I called up Dion, told him I knew Burroughs and Grauerholz. He knew about my festivals, so he asked me to be the publicist for the event.

In the meantime, on the evening before Saint Valentine's Day, Caroline and I went to see Nick Cave And The Bad Seeds at The Rialto, on Park Avenue. After the show we went down to the Foufs, natch. The Bimbo[2] was the barmaid that night.

Caroline recalls: "I was at the bar, waiting for my beer. Then Blixa Bargeld[3] comes up to the bar and orders a drink in English. The stupid Bimbo couldn't understand his English. So I translated and ordered his drink in French. Blixa went: "Oh my god, you're German!" and then he got down on both knees and kissed my hand. We continued yakking in German like that, at eye level[4]. Then Alan sidled up to the bar, at which point I left to mingle."

The Bimbo was making googly eyes at me. I smiled to myself, squinting and rubbing my chin conspiratorially, now entertaining the fantasy of organizing a threesome with her and Caroline.

---

1. Pronounced "Ah-tell-yay"; Transl: Workshop
2. Christened thus by Caroline
3. Of the band Einstürzende Neubauten—and also one of Nick Cave's *Bad Seeds* that night
4. Blixa was six foot one, against Caroline's five foot nothing

I asked Blixa's advice on how best to accomplish that. Hell, a rock star like *him* should know. He thought about it a bit. "The best way is, first you get in bed with the second one," he said. "Then, you call up your girlfriend and tell her to come over. When she gets there and gets over the first shock, there's a good chance it'll work."

I thanked him warmly. Meet Blixa Bargeld, *my Sex Coach*. I sleazed over to The Bimbo and asked her if she'd go for a threesome. Caroline was nearby. The Bimbo made a wry smile Caroline's way, but she wasn't looking. To make a long story droop, nothing came of it. *Thank God.*

And remember Ludivine? The 16-year-old I fooled around with in Lausanne? Well now she was 17, and flew all the way from Switzerland to my Losers Playboy Pad for me to deflower her. Except in a year she'd gone from being kinda cute to being definitely plain. I told her I was going steady now. We sat around in silence until the message sank in, and she smartly decided to shorten her stay in Canada.

I had one more last surprise stake to drive through my old sex vampire's heart. The Bimbo called me out of the blue saying she'd left her black belt wacko, and wanted to move in with me. I said: "Are you crazy?" She promptly agreed, and that was the end of blow-up dolls for me.

I went to Mario's apartment and asked to take a gander at his *Délire* manuscript. He looked all over the place, couldn't find it. Then it dawned on him: "I brought down a pile of newspapers to the basement this morning. I think it was in between the papers." I scrambled downstairs in a panic, to the room with all the garbage cans. There was Campo's piles of *La Presse*[5]. What luck—it wasn't garbage day yet! I saved one of the French language's capital texts. You're welcome. *Le Délire's* been reprinted here and there, but don't look for it in *La Pléiade*[6]. I ran out and immediately made a safety photocopy of the precious manuscript, which I kept.

For the momentous *Shotgun Paintings* show, I got the idea to put together an *Hommage à Burroughs* show at the Foufounes. It was to be

5. One of Montreal's major French dailies
6. France's hallowed literary series

my last hurrah as a scenemaker. I thought it would be a wonderful idea to bring Burroughs and Huncke together again, so I booked Huncke as one of the reading guests of the soirée. I passed by Bézy's and picked up my Burroughs books collection—the collateral I'd managed to pay off—and set up a window display of the Burroughs oeuvre at the bookshop *Ficciones*, which was near Oboro gallery.

I let Huncke stay at my apartment at The Losers Palace, and I stayed at Caroline's. Jack and I picked up Huncke at the airport in his old clunker, and brought him to my place. I left and they proceeded to down a bottle of Absolut vodka together, while Huncke told Jack stories from his book *Guilty of Everything*—Chicago in the Thirties.

Since I was busy with organizational duties, I didn't spend much time with Huncke, and asked Sylvain Forbes to take care of him. For a few days Huncke thus held court at my place, receiving his Montreal fans —including Mario, who was working on a French translation of *The Evening Sun Turned Crimson*. I counted on Forbes to keep Huncke company and supply him with choice substances. It was later reported that a young admirer who looked like James Dean gave Huncke a blow job.

⇝ When Grauerholz and Burroughs arrived at Oboro, we were given a private pre-vernissage tour of his paintings. We shuffled from painting to painting, stopping at each for Burroughs to explain the subject, or the painting technique he used. It mainly consisted in applying stencils or assembling a collage on a wood board, place a can of spray paint in front, shoot at the can, thus exploding its contents onto the shattered board[7]. He then applied more paint and worked in further details. The works on display had such titles as *Black Magic In Suburbia, Burning Heavens, Little People Autumn Leaves, Hell Is Where You Find It, Rx Morphine At Dawn*.

I remarked that he was wearing his *Commandeur de l'Ordre des arts et des lettres*[8] medal given to him by the French Ministry of Culture. In his trademark dry creaky drawl he harrumphed in mock irritation: "They gave it to *JERRY LEWIS!*"

---

7. See a demonstration here: https://www.youtube.com/watch?v=u02kFg_nxeA
8. Transl: Commander of the Order of Arts and Letters

Everyone bunched up and a photo was taken. The picture of me and Caroline next to Burroughs and Grauerholz is one of my most precious mementos. Caroline looks slightly terrified by it all. She left shortly, and I had to stick around, because I had to be at the Foufs in a couple of hours.

Burroughs and Grauerholz loomed like Olympian gods. I didn't talk much to them, because I was too in awe and intimidated in their overwhelming presence. I *did* muster up the courage to talk to James, and thanked him for dedicating himself to taking such good care of *El Hombre Invisible*.

Burroughs and I retired to a back office, with the night sky falling slowly over the Montreal skyline. I lit up a joint and smoked it with him. At sunset. In silence. I broke the stillness by asking about this mysterious drug called *Yage* he wrote about—pronouncing it like "gauge". "*YA-HÉ!*" he scowled at me—correcting my total ignorance. I dearly wished to disappear into a wall crack. To be in the presence of such an overpowering intellect was utterly terrifying.

For the *Hommage à Burroughs* show at the Foufounes that night, I had several events lined up, and the highlight was to be Huncke reading from his work. The poster reads ...

5 PM—launching of the latest issue of *Stamp Axe* magazine and screening of *Burroughs: The Movie* by Howard Brookner

7 PM—Inauguration of the software *Learning about William Burroughs* by the SCP

Starting at 8 PM, with "our indefatigable emcee" Jean-Luc Bonspiel:

Bernard Schütze reading excerpts from Burroughs' work

A tape of Burroughs reading *Last Words Of Hassan Sabbah* over a slide show of his books

Shooting Gallery: a performance by painters David Sapin, Christian Dion, Philippe Morin

Sculpture Sonore by Septyx Systems (Philippe Bézy)

The band French Bastards reading from Burroughs' *Le Métro Blanc* (White Subway), accompanied by their music

Monty Cantsin's performance *Inferno Neoismo*

〜 A Burroughs fan had put up a few artworks on the wall next to the bar for the occasion, including a *Dream Machine*, based on Brion Gysin's invention. I urged Grauerholz to bring Burroughs, but he didn't promise they'd show up. After a while, the fan took down his artwork and went home.

Then I saw bright lights in the staircase. It was a video camera crew walking up the stairs backwards. They were filming Burroughs and Grauerholz. Louis Côté had been bugging me for years: "Bring Burroughs to the Foufounes! Bring Burroughs to the Foufounes!" Well there we were, his wish—*and mine*—finally fulfilled.

Louis and I led Burroughs to a private room where Huncke was waiting. We had arranged between their armchairs a small table with a large bouquet of flowers in a vase, plus little piles of cocaine and rolled joints of hash and pot, to enliven their little get-together. The drinks kept coming too.

Burroughs sat down. "How ya doin', Herbert?" he drawled. "Not bad Bill," answered Huncke. "How're things with you?" They sounded like a pair of old Mah Jong cronies. Of course, it was tempting to play fly-on-the-wall, but we all backed off and let them catch up with each other in private. At a certain point Burroughs came out of the lounge and walked over to the edge of the mezzanine, and placed his elbows on the railing to listen to the proceedings of the soirée. He visibly enjoyed the event, and was particularly mesmerized listening to Bézy's *Sonic Sculptures*, which was reminiscent of Bill's cherished *Master Musicians of Joujouka*. Someone in the audience spotted Burroughs, and there was a roar of cheers and clapping. Old Bill waved back smiling, and there's a great photo of this unforgettable moment.

David Sapin explains his performance: "The sequence was entitled *Shooting Gallery*, and myself and Christian Dion hid in a tent on stage while pretending to use the shotgun to create a portrait of Mr. Burroughs. The shotgun sequences filmed for the *Homage to Burroughs* show were shot in a sandpit west of Mirabel airport, then later edited into a video loop that was presented at the Foufs."

Lastly, Herbert Huncke trundled up the stage and read excerpts from his new book *Guilty of Everything*. Which just *has* to be the best book title ever.

⇁ The following day there was a cocktail reception at Oboro. Vancouver artist Hank Bull was there, as well as Dubé and my American friend Laura Mitchell, who was there to interview Burroughs for arts magazine *Parachute*. Burroughs remarked to her: "You look just like Jane Bowles!" Caroline was a bit cowed by all the high-flying hoopla, and her profound distress was captured in a photo Dubé took of her.

At a certain point I corralled everyone, we all piled downstairs onto the sidewalk, and went over to *Ficciones* to see the display of my Burroughs books. They also had his latest book *Interzone* on sale. It was quite a sight to see the old man charging up Montreal's fabled *Main*, leading his disciples, madly swinging around his cane. In his beige raincoat he looked rather like a comical Monsieur Hulot.

We then convened to a dinner organized in Burroughs' honour, held at avant-choreographer Jean-Pierre Perreault's house on Sherbrooke, corner Amherst[9]. The creator of *Joe*—a work involving 32 dancers dressed like Magritte's skyfloating men marching in lock step—was away, and he'd graciously left his house at our disposal.

I was there ahead of schedule, busy checking last minute preparations, while anxiously awaiting the arrival of Burroughs and entourage. I heard a commotion, opened the front door and stepped onto the porch. And there was Burroughs in his trenchcoat, charging up the staircase ahead of everyone, thrashing his cane left and right as if

---

9. Now Atateken

clearing his way amid a throng in the narrow lanes of Tangier's Casbah, bellowing: "IS THERE ANYTHING TO DRINK IN THIS PLACE, SONNY???"

Of course, being the consummate Burroughs fan, I had one of his drinks of preference ready, and thrust it forthwith in his hand—vodka and orange juice. With *a lot* of vodka.

There were about fourteen of us seated at a long table. I still felt too intimidated to dare sit close to Burroughs, so Caroline, brother Bernard and I were at the end closest to the kitchen. Burroughs, Grauerholz, Daniel Dion and Hank Bull sat at the other end. Hank had curated an exhibition of Burroughs' paintings at his artist-run center The Western Front in Vancouver the previous year.

The chef preparing the sumptuous feast was none other than our eternally multitalented Jean-Luc Bonspiel, whose menu for this great occasion was the following:

First Course:
~ Tex-Mex Bean Salad.
~ Éperlans à la Romaine (Roman-style smelts).
~ Home-made Tzatziki, Taramosalata and bread.

Second Course:
~ Malaysian Dream Pot (The pièce de résistance).
~ Braised Binsi (stuffed Okra).
~ Saffron Rice with nuts.

Third Course:
~ A large combined salad with Buried Treasures (vine leaves, palm hearts, artichoke hearts "buried" in the salad), with Dijon dressing.

Fourth Course:
~ Fine cheeses, fruit.

Wine:
~ Aplenty

Also present at the dinner were American scholar Jennie Skerl—who wrote an insightful book on Burroughs—and a friend of hers as well as their lawyer hubbies. After the dinner, I pulled Bonspiel out of the kitchen to take a bow, and to come mingle with us. He recalls: "Iran Contra was raging at the time and two New York lawyers and their Burroughs groupie wives were there. I predicted that Ollie North would walk and the lawyer whose suit cost more than my lifetime wardrobe to that point said: 'We have something called The Rule Of Law'. I laughed in his face."

Bonspiel further confesses "I told Grauerholz I shoplifted all the fine cheeses, which made him uneasy."

⇜ As publicist I was fairly proud of my media scoop number two: I managed to get Burroughs' portrait on the covers of rival publications *The Montreal Mirror* AND *Voir* simultaneously that week—a publishing first.

On the morning of the official gallery show opening I organized a press conference. Burroughs sat at a table in front of the microphones, with Caroline beside him. She was the interpreter—which later turned out to become her lifelong career. So Burroughs was her first interpreting gig. Not bad—start at the top! Her copy of *Interzone* is signed: *"For Caroline, all the best interpretations."*

The press conference was well-attended by most of the important Montreal print media. I'd invited Josée Yvon and Denis Vanier to sit in, and they made a regal entrance, walking in dignified like a royal couple. Indeed, they *were* the prince and princess of Quebec's counter-culture. It was the last time I was to see them together.

⇜ The following day Caroline, brother Bernard and I flew on to Toronto, to catch a parallel showing of Burroughs' *Shotgun Paintings* at the Cold City Gallery, and also to attend a joint reading by Burroughs and Kathy Acker.

The reading took place at Toronto University's stately Convocation Hall. Surprisingly, Burroughs read first, followed by Kathy. It was strange to hear him start by saying: "It's an honor for me to be reading with Kathy Acker." He then launched into a series of texts that had me doubled over in laughter throughout his reading. People don't realize it, but in addition to being America's greatest writer of the postwar 20ᵗʰ century, Burroughs was also one of its great comedians. "Young people often ask me if I have any advice for them," he drawled in his inimitable dry rasp. "Avoid fuck-ups! Everything they have anything to do with turns into a disaster. Trouble for themselves, and everyone connected with them."

When it was Kathy's turn, she returned the compliment by saying it was an honour for *her* to be reading with the great William Burroughs.

After the reading, we were all milling around and yakking, and poor Bill just sat on a chair in a corner. If the ashen look on his face was any indication, he'd obviously enjoyed himself more in Montreal. The *Shotgun Paintings* monograph he'd signed for me said: *"For Alan Lord with memories of a great visit to Montreal."*

My one regret is that I didn't have the $100 to pay for copy number 23 of the *Black Magic In Suburbia* print series I'd asked Daniel Dion to set aside for me. Poverty sucks.

❧ Caroline and I, her brother Bernard and Rampike editor Karl Jirgens joined up with Kathy at Cameron House—a hip Toronto night-spot—where a Dr. John clone was growling out some hack blues at a Hammond organ. I was worried there might be some Torontonians I owed money to, so they went in first and Karl gave me the all-clear.

Kathy's beau that night was a big burly tattooed Black biker dude. *That* quickly dashed the secret hope I'd been entertaining of possibly engineering a threesome that evening. Caroline and I sat in a booth opposite from them, and I gave a nod her way. No doubt *he* could do a good job of smacking her around.

Caroline and I met Kathy for brunch the following day at the Delta Inn's restaurant, ostensibly to interview her. The taped interview quickly degenerated into chitchat and gossip. She said she loved to clothes shop in Paris' *Les Halles*, and that her favourite stores were *Kookai* and *Comme des garçons.*

❧ Karl let Caroline and I stay at his place, and he made us laugh with his funny poems, including *Where's The Dugong Gone?* Karl is a warm, beautiful, generous, creative soul, and a real mensch. To put it simply, the world would be a better place were there more like him. If an alien stepped off a flying saucer and asked me to bring it the best representative of Humanity, it would be Karl, hands down. In addition to being an all-around Good Guy, Karl slavishly edited and put out the avant-lit magazine *Rampike* for over 30 years, which featured the best of Canadian and international concrete poetry and tales from the nether limits of sanity. Karl is also one of the slim handful of people who ever gave me a break in life, publishing me when all I got were rejections. Not to mention the Ultimatum jerk he paid off out of his pocket for me.

⦚ To my unfathomable delight, Dubé came to the Losers Palace to rent an apartment from Rosalie. Lucky for me, one was available. I went in and checked out his new apartment with him. I rolled up the blind and looked out his window. I told him: "Dubé, stand at the window and don't move." I went back to my apartment and rolled up *my* blind. We were staring at each other face to face—our windows were exactly opposite from each other. "Mr. Random strikes again!" I declared, while Dube was going: "Crik crik crik, crok crok crok ..."

After laughing for a long while at the incredible absurdity of this moment, we both realized that Life, in short, was nothing more than a huge joke, and that it was really useless to worry whatsoever.

So now I was living in the same apartment building as my two most cherished friends. I'd run to Campo's apartment, snap up the latest page of *Le Délire* off his typewriter and run back to my apartment and read it out loud to Dubé. It was so funny and powerful, we had to pause in between our doubled-over guffaws to reflect in stunned silence at its devastating moments of existential lucidity.

Then I'd start all over again, running to Mario's place, hovering anxiously waiting for him to finish the next page, like a trembling junkie waiting for his next fix. As the paper edged out of the typewriter I yanked it out and bounded the steps to go read it to an eagerly awaiting Dubé. "Those were good times," he said, reminiscing years later.

Mario's *Délire* ranks as one of my favourite texts in all of literature, French or otherwise. It's up there with Rimbaud's *Season In Hell* and Lautréamont's *Maldoror*. Each time I re-read it, I experience the same primordial shock. Only Burroughs beats it. Sorry folks, but I like my literature very strong, dark, and no sugar.

Le Délire is a stillborn epic novel that alternates shocking phrases and confessions of carnal baseness with astounding philosophical revelations that leave you breathless. I can't help thinking this is exactly what Rimbaud achieved in his lost masterpiece *La chasse spirituelle*[10].

So finally, The Losers Palace had become our *Beat Hotel*. All three of us laid down our key literary works there, and read them out loud to each other, choking with laughter. It was at Mario's *Castel Rosalie*, apartment 23, that I served my stint as a seedy bum, a doomed poet, a hungry artist, a welfare loser, a broke musician.

It was the best time of my life.

---

10. Transl: The Spiritual Hunt

23

ON THE ROAD IN FRANCE AND CATALUNYA

I was looking forward to the VDMS tour in France promised by our manager Luc Natali that summer, and planned on bringing along Caroline. I soon began suspecting it was *not* gonna happen. Then, during a magical night at my Losers Palace apartment with Caroline, Dubé, Tristan and Campo, snorting good coke and reading from *Le Délire* out loud, we all wound up running around nearby Parc Lafontaine until the early morning. Stretched out on the grass, looking up at the few stars that managed to poke through the light pollution haze, I got a sudden eureka flash. My *Frogs* bass player Denis Duran told me he was planning on hanging out with his family in Provence that summer, and said I was welcome to stay at his sister's sprawling country house. I turned to Caroline and said: "Screw VDMS. We're going to France! We'll go to Paris, then stay with Denis in Provence, and then go down and stay with Ríus in Barcelona."

Miraculously, I got a translation contract from Traductor—the translation company Caroline worked for—just in time to provide money for the trip. It was a technical translation for Circo Craft—a company that made printed circuits. I needed a computer to work on, so Traductor lent me a Mac. The owner was a sleazy fat fuckface who notoriously paid late or not even at all, so I held the Mac hostage until he provided me with a certified bank cheque. Jack came with me in the VDMS Econoline, and only after I'd cashed the cheque did we open the doors and let him have the Mac back. With the proceeds I also bought Caroline a cool black leather jacket.

ϟ On May 26th—the evening before we left for France—VDMS gave a show at the Foufs, *with my Frogs as the opening act.* Yes folks, I had double-shift that night. As you can imagine, I was thoroughly drained, and after that ordeal I made it to Caroline's table on the outside terrace, where I plonked down my sweaty exhausted carcass to cool off, my back against the floor slab of the very structure I'd designed for no pay.

Gagnon later pointed out to me that Bonspiel had taken off with our Frogs' fee. Fair enough for me—it was payback for the money I owed him. But how about the *other* Frogs? That's the sort of assholery that was par for the course in music, and which I'd had enough of by then. That was to be the last show for The Frogs, and the start of my countdown to blowing off VDMS for good.

ϟ Mario had two plane tickets to Paris—one for him and a spare. So he gave it to Caroline and we all landed in Paris the day after my double gig. Caroline and I settled in a hotel in the seedy red-light district of Pigalle, where shady gentlemen invited strollers to enter the narrow doorways of titty bars under blinky red light marquees. We stayed there a few days and once even got out of bed at 4 PM, shocking the chambermaids and desk clerk. Even the French had their limits of decadence they could tolerate.

After booking our room, Caroline and I went to a recording studio near Place d'Italie, where the Garçons Bouchers were laying down vocal tracks. Luc Natali let us in, and I plonked down a huge bottle of duty-free Jack Daniels on the mixing board—the coveted drink of French rock n' rollers. They were in the middle of recording their paean to wine—*"Du Beaujolais, du bon et du bien frais…"*[1] Hadji-Lazaro happily poured the Jack into cups passed all around, as we kicked back to listen to the tracks taking shape.

Lazaro invited us to a monster show of his Garçons Bouchers a few days later at Paris' legendary Olympia. The legendary concert hall had once hosted the likes of Édith Piaf, Brassens, Jacques Brel, Ferré, and *La*

---

1. Transl: "A good Beaujolais, fine and very fresh"; Hear it at: https://www.youtube.com/watch?v=X06TM8dIEg4&t=8s

Gréco—not to mention the Beatles, Stones and Johnny Hallyday. It was strange to see the stately theatre packed to the gills with rowdy punk revelers pumping their fists in the air, amid raucous shouts and yobby whistling.

↗ Waking to our first morning in Pigalle, we were served breakfast in bed, and then we went out to buy morning beer for Mario, who was staying at the more upscale Opéra Cadet hotel—an eight minute walk from us.

Mario greeted us naked and still drunk from the previous night. While shaving in the dark, he recounted his hassles with "a Moroccan fag" he'd met, and cut his ear. He was bleeding like a pig, and Caroline somehow managed to stop the bleeding. He had a big wad of bandage stuck to his earlobe, with a stain of blood on the cotton gradually getting bigger and bigger. We walked around like this in Les Halles, with a blood-stained bandage dangling from Mario's ear, like a gross 6-inch earring. Whenever we passed a stunning Parisienne—which was every block—Mario got excited and gesticulated, loudly yelling "woo woo!" Caroline was mortified and fled to visit her best friend Jeanne. I was to meet up with her later at the Jardin du Luxembourg—"and by then," she added—"hopefully, *Marioless.*"

After wandering in the Latin Quarter, Mario and I finally decided to visit the tomb of his great hero Baudelaire, which he hadn't managed to find on his previous trip. Before arriving at the Montparnasse Cemetery, we picked up a bouquet of fresh flowers and a sixpack of beer—Kronenbourg 1664—to celebrate our dear Charlie B. Along the way we passed by Campagne-Première street, because Rimbaud had lived there—in a lodging at the corner with Boulevard Raspail. Which in his day was called *Boulevard d'Enfer*—Hell Boulevard. Rimbaud had spent a season there—get it?

Of course, Paris lacks no stellar literary landmarks, and on Rue Campagne-Première you also have the Hotel Istria. We sauntered in like a pair of eager schoolboys and asked the desk clerk if Rimbaud had once stayed there. We were told: "Non, but Marcel Duchamp and Man Ray, oui." Bam! After that, we went to lay our flowers of evil on the tomb of Général Aupick. Because you see, there *is* no such thing as the "grave of

Baudelaire". That's where our poor Charlie lies—sandwiched between the bones of his hated father-in-law, and that of his beloved mother.

As usual, there were some offerings already deposited on the grave: dead flowers, stems of burnt-out incense, a wet joint. We respectfully deposited our flowers, drank a few beers and Mario recited from memory *La Vie antérieure* from *Les Fleurs du Mal*[2].

Just as we were finishing our last beer can, a girl slinked up and joined us at the tomb. With her shiny long black hair and olive skin, she looked straight out of a Gauguin painting. And she began reciting the very same poem from memory! She told us she was an American student—from Hawaii—which naturally explained her Polynesian complexion. Who could have wished for a more marvelous surrealist encounter? Some days just turn out to be fabulously magical.

I brought Mario to see the tomb of Tristan Tzara—which is a headstone's throw away—and then took him to the other end of the cemetery, passing by the ridiculously pretentious bust of Sainte-Beuve. He was a writer, critic, and Baudelaire's more popular, established and mediocre rival—now eminently forgotten. Karmic revenge can be such a wonderful thing.

Our trip through the enchanting *Cimetière Montparnasse* ended at Baudelaire's Cenotaph—where, hanging over a stone effigy of the poet lying in state—is the striking sculpture of a darkly brooding young man, absorbed in his lugubrious thoughts. At that point I went over to the nearest tree, and banged my head slowly and repeatedly against the tree trunk. My sensory overload that day had been a tad too much.

And that was my best day ever with Mario.

༣ At the cemetery's exit we took leave of each other, and I met up with Caroline, who was waiting for me on a bench in the Luxembourg Garden. We visited the Place des Vosges and wandered around Le Marais, losing ourselves among the magnificent 17th century residences.

We then took the long subway ride to the Communist-run working-class suburb of Bagnolet, where Mano Negra was giving a show in a huge hall. They were starting to get big by then, and while entry was free for

---

2. The poem Past Life from The Flowers of Evil

the kids from Bagnolet, the well-off *fils à papas*[3] *who had to cross all of Paris from the better* neighbourhoods of Paris had to pay.

Caroline and I were waiting in line to get in. Then Manu Chao passed by on the other side of the crowd-control gates. "Hey Manu!" I shouted. He stopped and said: "Hey, ça va toi? Suivez moi!"[4] And he led us out of the line to a choice place off stage left. And *La Mano* did not fail to give another killer performance.

Since the purpose of this book in part is to educate the Anglocentric world to the superlative non-English speaking artists of which it has no clue, let's take a well-deserved page for me to tell you about Manu Chao. In 1998 he released a solo album called *Clandestino*, which made him the Bob Marley of the French and Spanish speaking worlds. It wound up selling over 5 million copies worldwide, but that's not the point. Although there are some songs in French and English, with a smattering of Brazilian Portuguese, the album is sung mainly in Spanish. Across South America, he is seen as a rock god, and when in 1999 I lived a year in Santiago, Chile, whenever I mentioned to young people I knew Manu Chao, they'd sidle up to me to touch my arm.

By the early '90's, Chao's Mano Negra was on the cusp of U2-like stardom. But instead of continuing to complacently tour Europe in relative comfort, he decided to drag the band on a grueling hitch-hiker's tour of Latin America—a perfect storm that would break up any band.

After they abandoned him, Manu Chao continued careening randomly throughout South America for over three years—discovering the continent much in the manner of Che Guevara. He busked around and played in bars, taping songs on his laptop along the way. The result was *Clandestino*—in which he amazingly managed to capture the plaintive sights and sounds and sadness of the Andean highlands, and the very soul of humble indigenous families huddled in a hammock in their earth-floored straw-roofed huts. It is the *Blonde On Blonde* of this red-earthed oppressed land, to me the most poignant and touching album ever made. And to fully *get it*, you need to have witnessed the humility

---

3. Transl: Spoiled brat scions of wealthy families
4. Transl: "Hey how are you? Follow me!"

and self-effacing life of the soft-spoken folks eking out their everyday struggle for dignity. Quite simply, for me, *Clandestino* remains the best rock album of all time. And the Beatles can shove their goddamn privileged Pepper up their ass. The story behind this admirable man and his album was perfectly captured 15 years later in *The Guardian*[5].

↗ Now it was *meet the parents* time. Gulp. We met up with Caroline's parents at a Chinese restaurant in Paris' Chinatown, the *13e arrondissement* off Place d'Italie. Caroline's father was a distinguished-looking German diplomat, close to retirement. He looked a lot like Beatles producer George Martin. And her mother was a cute snow-haired prim respectable matron—a Québécoise who'd met her dashing future hubby when she was a secretary in 1960—back when living in Paris was very cheap. Their daughter was now with this louche guy in a leather jacket, and uncharacteristically wearing one herself.

"*So* Mr. Lord, what *is* it that you do exactly?" her father enquired, looking at me eagerly, puffing at his pipe. "Er ... I ... uh ..." I didn't know how to answer this simplest of questions. Caroline came to my rescue: "He's a *bauingenieur*, papa!" I nodded. "Y-yes, that's right. I'm a building engineer!"

We also made a quick trip to meet her *opa*[6] in Bonn, who by then was living in a high-end old folks' residence. He talked to me animatedly in German, and I just nodded in agreement: "Ja ja, natürlich!"[7] Word was he showered gifts upon the shapely nurses who took showers with him. By all evidence, the randy Schütze gene lasted at least to age 87.

Before leaving for the south of France, Caroline's old *lycée*[8] pal Jeanne dropped by to see us in our Pigalle hotel room. They sat on the bed with their backs against the bedboard and giggled, reminiscing about old times together. Jeanne's father was the famous filmmaker

---

5. https://www.theguardian.com/music/2013/may/09/manu-chao-clandestino-culshaw
6. Transl: grandfather
7. Transl: "Yes yes, of course"
8. High school

Marcel Ophuls, who made *The Sorrow And The Pity*, while her grand-father was Max Ophuls, who made *La Ronde*. She wanted nothing to do with film, and wanted a low-profile life—far from her monster of a father, who terrorized her mother. Jeanne was brilliant, and whizzed through the oppressive and eliminative French school system with top grades, but wound up choosing a simpler life as a schoolteacher in rural Normandy, where she raised her son with pianist husband Emmanuel.

The following day we went to Gare Montparnasse and took the TGV[9] to Avignon in the south of France. It was strange to see the countryside whizzing by at 320 kph, with bereted peasants in the coaches contentedly chewing pieces of bread and slices of salami cut off with a pocket knife, as if they were calmly lunching at a rough-hewn table next to the barn.

From Avignon we took a bus to Cavaillon, where we waited for Denis to pick us up. Finally, we were in the deep south of France, lolling at a café sipping a cool *Ricard* in the shade on the sidewalk, watching kids spluttering by on their *mobylettes* under the lazy sun. Denis showed up in his *deux chevaux*[10], and brought us to his sister's house in Les Borrys—a big farmhouse in the middle of nowhere. A good part of Denis' extended Vietnamese-origins family was there, including his French brother-in-law who was a smiley long-haired hippie smurf tending to his mushrooms. The kind we eat. Their toddler happily traipsed around the huge garden in his Pampers, cooing and occasionally yelping in delight at the sight of a passing butterfly.

≷ I managed to rent a car with no credit card and an expired Quebec driver's license, that I waved under stupid Avis France's wine-veined red-bloated noses. And off we went to explore Provence.

Driving under the hot *Midi* sun, I spotted an orchard ahead and pulled over to the side of the road. I hopped out, jumped a low stone wall and ran over to a squat tree. "Watch this!" I yelled to Caroline, and craned my neck to eat a cherry right off the branch. At a roadside stand we bought a paper bag of cherries and spit the pits out the car window

9. France's bullet trains
10. A Citroën 2cv

laughing, with Mano Negra's *Patchanka*[11] blaring all the way to Arles. We had not a care in the world.

We wound up visiting Arles, Nîmes, Uzès, the Pont du Gard, Les Beaux, Aigues Mortes and swam in the Mediterranean at Sainte-Marie-La-Mer. Mid-May to mid-June is the perfect period to visit Europe—no tourists or vacationing locals yet—so the shopkeepers, hotel and restaurant staff are *thrilled* to see you.

While wandering in Nîmes, we saw a sign in front of a small club. It said *Les Garçons Bouchers Tonight*. Huh? What a strange coincidence! So that night we turned up for the show. There was no one in the audience. The place was empty. Apart from me and Caroline, there was the huge Hadji-Lazaro, his musicians, Luc Natali, and about *two* spectators. After the packed show at the Olympia, what a contrast! They were all visibly depressed. We sat with Natali and Lazaro and paid them a beer. They had no money.

While waiting for the show, the DJ put on a song that sounded vaguely familiar. Holy shit—it was *Les Grands Boulevards*—from my 1980 *Johnny Frisson* album. I went over and ducked into the DJ booth. "Hey," I said, "that's *me* playing the guitar!" The DJ exclaimed: "Cool man, I *love* that album!"

⤳ We fell in love with the small town of Uzès, and I admired Caroline's elegant strokes as she swam in the icy waters of a stream cut in the valley. Then in Arles, after a walk in the Roman cemetery of Alyscamps at seven in the morning, we sat down for coffee at a café and read horrified about the Tiananmen massacre in *Libération* and the *International Herald Tribune*. I'd been closely following the inspiring pro-democracy student protests in Tian An Men Square, and was furiously outraged when the Chinese criminal thugs in power quite literally crushed the movement. The bastards' "Peoples Liberation Army" tanks ran over kids sleeping in tents in the middle of the night, killing over 1000. I never forgot that, and unlike the mindless worshippers of *business at any cost*, I never saw China as anything other than a grave fascist menace to Humanity.

---

11. Hear it at: https://www.youtube.com/watch?v=u_Iu0u9IBxw

⇁ We crossed the Pyrenées into Spain in an excruciatingly slow *Renfe*[12] train. We passed through Port Bou, where in 1940 the German Jewish philosopher Walter Benjamin preferred killing himself, instead of falling into the hands of the Gestapo.

I dragged Caroline to see the astounding *Teatre-Museu Dali* in Figueres, but we couldn't even get in. Busloads of elementary school kids had invaded the place, turning it into an unbearably loud screechy kiddie hell hole. Furthermore, Caroline was fed up being landlocked in a hot dusty town and wanted to see the sea, so we made a beeline to Roses, where we rented a hotel room on the beach. How could I ever forget our romantic walk hand in hand along the beach at sunset ... punctuated by the violent slappings of a freshly-caught octopus being tenderized on the rocks by a gruff fisherman.

No doubt inspired by that brutal sight, we went to a local fisherman's wharf café and sat down to eat a dish of *pulpo*[13], which was served to us reluctantly by the owner, glaring at us tourists in contempt. We then loitered watching the crusty oldsters with burnt necks prepping the boats for night shrimp fishing, their young apprentices shouting and laughing while throwing aboard provisions, equipment, nets and thick ropes. At dusk the flotilla boats departed one by one, to the sound of seagulls and gurgling diesel engines, with the last rays of the sun dancing on the waves.

⇁ We continued on our route to Barcelona, where we lost ourselves in the Barrio Gótico[14], feeling like we were in the 14th century. Our medieval reverie was broken as we exited into 20th century traffic, passing by a building still riddled with bullet holes dating from the Spanish Civil War. I was thrilled to show Caroline Antonio Gaudi's Casa Battló, Casa Míla, and Parc Guëll. We climbed the towers of the unfinished Sagrada Familia to observe the work still in progress, then sat at a café at the end of the day, watching people returning from work, or shopping for food with their kids in tow.

---

12. Spain's national railway company
13. Boiled octopus, Galicia style
14. Old Gothic neighbourhood

We took the 45-minute bus into town daily from Castellar del Vallès—a small town 39 km north of Barcelona—where we were treated like royalty by Ríus and his second wife Pílar. She made us all kinds of delicacies, including *Pa Amb Tomàquet*[15]—a simple yet delicious Catalán specialty consisting of grilled slices of bread rubbed with fresh tomatoes, and drizzled with olive oil.

Ríus had a spanking new black Mercedes sedan, but never offered to ferry us into town with it. When I later described Ríus' car to my father, in a pathetic fit of one-upmanship, my 72-year-old dad rushed out and bought himself a powder blue Pontiac Firebird Trans Am. Moreover, it had a humongous black eagle painted on the hood, which in cartalk parlance is called a *Fire Chicken*. There was no sight more ridiculous for folks stopped at a red light to glance sideways and see this shrunken old man sunk in a bucket seat, straining to see above the steering wheel of his muscle car. My mother always wondered why everyone found them so funny.

≳ By the time we made it back to Paris, Caroline and I were dead tired and dead broke, and had to stay at her cousin Stefan's apartment. As we moped along utterly dejected to his place, staring at the sidewalk instead of the graceful Parisian skyline, we came upon a miraculous 100 Francs note[16]. Which covered the cab ride to the airport.

Once back in my Montreal Losers Palace flop hotel, after shooing away the cockroaches I looked up *Les Borrys* in a Michelin Guide. Without knowing it, we had been only 7 kilometers from the ruins of the castle of the Marquis de Sade. Damn!

So here I was, home and poor again. Out of desperation I sat down and wrote the song *Bonyeu*[17], in which I implored God to gimme a job.

While waiting for my tongue-in-cheek divine invocation to take effect, I hunkered down and resolved to finally compose my new computer cut-ups software *Scissors*, in order to write my prose poetry opus

---

15. Tomato Bread
16. About $20 ($45 today)
17. Transl: Hey God

Le carnaval tragique—which ends with a 21-page poem[18]. Whereas before I had to type every word beforehand into array cells, with *Scissors* I could now input a text file of any length. It counted the words, then calculated the array size needed to store the input text, then spit out a torrent of random cut-ups until you pressed STOP. It was a small *hallelujah* moment for me.

ᘔ By September I was sick to death of being poor and was desperately looking for a job. I went to Lachine—a desolate industrial park on the city outskirts—to apply for a job at Tri-Steel, where I'd be designing (ugh) hydroelectric powerline towers. Not too glamorous, huh?

The secretary asked me to sit in the waiting room. I passed a sign which said WELCOME TO THE CHINESE PEOPLE'S DELEGATION. Then a horde of geeky white-shirted Chinese piled in through the door and were led by chuffed executives into a boardroom.

"What the hell *is* this?" I was thinking. "Are these cocksuckers schmoozing those murderous pricks to build hydro towers in China?" I was stewing in anger, feeling powerless. "I'm a Neoist," I finally reminded myself. "What would a *Neoist* do in a situation like this?"

I charged into the boardroom meeting, and ran around yelling in fake Chinglish "BANG! BANG! TIEN AN MEN! YOU KILL STUDENTS??? BANG! BANG! TIEN AN MEN, TIEN AN MEN!"—I took them all by surprise. The Tri-Steel execs froze, and before they could react I bolted out the door and scrammed the hell off, squealing the tires of my Fire Chicken Camaro, like Steve McQueen. I raced along on the highway, crying tears of rage and desperation. And I sure hope I killed right there and then any prospects those fuckers had of getting a contract with China. At the very least I embarrassed the hell out of them and they had a lot of explaining to do to their wonderful delegation. What a Werrcome indeed!

ᘔ To my surprise, that fall Caroline enrolled in a Comparative Literature Master's degree program at McGill University. I sometimes drove her to her classes in the Fire Chicken. She was so embarrassed, I

---

18. See Appendix—Selected Texts—for an excerpt

had to drop her off on McTavish well below the Student Union building. She got along fine and made a slew of new friends. They were all girls in her class, and gave parties often, which we never failed to attend. I loved to needle these serious gals, and called them *The Masters Chicks*—which to my great delight brought me howls of protest.

Me, I still had no income. No job, no fortune, only a bit of VDMS fame, completely useless. Walking around town with Caroline, I was often recognized by someone across the street, yelling "hey Alan!" I'd peer closely at them and realize it wasn't someone I knew. "You're famous!" Caroline chirped. I didn't like the feeling—my street anonymity was being violated. Being recognized by strangers and shouted and waved at on the street like that used to creep me out. Who wants to be famous? Fame is like coke—every 15 minutes you need another 15 minutes.

24

THE END OF MY ROAD TO RUIN

I guess God must've heard my plea for a job, because sometime in October I got a call out of the blue offering me one. The Groupe SM company (yup) was looking for an expert in computer analysis and design of concrete structures. A good Samaritan draftsman from the old Norsk Hydro project tracked me down and gave them my name. So overnight I went from being a welfare bum to making $45,000 a year[1]. I wrote a letter to the Welfare people, thanking them for their support during hard times, saying I didn't need their cheques anymore.

After a couple years of a precarious, chaotic lifestyle earning peanuts on the music scene, it was a novelty and a relief to have a steady paycheque again. Have I already used this line? Well it sure comes in handy.

⊃ I was now the lead structural design engineer for the Montreal Biodome—a $45 million project[2]. Housed under the Olympic Installations' original Velodrome roof shell, the Biodome was to be an ecosphere and environmental documentation center, featuring several live animals in painstakingly recreated natural habitats. My tasks included the finite element analysis and concrete design of the Biodome's complex structures. These included the St. Lawrence Seaway Basin (a huge aquarium with panoramic window), plus the Polar World, Boreal Forest and Tropical World exhibits. The challenges posed by this unique project called for creativity, and I wound up pioneering custom

---

1. $96,000 a year today
2. $90 million today

techniques for the support of towering shotcrete[3] artificial rock cliff formations. It was a very rewarding experience for me to work with landscape architects, and translate their wishes into reality. The surface of the "rock formations" and some of the trees which were artificial were worked out like putty and then painted by hand once dry.

For my complex structural analyses I chose an advanced software called GT-STRUDL, which was run on a VAX computer. The operating manual came in four fat binders. The software was so complicated that we had to bring a specialist up from Georgia Tech in Atlanta, and he sat next to me for three days, until I could learn to run the program and print the results on my own. Although the VAX was powerful, a run of the 3D finite element model analyses of the Polar World took 24 hours. So if I forgot a comma, or wanted to change anything, I had to wait a whole 24 hours to try again.

Much to my chagrin, I soon discovered that the arts weren't the only domain rife with asshole divas: when addressing journalists, my bean-counter boss elbowed me aside and brazenly took all the credit for my arduous design work.

❧ In early November, Caroline and I started hanging out weekends at her parents' house in Magog—a small town 125 km from Montreal. What a relief it was for me to be all cozy in the wood-paneled Schütze family basement, watching TV together. A quiet sanity reigned here, unlike the way I grew up. There was no dysfunctional screaming at each other, no sobbing kitchen drama crises ever. I was used to tufts of armpit hair sticking out of a wifebeater, as my dad lurched across the dinner table to stab at a forkful of salad straight from the salad bowl. I was ever fearful of protesting this disgusting habit of his, lest I wish upon myself a prompt slap upside the head.

No. *This* household was a proper, civilized family. White-haired owlish Mom knitted with her feet propped on an ottoman while chain-smoking her cigarettes, and Papa puffed contentedly on his pipe, painting tin soldiers for his next historical diorama. We watched the Berlin Wall come down live on TV. Papa Schütze was all excited that his

---

3. Concrete sprayed at wall surfaces through a hose

fractured hometown of Berlin—his *heimat*—would soon be made whole again. A feeling of great hope was in the air, World Peace just in time for Christmas. Tranquility Base here, the beagle has landed. To sleep soundly as the quiet snow falls softly outside.

≥ Right before Christmas, Jack booked VDMS in what turned out to be our worst show ever—the absolute bottom of our "career" in music. By a miserable night of sub-zero cold, he had us opening for a thrash metal band called *Gorguts,* in a tiny nondescript venue in Sherbrooke. Their hardcore fans didn't even know who we were or even cared, they were just waiting for the moment to start nodding caveman-like, sweeping their shoulder-length hair back and forth, in time to the pummeling "music" of their grunting heroes, equally nodding caveman-like, sweeping back and forth their shoulder-length hair.

After this wondrous evening we all shot Jack dirty looks, and I was glad I could slink off to a warm bed in nearby cozy Magog, instead of having to slog the 155 kilometers back to Montreal, utterly fuming and stewing in Jack's toxic juices. There was no New Year's Eve show at the Foufounes that year, and a damn good thing too.

I was looking for a way out. Meanwhile, sporadic VDMS shows went on. The Bimbo had taken to the annoying habit of sitting on the edge of the stage beside me, as if she were my moll. And she did this fully realizing I was with Caroline. How embarrassing.

I was getting bored while playing guitar during shows. I noticed guitar geeks starting to cluster at my feet, trying to make out what I was doing on the fretboard. So to amuse myself I began kneeling at the edge of the stage and jut out my fretboard to show them my handiwork, making surprised faces as if to say: "Oh! So *this* is how it's done!"

During the breakdown of the set after a show I searched all around backstage for my beautiful tan leather satchel storing my effects pedals and guitar cables. It had been stolen. Another omen of end times for VDMS.

≥ The cockroach situation was getting out of hand at the Losers Palace. I became afraid of turning the light on in the bathroom and scaring awake the little bastards in the tub. I was making good money now, and didn't have to put up with this anymore. So that spring I rented a huge two-bedroom place on Fabre below Mount Royal, where my by-then meagre possessions suddenly had a lot more breathing space. Caroline helped me decorate, but it was a fruitless endeavour. I was always at her place anyway. So logic dictated that I make *The Big Move* into her place on Cartier.

Dubé stayed a while longer at the Losers Palace, but was soon expelled for missing rent payments. Good old trustworthy Mario went over and broke the lock, and Dubé managed to retrieve his stuff from the apartment.

What with my day job and life with Caroline, I now saw Mario less and less. When I did, with his constantly red eyes and thinning frazzled afro sprouting out the sides of his bald dome, Mario looked increasingly like some sort of weird bug. And believe it or not, after a solid eight years' residence, he too managed to leave the Losers Palace.

Speaking of his favourite movie *Barfly* in *Le délire*, Mario said, "I was Mickey Rourke looking for his Faye Dunaway." Well he finally found his Faye Dunaway—another drunk by the name of Réjane. She saw him fall off a stool in a bar and said, "That's the man for me."

Apart from drinking beer and wine, she was also a pothead who smoked awful homegrown Quebec weed all day, like all losers did here. It gave you a crappy mild buzz which could've been mistaken for a slight headache. Campo and Réjane moved into the first of a series of same-looking hovels, on Marie-Anne near Mentana. Wherever he lived, the place wound up reeking of nicotine-yellowed walls, stale beer and poverty.

At a party given by Réjane's son, Caroline and I watched transfixed as a teetering Mario bent over to light his cigarette off a candlestick. We looked at each other in panic, absolutely certain he was going to fall over and set his frazzled hair on fire. *But no!* He managed to stumble away, puffing at his badly hand-rolled cigarette falling apart. He made his own, because it was cheaper. In order to save money on their tight welfare budget, Campo also started making his own beer, but he only succeeded in poisoning himself.

I soon gave up on seeing Mario, because I couldn't even hold a conversation with him anymore—Réjane was always there, and she just couldn't shut up. In truth she was a simpleton, who exasperated even Mario.

⇋ One evening at the Spectrum after Pigalle had played, I went over and talked to François Hadji-Lazaro, who was busy rolling up a cable. I asked him: "So, do you plan on putting out a next album by us?" He shrugged, "Do you have one ready?" Good question.

Anyway, by now my life was pointing ahead, away from the old ways and the old friends. Fundamental change was in the air, and the VDMS boys sensed it too. Bonspiel didn't bother showing up for a gig we had at the bar *Le Magog* in Sherbrooke. The show was even more shambolic than usual, and we resorted to inviting fans in the audience who knew the lyrics to come and sing at the mic. Management refused to pay us, and rightly so.

Bonspiel says: "Our last show was at the Foufs in May of 1990 and it really felt like it." After packing up the gear I told the boys not to call me ever again to do any shows. That was it, I was throwing in the towel, hanging up my skates, pulling up my socks. I wanted to concentrate on my Biodome project, and settling down to a normal life with Caroline. I was now nearly 36 years old and finally smartening up. I stopped doing drugs. The time for fun and excess was over. *That* had become boring now. Throughout the Eighties I had the time of my life. Now it was time to change it.

⇋ The end of VDMS was also the end of our erstwhile manager Luc Natali. After riding on our coattails for over two years, he now found himself without wheels. When repossessing our VDMS Econoline, we found stuffed in the glove compartment a crumpled pile of unpaid parking tickets Natali had left us, totaling $600[4].

In the final analysis, VDMS didn't work because JM and I were pragmatic realists who wanted to forge ahead, while Jack and Bonspiel were self-sabotaging knee-jerk contrarians. When four feet are on the gas pedal and four feet on the brakes at the same time, the *char* won't be going anywhere. The way I explain VDMS to American friends is thus: imagine if the Sex Pistols had remained at the Marquee Club in London, known only to a couple hundred rabid fans.

Today, VDMS' renown has attained near-mythic proportions. In

---

4. $1200 today

2017, Francoeur had me guest with his reformed Aut'Chose on a couple of songs. Backstage I was yakking with opening band *Les Hôtesses d'Hilaire*[5]; when they learned I was in VDMS, they gave me the full "we're not worthy" treatment. Bands have covered our songs, and in 2020, *Le Backstore*'s Pat and Numa got together to issue a deluxe limited edition live album on coloured vinyl, complete with T-shirts and badges. Then in 2021, vintage Quebec rock afficionado Yannick Roof reproduced and re-issued our original *Boucherie* album. Incredibly, after thirty years plus, our mojo's still risin'. Witness recent fan comments on Facebook:

> "VDMS, that was something. I think no one could come out of one of their shows being left indifferent. The same can't be said of many other bands."

> "*Sophie Stiquée* will always be the test to pass when I receive new guests. You don't like it? You don't understand? Well then *fuck off.*"

We did a comeback show in 2008 to a packed Café Campus. Joe Bébel said: "I've been waiting 19 years for this!" It was also the last time Philippe Côté would get to jump onstage and crash a VDMS gig. He died of cancer in 2011.

⇄ I'd been slaving away on the grueling structural analyses of the complex structures of the Biodome since October. We were now in May of 1990, and the pressure was full on to wrap up the designs, because construction had to start. I couldn't take it anymore. I went to my boss' office, sat down and calmly told him: "Listen. I'm giving you two choices. Either I quit now, or I take a week off and go to Guadeloupe." He looked at me all surprised. He said: "Go to Guadeloupe".

Fred Mignault was down there working in a neon shop with his partner Jacques. They had a good thing going. With tropical hurricanes

---

5. Pronounced "Lay Oh-tess Dull-air"; Transl: Hilarious Hostesses—phonetically, it also reads "Flight Attendants"

blowing through the island regularly, smashing everything in their path—including the neon signs of bars and restaurants—business income was guaranteed for life. They lived above the shop in a big house, and I had an open invitation to stay there anytime.

So I gave Fred a call. He was thrilled, and asked me to bring him the two things he missed the most from back home: a huge jar of Kraft peanut butter, and a huge pot of Cheez Whiz—which in his Québécois *hack-cent* he endearingly pronounced "Cheez Wheeze".

Fred and Jacques picked up Caroline and I at the airport and brought us to a restaurant on the beach. It was already dark. First thing I did was strip off my clothes and run out into the warm surf. Then we sat down at a table and drank a beer with our feet in the sand, waiting for the food to arrive. Jacques was an amiable scraggly Frenchman with collar-length hair, and he was wearing a cool flowery Hawaiian shirt, similar to mine. I looked at Jacques and said: "I like your shirt." He said: "I like yours." On cue we stood up, took off our shirts and swapped them, laughing like loons.

Caroline and I had trouble sleeping at night. There were roosters in the farms all around, and to our horror we found out that roosters don't only crow at dawn, but also throughout the night—just often enough to wake you up again after you've finally gotten back to sleep. What the hell, we didn't need to be alert to loll around on the beaches.

After spending a few days on the beach and eating shellfish, Jacques asked me if I knew Excel. "Sure I do," I said. "I'm a bloody expert!" He wanted me to show their accountant how to use the damn thing. He was a nice young local, eager to learn. I took a look at his computer. It was a 286 PC. I said: "What are you doing with *that*? We're up to 486's, and even *Pentiums* now. You should at least get a 386!" In his Créole accent he replied: *"Oh non non ... c'est twoh vite!"*[6]

Speaking of *too fast*, Fred drove us down to visit the capital of Pointe-à-Pitre. He was driving way too fast—beyond his driving abilities—yakking and careening all over the place on the road. The fucker nearly killed us. Why is it that people who don't know how to drive always go too fast? I told him to stop and took over at the wheel. I'm

---

6. Transl: "Oh no no ... it's too fast!"

not crazy about driving and normally find it a chore, but I must confess that driving along winding roads amid palm trees is one of my life's pleasures.

Caroline and I were really enjoying the sea and sun. But not Fred. He sat on a beached log smoking cigarettes, moping and frowning, his toes digging around in the sand. He clearly wasn't happy in this paradise. To him it was only a strange land. He soon returned to Montreal, and found happiness making his neon sculptures again and doing performances at the Foufounes, surrounded by his old friends. To this day.

⇚ In June I was invited to give a presentation on my Montreal Biodome at Georgia Tech in Atlanta, during a four-day conference on GT-STRUDL. It coincided with Caroline's birthday, so while I was at the conference, she celebrated her birthday, getting plastered on pitchers of Frozen Margaritas in the cool shade with Joyce—one of her *Masters Chicks* pals. I joined up with them later and we went out to dinner. During our stay, Caroline and I explored Atlanta and caught a big MLK party and fair. On the bus, elevated MARTA[7] trains and the fair itself, we were the only two white faces in a Black sea, and thoroughly enjoyed ourselves, sampling the soul food and buying some crafts. When reporting our day's outing to Joyce's friends in the whitebread enclave of Little Five Points, their faces blanched from shock. They thought we were completely insane, "risking our lives like that."

⇚ That June, Dubé and I got together and created a *Third Mind*—we founded *Le Groupe Absence*—a pseudo-corporate entity that subverted a culture so cherished by Anglo-Americans: *Corporate* Culture. Our goal was to exasperate business-inclined folks with newsletters, slogans and catch phrases even more ridiculous than theirs[8].

We were soon joined by Tristan—who wanted to put together an opera called *Ultramar*[9]—as well as John Berndt in Baltimore, and Florian Kramer in Germany, who got it immediately and dove right in.

---

7. Metro Atlanta Rapid Transit Authority—which the gallant suthern gentlemen dubbed Moving Africans Rapidly Through Atlanta

8. See Appendix—Selected Texts

9. A chain of gas stations in Eastern Canada

Dubé came up with a brilliant logo for us: A set of chevrons, with one stripped off each year, until none would be left by the year 2001—the planned end date of *Le Groupe Absence*. Business cards were printed for all.

Dubé's specialty was digital drawings subverting company logos, such as *King Burger*, or melding the Chrysler and Mercedes logos. I worked on a wall-sized painting that spelled *Apple* using the IBM logo font. It was all good tongue-in-cheek fun. We drove Phil Côté nuts. "*What* is Le Groupe Absence?" he kept asking in frustration.

The fun ended when Dubé's penchant for all-consuming compulsions veered to becoming a novelist. For some reason he became obsessed with the writer Christian Mistral, who'd created a stir with his novel *Vamp*. Dubé now wanted to prove that *anyone* could write a novel, by writing one himself. So he wrote the novel *Gloire*, which was eventually published, under his new name Joseph Jean Rolland Dubé. His next literary effort was a light tongue-in-cheek book called *Le fanfaron*—which Tristan absolutely despised. Once, Dubé called on Tristan accompanied by his girlfriend, and Tristan began insulting Dubé from the top of the stairs—yet he thoughtfully paused to politely acknowledge his girlfriend with "bonjour miss, very pleased to meet you!"

Well, what do you expect from a Neoist? Tristan could be dismissive, even with his own friends, evidently. "L'art, ce n'est pas de l'Art"[10] was his best quote at the time.

➤ The Ramones were playing at the Rialto on July 4th. How appropriate! I dragged Caroline over to see them, gushing: "They're the greatest live band in the world … you'll love 'em!"

What a disappointment. Dee Dee was gone by then, and they now played the songs at twice the speed. They played so fast that Joey had to skip every second word and gulp out their once-classic songs—now totally ruined. I was shocked. I was speechless. What the hell happened? My guess is they felt they had to keep up with the dime-a-dozen speed

10. Transl: Art is not Art—meaning: what's hung on gallery and museum walls ain't the real thing

metal cretin bands they'd spawned. Pathetic. I frowned and grabbed Caroline's hand. "Come on, let's get out of here. They ain't what they used to be."

It was the end of an era. The Ramones didn't get it, but I sure did. Like Giorno said, "Things that work in one decade don't work in the next."

⇐ At our place on Cartier street we never lost our reputation for throwing the best parties—whether it was Bernard downstairs, or us upstairs. During a rather raucous party deep in the summer, both apartments plus back yard were packed to the gills, and Jack and Bonspiel started having an apple fight, lobbing the red missiles at each other across the back yard. I brought Bonspiel upstairs and showed him my song *Bonyeu*[11], and we gleefully sang the song VDMS never got to do.

I'd invited my 71-year-old mom to the party, and marveled at the amazing energy she still had. She was still going gangbusters at 3 AM— yakking, joking and pulling the flagging young 'uns off the couch to get up and dance frantically with her. We later learned the source of her secret powers: someone had brought a cake baked with pot, which she'd very much enjoyed.

As dawn came around and the revelers had mostly left, Caroline said she saw the grinning face of Phil Côté rolling around in the tomato plants, fucking the icky Tree Lady in the dirt. We'd baptized this weird, gaunt East European yuckie witch *The Tree Lady*. You'd find one of these haughty mysterioso Nico-wannabe bohos at *every* party. The revolting sight in the tomato patch creeped out Caroline no end, and placed a definite kybosh on any further attempts at freewheeling entertainment at our place.

⇐ In November, Caroline and I decided to spend a long weekend in New York, to get a much overdue art overdose. We saw a Frida Kahlo exhibit, new robots by Nam June Paik, and Arman's accumulations— this time consisting of dozens of huge paintings with just artist's tubes

---

11. I gave it to Les Colocs in 1995 and it became a big radio hit: https://www.youtube.com/watch?v=BJpyEGj9jjA

of colour squirting out long wiggly lines of paint. I was very disappointed by this Low Effort Art of his. We also caught an exhibit of Dada leaflets and posters, Jeff Koons' big dumb chrome rabbits, the *High & Low* show at MoMA, and a huge Dennis Oppenheim show with a cool machine that shot skeeter pucks at a large target in a corner, smashing them crumbling into a pile.

We checked into my favourite hotel—the stately Gramercy Park Hotel, which they've *boutique* ruined since—and of course the first thing I did was to ring up Huncke.

"Hey Alan! Where are you?" he asked, excited. "I'm at the Gramercy, Herbert!"—"I'm coming right over," he said. "Okay," I said, "meet me at the hotel bar in twenty minutes."

I knew why he was in such a hurry to meet me, and I was ready for him. I went downstairs and in no time Huncke ducked into my booth. I ordered drinks and we both started yakking a mile a minute—we had a lot of catching up to do.

Then there was that awkward pause in the conversation I'd been waiting for. "Listen man, I'm kinda short, could you lay some bread on me?"

"Sure thing, Herb," I said, whipping out the deuce twenties I'd been clutching under the table for him, waiting for the appropriate moment. "Oh man, great!" he exclaimed. "Thanks a lot, man. I sure need that right now." It was a Saturday, which of course leads to Saturday Night. He said: "Hey, there's a party at a friend of mine's—Matt Radz— at the Chelsea tonight—you wanna come? Gregory Corso will be there."

Well, I sure wasn't about to pass up the opportunity of getting to meet another legendary member of The Beat Generation now, would I? Caroline and I followed Huncke, who was sauntering at a quick step. We stopped at a corner red light and I turned to him. "You're so mushable"—explaining this was our expression for *cuddly*. The light changed and we hurried across the street to the Chelsea, with Huncke repeating "*mushable!*"—chuckling in disbelief.

We passed the grumpy manager hidden behind plate glass and the "Hotel Rules" signs in the lobby, and walked up the grubby steps of the Chelsea Hotel, carefully side-stepping the dead inch-long cockroach on its back, its skinny brittle legs pointing upward.

Matt Radz was an amiable grizzly, bearded, bellied freelance jour-nalist and erstwhile poet. All night he kept repeating his same one and only poem to one and all, without the least prompting from anyone. The poem had something to do with the crystals of the mind melting in the rainbows of eternity.

His apartment was full of exotic furniture and trinkets, shadow-play puppets and umbrellas he'd just brought back from a trip to Thailand. My guess is he was hoping to fob off some of the stuff to his guests.

I didn't realize it at the time, but Matt Radz was the one who'd interviewed me for a full-page article in the *Montreal Star* back in 1979, when I was the latest up-and-coming punk rock star on the block. There's nothing worse than fame and no fortune. I loved what Kerouac said: "Fame is old newspapers blowing down Bleecker Street."

Corso, wearing a baseball cap deep over transfixed eyes atop a grin-ning beard, was huddled watching a baseball game with his cronies, barely a foot away from the TV set.

I figured I'd leave him alone. I turned to Huncke and asked, "Hey, is there any place around here we can score some pot?"

"Sure," he said, "follow me." We made our way down to a lower floor, and he knocked on one of the Chelsea's dark, creepy anonymous doors. A too-skinny kid with long scraggly hair opened the door and let us in. He was living in the tiniest apartment I'd ever seen—it was like a walk-in closet. He jumped onto his bed to make room for us. We had to squeeze by between the "bed"—a mattress atop a huge chest with drawers—and a wall of audio cassettes, carefully catalogued in boxes and shelves on the opposite side of the cramped room. There was a cruddy sound system and weird clunky boxes of hand-built electronic devices. He looked like a gearhead Rasputin, or technological monk. As he prepared our bag of pot, I marveled at his vast collection of Blues—obviously he was very erudite musically. Wow! He had the com-plete box set of Robert Johnson. "I never heard an original Robert Johnson," I explained. "Could you put something on—Crossroads?" He put on the song I only knew through Eric Clapton's Cream.

As is the tradition when buying dope from a kindred spirit, we toked off a huge joint graciously rolled for us. We sat back and smiled at each other, nodding appreciatively at the plaintive music eked from Robert Johnson's cut-short life of rambling tirelessly across the Mississippi Delta. He was the first original member of the famed *27 Club*.

I was finally in the middle of one of Huncke's stories, populated with one of his strange and wonderful characters, whose existence normally we'd barely notice and pass by without a glance, were it not for someone as sensitive a human being as Huncke taking us by the hand and sitting us down a minute.

↗ George Herbert Walker Bush rang in 1991 with the brutal air campaign of the Gulf War. The spectacle on live TV totally traumatized Caroline and I, as much as it did everyone else. Another thing traumatizing Caroline was her pudgy thesis director—we'll call him *Professor Kreepotkin*. He was a typically cryptic East European with round glasses, who'd perfected his ominous demeanour behind the Iron Curtain. He looked like Vyacheslav Molotov, and prodded Caroline unrelentingly with his narrow piglet eyes: "*So, Miss Schütze,* how is your thesis comingk along?" He pushed her to study Bertolt Brecht's *Lehrstücke*—tiresome didactic plays in which she had zero interest. Like many a prof, Kreepotkin just wanted to take credit for her work. Completely disgusted, Caroline dropped out of her Comparative Literature program. One more year of that would have succeeded in obliterating her love of literature. Ultimately, Caroline didn't know why she went into Comp Lit in the first place, and just wanted out from the academic world. Unlike some of the Masters Chicks, she was no faculty groupie interested in the Lit department intrigues, cocktail party gossip and endemic cattiness.

Back at SM, by May the Biodome was completed, and I was just doing crap rehab work on dinky buildings and shit. Just like all bosses, mine started giving me dirty looks because of the paucity of any real project work, and I started checking the exits instinctively. By now both Caroline and I felt at the end of our respective roads. And what better solution than to postpone an inconvenient existential reckoning by taking a nice long holiday in Mexico?

We landed in Cancún and quickly scudded down the coast to the rougher Playa del Carmen. Back then the coast wasn't overdeveloped like today, and we stayed in a $15 a night cabaña on the beach. We were so excited we drank too much tequila, and Caroline retched her guts out on the sand floor. It was our first hint that she couldn't drink alcohol no mo'. We then stopped for a swim and a quick Corona in Chemuyíl, and wound up renting a very spartan cabaña on the beach in Tulúm, which was practically a tourist-free village back then. There was ONE public phone in town, and to order a Western Union moneygram, I had to ride the 6 km from the beach on a rickety bicycle under a beating 40° C sun, stopping periodically to wet a towel with water from my canteen and wrap it on my head.

We visited the major Mayan sites of the Yucatán except for Chichén Itza, which we shunned because it had been "improved" for the tourists. We met Americans and hopped into their VW Beetle to Coba, and walked for hours in the stifling heat and overwhelming humidity of the jungle, keeping an eye on a pack of wild dogs that followed us with interest in the bush. We climbed to the top of a pyramid, to see there was nothing but jungle in all directions, other than the other Coba pyramid sticking out of the jungle canopy.

For transportation we used the same buses and makeshift taxis as the locals did. We even made it to the grottoes of Loltún by hitching a ride in the back of a bone-rattling open truck ferrying workers to the fields. It was very refreshing to explore the caves, whose vaulted ceilings, sculpted by nature in a river of rock, were as tall as Gothic cathedrals.

In the ruins of Uxmal there was not the least wisp of wind in the horrendous 45° C air, and we had to wait for the sun to duck behind a cloud before sprinting over to the next building complex. While waiting, we watched two iguanas battle ferociously in the heat.

As we climbed the steep 60° steps of the Pyramid of The Magician, I was wondering why there was a heavy iron chain running up the steps. As we got to the top and I swung around to see the sheer drop, I yelled at Caroline: "There's no fucking way I can get down—they'll have to send in a helicopter!" I soon realized the only possible way back down was to shimmy carefully over to that chain, and hang on for dear life as we edged back down the pyramid one step at a time. The priests had calculated those steep angles to allow victims' carcasses to tumble down easily, once their pulsating hearts had been ripped out.

Between the small towns of Muna and Ticul, we found ourselves in a crowded second-class bus—swaying and holding onto our straps—when an old blind campesino began to sing an overwhelmingly poignant song on his guitar. I was suddenly plunged into a monster state of illumination, with tears welling in my eyes. I had an epiphany—comprehending Life all at once intensely, and grasped how obvious it should have been all along—the simplicity and humility and perfection of existence as it stands on this Earth—and the realization that everything was—and would, forever be fine.

Palenque was considered the most beautiful of all the Mayan sites, its Paris. We took the bus to Chiapas with the locals and their poultry, and I was squeezed in back next to a drooping old man; I was certain he wouldn't last the journey. We disembarked at our destination at five in the morning after a fourteen-hour journey, completely exhausted, dizzy, confused, disoriented, and enveloped in the fog of interrupted sleep.

Stepping off the bus we were immediately greeted by a totally paralyzing surrealist sight: a young man was painfully pushing up the hill a wheelbarrow overflowing with pieces of a freshly butchered pig, its severed head nodding on a heap of pink limbs ending in bloody tips, its nose haughtily upturned, and rubbery ears jiggling at each bump in the uneven road, like the wings of an airline jet suddenly flexed by a violent air pocket.

⇝ We made it to the enchanting town of San Cristóbal de las Casas, and hired a guide. We galloped on horseback through the fields in the mountains of Chiapas at 2200 meters above sea level, among the Tzotzil Indians guarding their goats, and with a crowd of barking dogs nipping at our heels. The guide took us into the Church of San Juan de Chamula, where we saw indigenous folk kneeling on the ground among candles and pine branches, praying in a soft, touching mumble, hand applied to their cheek.

The Mayans took only what they liked from Catholicism, and melded it with their religion. They prayed to Saint John the Baptist—not Christ—they rejected the idea of worshipping a dude being tortured on a cross.

We saw a woman rubbing an egg on the lower back of her baby, praying in front of an altar that contained several saints placed in glass boxes. A mirror was hung around each saint's neck, so that the saint could recognize whoever it was that was praying in front of them. Only then could they grant that person their wish—say to be admitted in heaven after death, or to protect their child from illness.

We couldn't have been admitted into that church without our guide. He placed an offering of a few dollars on the floor in front of the shaman priest, and we knelt before him amid the candles, flowers and incense. He murmured a prayer and then gave each of us a small cup of *Posh* to drink—a potent spiritual elixir of god knows what.

We'd lucked out, because starting that December, Chiapas became an off-limits war zone—the Zapatista uprising had finally ignited in San Cristóbal de las Casas. Now we knew why we'd been ordered off the bus at gunpoint at military checkpoints, and why groups of women were squatting on blankets under banners and placards around the cathedral in protest. We definitely felt some sort of trouble was looming, and witnessed the swelling agitation which exploded into the Zapatista rebellion.

Returning from our trip to Mexico still in a daze, I finally resolved to finish my goddamn *Carnaval Tragique* already. Which I did. On the job. My three-years'-labour computer cut-up opus was warmly received by my huge fanbase of three people: Campo, Dubé, and Tristan. For his part, Lotringer's reaction, with calm near-paternal pride, was "c'est bien"[12].

Campo called it "génial"[13] and years later surprised me by reciting the opening line from memory. Dubé really obsessed over it, calling it "a plea for the total liberation of the individual"[14]. He adopted certain phrases as part of his fetish vocabulary, often repeating: "On part pour Mars!"[15] out of the blue. As for Tristan, *his* choice phrase was: "Après Mars, Vénus!"[16] and told me: "What could you possibly do after *that*, Lord?"

---

12. Transl: It's good
13. Transl: Brilliant
14. He said in French: "Un plaidoyer pour la libération totale de l'individu"
15. Transl: On to Mars!
16. Transl: After Mars, Venus!

Unfortunately for me, a Parisian publisher later begged to differ in opinion.

⌐ The trip to Mexico had been a great respite, but Caroline and I were still both sick of Montreal, our families, friends, the whole loser Foufounes mentality, my job at SM, her studies and hand-to-mouth freelance translation contracts.

Caroline's cousin Stefan in Paris called, saying his employer Deutsche Bank was transferring him to Dusseldorf, thus freeing up his apartment, which was halfway between l'Opéra and the Gare du Nord. Caroline and I took one quick look at each other and yelped: "We'll take it!"

We held one big last farewell party on Cartier, and the whole gang was there: the VDMS boys, Tristan, Sapin, Campo and Réjane, Dubé and the SCP boys. Little did I know it was the last time we'd all be in the same room together.

Caroline and I stuffed our belongings into two huge suitcases and bid our crappy white wintry Canadian wonderland goodbye. We landed at CDG[17] with $10K in savings[18] that were to suffice until we secured gainful employment. I brought along my guitar I don't know why, and also my PC with the idea of selling the SAFI structural analysis software over there.

---

17. Paris' Charles de Gaulle Airport
18. $19K today

25

ESCAPE TO PARIS, ESCAPE FROM PARIS

Mid-January 1992, Caroline and I moved to Faubourg Poissonnière corner Général Lafayette, roughly midway between the Opera House and the Gare du Nord train station. We were so thrilled when entering Stefan's apartment that we immediately unpacked our bags in an adrenaline rush, and zoomed out to walk around our brand new neighbourhood. The jetlag soon caught up with us and we returned to conk out fast asleep.

So yes, we flung ourselves unthinking at this unique opportunity to live in a cramped one-bedroom apartment. It was ridiculously tiny, with an even tinier kitchen that two people couldn't fit in at the same time. But at least we were in Paris!

The first person to drop by to see us was Sylvère, who happened to be in town visiting his daughter. I asked him if he knew anyone we should meet, and he gave me the phone number of Nina Zivancevic—a Serb poet who'd been Allen Ginsberg's secretary. I called her up, and she invited us to her poetry reading in a basement cave that had stone walls curved into a vault. We made the acquaintance there of Nina's friend, expat American artist Sigrid Sarda, who along with her boyfriend Michel, became our great friends.

Paris was a cultural Disneyworld, and Caroline and I had a lot of running around to do. One of the first things we did was to go see the *Opéra Bulles*[1] exhibit at the impressive new Parc de la Villette complex

---

1. Transl: Bubble Opera; meaning the "bubbles" containing dialogue, found in cartoons and graphic novels; see photos of the exhibit at: http://www.lucie-lom.fr/site/scenographies/opera-bulles/

in the 19th arrondissement. You wandered through rooms with giant bookshelves and walked across giant open books as if you were Alice in Wonderland. Each room was populated with the different figures of France's well-known comic books—Lucky Luke cowboys, Astérix Gauls, Brétécher, etc. In each room was a nook where you could sit and read from a comic book or graphic novel chained to your armchair. Lastly, the exhibit ended in a cavernous hall in which they satirically recreated a *"French on Vacation"* beach scene in exquisite detail, complete with a cruddy gross public bathroom Caroline laughingly recognized from her icky overcrowded beach vacations in France as a teenager. The French really had a knack for putting together such amazing exhibits.

≳ I called up Luc Natali and landed a small gig translating presskits for Boucherie, but under Hadji-Lazaro's wary eye. The money I made paid for a lowly meal at a bistro. It was clear I couldn't make a living from that.

I also deposited my *Carnaval Tragique* manuscript at *Les Éditions Blanche*. They'd published Kathy Acker. After a few weeks the verdict came back: "C'est une bombe, mais est-elle bien amorcée?"[2] It was rejected, and I didn't push it any further. I suspect being a complete unknown was my fatal crime. I was a nobody, and didn't have the inclination to start tirelessly building a cult following and carefully nurture some stupid purple-haired tattooed "persona".

By the end of February we were starting to get worried about our dwindling reserve of cash. After a few panicked phone calls, Caroline landed a job as a translator thanks to Gene—the dad of her old *Lycée* friend Anouk—who worked at Salans, Hertzfeld & Heilbronn. It was a posh international commercial law firm with such clients as Chanel and Pfizer. Gene had longish hair, dressed and looked like a hippie, but was in reality an ambitious, no-nonsense, international corporate lawyer—very rich and high-powered. As we eventually learned while living in France, you got ahead only by adequate *pistonnage*[3].

But never mind those petty earthly concerns ... because then there was ...

---

2. Transl: "It's explosive, but is the bomb well-primed?"
3. Transl: Connections

THE DAY WE SAW GOD

Yes! It happened on February 29th—a Saturday. That afternoon we went to *Les Tribus ou l'Europe*[4]—a two-day international colloquium on the brutal civil war going on in Yugoslavia among the Balkan "tribes". It was held at the Palais de Chaillot—the famous spot where Hitler took a selfie with the Eiffel Tower. In attendance were a slew of intellectuals, including Bernard-Henri Lévy, Alain Finkielkraut and filmmaker Fernando Arrabal, of *Viva La Muerte* fame.

As Caroline and I entered the building, we found ourselves walking a few steps behind a man a few inches shorter than me, with a bald pate. People on our flanks were making a fuss, pointing cameras at him. Then I recognized the bald pate. Holy shit, it was *French President François Mitterrand*—or *Dieu*[5]—as many snickeringly called him. We continued following him into the hall, and I felt sheepish with his bodyguards eyeing me suspiciously. Caroline and I ducked into some seats, and Mitterrand strode imperiously up onto the dais, brushed away the conferenciers and took over the proceedings. The fucker crashed the conference! He droned on interminably, attempting to justify his glaring lack of action in Europe's greatest crisis since World War Two. He eventually left, and the invitees went back to giving their scheduled talks. After the conference I got to chat a bit with Arrabal.

Ƨ Among the many things that illustrate how civilized the French are is the fact that their lunch hour at work is a whole *one and a half hours*. No American-style gulping down a quick sandwich at your desk, or skipping lunch entirely for *this* bunch. In fact they encourage you to go out at noon and enjoy a meal at a local bistro, by issuing you a dozen *Tickets déjeuners*[6] along with your paycheque. So I'd often pick up Caroline at Salans, we'd eat unhurried at a bistro, and then we still had time to either take a walk or laze on a bench in the nearby Tuileries garden.

In an attempt to sell my SAFI software I went to a construction

---

4. Transl: Tribes or Europe?
5. Transl: God
6. Meal vouchers, respected by most restaurateurs

engineering trade show called Bâtimat, but quickly saw that the competition was decades ahead, so that was the brutal end of my career as an engineering software salesman. I started looking at applying for an engineering job.

Disenchantment with life in Paris began creeping up on us. Caroline had to develop sharp elbows to fight her way into the packed métro[7] at rush hour, her nose pressed against the reeking armpits of arms raised to clutch the swaying straps. Then getting home to our apartment after a long day of work, Caroline had to take our cramped two-person klunky elevator, which usually smelled like the homeless bag lady who rode it up and down until the tenants chased her out of the building.

A good night's sleep in Paris was impossible. You were ripped from your sleep by a motorcycle zooming down an empty boulevard in the dead of night, then the *éboueurs*[8] at dawn. No wonder Parisians were such an irritable, hostile lot. Their national sport was making life hell for each other.

In order to get a good night's sleep, most Parisians took sleeping pills. In fact they had the habit of taking handfuls of pills for any and all ailments, real or perceived. Caroline and I refused to take sleeping tablets, so we resorted to *Sleepytime Tea* and other organic concoctions. Which made you get up to pee in the middle of the night—so much for that.

⇜ Our apartment had a large back window with a view on a big interior courtyard that was ringed with the tall apartment buildings all around, with similar back windows. This permitted us to hear screechy violin lessons, couples' quarrels, and whatever was playing on TV. While watching the 8 o'clock news one day I told Caroline "watch this" and muted our TV. It was still perfectly audible from the reverberating broadcasts from neighbouring windows in our collective canyon of urban misery.

---

7. Transl: Subway
8. Garbage men, with their noisy trucks picking up and emptying dumpsters

In the middle of the courtyard was a mysterious one-story house with a Mercedes parked next to it during the daytime. On sunny days the car alarm was always going off. I had fun dropping eggs onto it, cupping my ear gleefully to hear a delightful "POK!" That strange house was busy mainly in the middle of the night, and we were often woken at 3 AM by the echoes of tipsy giggling floozies and the clip-clops of their unsteady high heels reverberating in the back yard, accompanied by their lout no-neck suitors guffawing loudly. Sheltered by the dark anonymity of the block, I yelled with the best working-class Parisian accent I could muster: "Ta gueule, connard!"[9] A guy yelled back: "Qui a dit ça? J'te fous une balle dans la tête!"[10]

Most Parisians live in cramped apartments—that's why they're always sitting outside in cafés—they can't stand staying at home. We were no different, and escape was near impossible. On the first warm day of spring we decided to pack up a picnic and go spread a blanket on the grass in the Buttes Chaumont park. When we got there we saw that half of Paris had already gotten the same brilliant idea—the goddamn place looked like Woodstock. We wandered around for a long while before finally finding ourselves a square yard of unoccupied green grass. You see, that's the problem with Europe. You just can't get away from people. It's too densely populated. Just like New York, Paris is loud, agitated and noisy, 24/7.

Unlike most Parisians though, we had a secret escape plan up our sleeves. Our only respite from Parisian hell was Caroline's Uncle Walla's house near the quaint village of Saint-Rémy-les-Chevreuse—the last stop on the blue RER B line[11]. All the while we lived in Paris, it was the only place we could get a good night's sleep. There was a garden in back that ended at the small stream of l'Yvette, beyond which lay a peaceful vista of lush green pastures with cows leisurely munching on grass. It was as idyllic a spot as you could wish for in the area, but we had to space our visits with care, in order not to overstay our welcome.

---

9. Transl: "Shut the fuck up, asshole!"
10. Transl: "Who said that? I'll put a bullet in your head!"
11. The RER is Paris' network of trains to the suburbs

≈ I got lots of job interviews, but at a certain point it dawned on me that I was merely an object of curiosity for them as a Canadian, and that they only wanted something interesting to say about their day at the nightly family dinner table. And so went my weekly trek to La Défense[12] for yet another mutually entertaining fruitless job interview. After a while I gave up, glomming onto the clever Catch 22 of the French immigration system: to get your papers you needed a job offer, and to get a job offer you needed your papers. Got that?

≈ During a weekend Caroline and I went to the *Salon du livre*[13] at the impressive *Petit Palais*, which was built for the 1900 Universal Exhibition. To my great surprise and delight we happened upon Paul Virilio, whose *Pure War* I'd read thanks to Semiotext(e). As he was signing for us a copy of his new book *l'Écran du désert*[14]—about the recent Iraq war— I remarked, "Ah, Monsieur Virilio … we have a friend in common!"

"Oh? And who might that be?" inquired the man. "Sylvère Lotringer," I said. "Well then, we must get together!" he exclaimed, scribbling down his phone number on a scrap of paper. Sylvère's death in 2021 reminded me of how much he touched people's lives and brought them together in such unexpected ways. Without him, I wouldn't have met Caroline through her brother Bernard, and we wouldn't have produced our wonderful son Nico.

Virilio was a curious little man, very vivacious. He could have passed off as the cheery village priest in any corner of France. Except he started out as an urbanist, quickly becoming a sought-after "public intellectual"—something France has an abundance of—and which the rest of the world sorely lacks.

Through Semiotext(e)'s translations, he became known for his books *Pure War* and *Speed And Politics*, by which he illustrated his notions of *Dromology*—that speed was the dominant factor in our frantic modern civilization. Funny enough, Sylvère snickered: *"Mr. Speed*

---

12. The office-tower business district just past Paris' city limits
13. Paris' yearly book fair
14. Transl: The Desert Screen

putters around in a *Deux Chevaux*"—a dinky little Citroën 2cv—powered by an engine that gave it a vertiginous top speed of 100 kmh.

So with Virilio, as with all Frenchmen, a Canadian always elicited curiosity—and especially in my case, a Canadian *engineer*. Much to the dismay of *Québécois* nationalists, the French considered us *French Canadians*—or even worse—just *Canadians*. I'd start talking to any Frenchman in the best Parisian accent I could mimic, and they'd immediately go: "Ah, vous êtes *canadien*?"[15]

For our first meeting I stood up *Speedy*. Yes, me—normally a pathetic, pathologically punctual guy—stood up *Paul Virilio*. Unforgivable, I know. You see, in my half-hearted attempt at becoming gainfully employed, I'd gone to the southern suburb of Le Petit Clamart for a job interview. This involved taking the yellow RER C train from Gare Montparnasse. Getting back in time was an utterly complicated mess of RER line switchings, and *bref*—as they say in France—I missed meeting Virilio at Paris' famous literary watering hole *La Coupole*. What a fucking idiot!

After an effusively contrite, embarrassed phone call he graciously re-invited me to La Coupole. I made damn sure not to mess up my *second* chance. I showed up way too early and sat for a Jack Daniels at the bar. Soon, a breathless Virilio charged in to join me. He ordered a modest *Kir*—that favourite of non-alcoholic Parisians.

I gave him a copy of my *États Limites*, and explained to him that the "ultra-rapid texts" section had been inspired by his work. He took it and thanked me, but admitted he was more fascinated by the fact that I was an engineer, insisting it was a very important thing. He surprised me by adamantly declaring, "Lire et écrire, c'est bien, mais c'est pas assez. Il faut bâtir, enseigner, transférer nos connaissances, former les gens"[16].

On that occasion we discussed the unavoidable topic of the day: the civil war in Yugoslavia—which by this time—spring of 1992—was starting to heat up. He explained that during Tito's reign, a vast

---

15. Transl: "Ah, you're Canadian?"
16. Transl: "Reading and writing is fine, but it's not enough. We must build, teach, transfer our knowledge, train people."

underground network of armament and munitions bunkers had been built throughout Yugoslavia, ready for guerilla warfare in case of a Soviet Czechoslovakia-like invasion. Thus, once hostilities began after Croatia's declaration of independence, each warring side had massive readymade arsenals at their disposal. Virilio was an unstoppable torrent of exhilarating knowledge, and I regretted not having a tape cassette to record all of this amazing stuff pouring out of him.

↗ In April I had to go back to Montreal to have my French visa renewed so I could stay longer in Paris. The first thing I did in Montreal was to call on Mario. And of course, he had a new story for me. He said he'd been picked up by a couple in a bar. The morning after their threesome, the satiated beaming couple treated their new pervert darling—who was wearing one of their silk bathrobes—to a luxurious breakfast of champagne, cakes and fruit. When the time came for Mario to leave, the couple implored him to stay, and began bawling big heartbreak sobs, inconsolable over their lost love.

I called up my old SM boss just to touch base, and he suggested we go over to see the Biodome, which was nearing completion. As we came off Jacques Cartier bridge and drove up de Lorimier street, we stopped at the red light, corner of Ontario street. A wobbly, disheveled bag lady staggered across the front of the car. "Ouarche![17], did you see *that*?" he said. I felt like blurting out: "B-but ... it's *Josée Yvon!!!*"

That was the last time I ever saw her.

I couldn't leave without bidding farewell to Mario. "Ah ... um ...," he stopped to ponder, "you're going back *home* ... to *Paris* ... that's where you *live* ... ah ... um ... *you live in Paris!*" As with all Quebec intelligentsia, he still harbored the aching romantic notion that living in Paris could only be a dream.

↗ Between March and June I made a total of sixty job applications. I couldn't get a job, and all the time we were in Paris, Caroline couldn't even afford to buy herself a new blouse on her salary. To add insult to injury, on her way to work she had to pass by the fashionable Rue

---

17. Transl: "Yuck!"

Saint-Honoré and run the teasing gauntlet of Hermès, Louis Vuitton and Balenciaga, seeing in the shop windows all the clothes she couldn't afford.

For my food shopping needs I had started out buying expensive milk-fed veal at the pricey Félix Potin down the street. Then on Caroline's "advice" I graduated to the more reasonable Franprix further north. By now though, I was joining the plebs shopping at the depressing bargain-basement Ed on Boulevard Rochechouart. To this day Caroline can't eat a Salade Niçoise. It was cheap to make and I finally made it once too often.

We had to face the depressing fact we were poor. Caroline's birthday was coming up and I had no money to buy her anything. So I went to a pawnshop at Nation and sold my 1970 Les Paul Junior Custom guitar with single-coil pickups, and with that money I bought her a slew of Chanel cosmetics. It wasn't romantic, it was desperate. I sold my prized Les Paul for $400, and now if I wanted it back it would cost me $3500.

The French have an expression—*la galère*[18]. Well, we were tired of *galérér*, which is what you do in Paris when you're not rich. When you're poor in Paris, life is no fun. You feel crushed by the wealth you see all around you.

≥ I continued exchanging a few letters and phone calls with Virilio, and I was reconvened to another meeting at La Coupole. This time I brought along Caroline to meet *The Little Man*—as she fondly used to call him. After a few drinks he asked us: "Would you like to meet *Atom Egoyan*?" We shrugged. "Sure, why not!"—so we tagged along with him to his first encounter with the famous Canadian filmmaker. As we walked briskly through the streets of Paris, trying to keep up with him, he exclaimed: "Atom! Atom! ... j'aimerais ça m'appeler Atom!"[19]

At the door of an upscale apartment in I-don't-know-which-fucking-*arrondissement*—a chichi *bourge* hostess warmly greeted Virilio, after which she turned to us two Canuck peasants and inquired, with

---

18. Transl: Chained to an oar in a slave galley
19. Transl: "Atom! Atom! ... I would *love* to be called Atom!"

a big haughty smile, blinking her heavily mascara'd eyelashes, "*Et vous êtes?*"[20] Caroline and I looked at each other in panic. "Uh . . . we're with *him!*" we said, pointing to Virilio.

Egoyan was there, neatly dressed all in black: black jacket, turtleneck sweater, pants and shiny patent leather shoes. He looked exactly as you'd expect a famous filmmaker to look like. He was particularly interested in a recent book Virilio had written called *l'Oeil de la caméra*[21]—and discussed it with him animatedly, flipping through the book on his lap.

Caroline and I didn't know what to do with ourselves, so while Virilio was engrossed with his tête à tête with Egoyan, we slinked off to inspect the exclusive signed editions of Peter Greenaway prints hanging on the walls.

Egoyan's wife Arsinée Khanjian joined us and we started chatting about Toronto, Montreal and all things Canadian.

Of all the things Virilio said to me, one thing stuck in my mind, because it was so surprising. He stated: "Je déteste l'Amérique mais j'aime les américains; j'aime la France mais je déteste les français."[22]

⟋ Hanging out with Virilio at La Coupole was all fine and dandy, but life in Paris had definitely soured for us, and was accompanied by the attendant bickering that financial stress entails. Unpaid bills started piling up, then I was scolded by a Credit Lyonnais clerk, saying that my daily *cent balles*[23] ATM withdrawals were too frequent (yes, I suppose in France they made it a business of theirs). And then finally the supreme insult: the ATM gobbled up Caroline's *Carte Bleue*[24]—the universally crucial bank card without which your life—financial and otherwise—no longer existed. Caroline was livid, and had to howl at the haughty bank manager to get it back. Meanwhile, I now withdrew *200 balles* at a time to avoid any further clerkly opprobrium.

---

20. Transl: "And you are?"

21. Transl: The Camera's Eye

22. Transl: "I hate America but I like Americans; I love France but I hate the French."

23. 100 Francs—about $25 ($46 today)

24. Transl: Blue Card

One Friday evening we were invited to dinner by Anouk at her dad Gene's stately house in Saint-Nom-la-Bretèche, just northeast of Versailles—45 minutes from Paris by train. And yes, the suburb was as upscale as it sounds. The meal and drinks were lavish and a welcome distraction from our daily paupers' lives, but as the evening wore on, no invitation to stay overnight was forthcoming. A Chevreuse 2.0 it was not to be. Caroline was furious at her friend, whereas I felt merely defeated and insignificant. We managed to catch the last train back to Gare Saint-Lazare, and trundled glumly back to our lowly digs late in the night.

❧ *Paris is so romantic*, isn't it? Well, we knew better by now. It's a hot, dirty, smelly, overcrowded, surly, gridlocked, polluted, expensive hellhole for those who aren't rich or just passing thru with a load of tourist cash, and are actually stuck living there scuffling to make ends meet. If you work there, you're poor. You have to fight your way through the subway crowds at rush hour, observing the rats cavorting merrily around the tracks, or watch in horror as a homeless woman squats to pee on the subway platform right across from yours. On your lunch hour you'll be in a packed café trying to bring a fork to your mouth, and your elbow gets jostled by the irate waiter bending over to shove a plate of food at another customer.

The dreamy accordion-wafted beret vision of Paris presented to you by fantasy-pimping American filmmakers like Woody Allen—who never actually had to live and work and struggle there—is laughable bullshit. Funny, there are never any crowds or traffic or yelling Frenchmen or homeless tents or milling migrants in *their* movie scenes.

The once-quaint existentialist Left Bank has become a scuzzy Kebab Stand Gap Kids Burger King tourist trap oasis, best avoided. In the beautiful public gardens you can smell the urine of centuries of tramps and pervs, and if you're walking the streets, marveling at the stupendous architecture instead of inspecting the sidewalk, you'll step on a creamy lump of dogshit.

And then there's the Parisians. Their national pastime is to make life unbearable for each other. If you're too friendly with them they'll take you for a fool, an insignificant bumpkin. To be taken seriously you have to be a demanding haughty crabby asshole, who might be rich and connected enough to make *their* life hell.

The last straw for us was *le quatorze juillet*—the French national holiday on July 14th—Bastille Day. The streets were crowded, full of revelers setting off huge firecrackers that sounded like bombs going off, and this went on well into the night and the next morning. We didn't feel like celebrating anything. We felt lousy and broke. Caroline was in a dead-end job with no advancement possible, and yours truly was truly nowhere. To boot, we'd passed the end date on my visa and I was now on French soil illegally.

We'd had our fill of Paris, and decided to return to Canada that August. We missed the open spaces, and miles of hiking in the woods without seeing a soul. Like my painter friend Jacques Diard[25] said, "Ils devraient nous *payer* pour habiter Paris!"[26]

In the end, we lasted from January 15th to August 9th in Paris—barely seven months. Sure, we looked like idiots coming back home with our tails between our legs, but we were running out of greener grass to jump into, trying to escape from the pan. However, we *did* come away with one positive development from our Parisian fiasco: one day at Salans, Caroline was asked if she'd given any thought to becoming an interpreter. This stuck in her head, and she eventually entered the intense two-year Interpretation Program in Ottawa, and finally found her calling as a conference interpreter—a rare profession in which she excelled, and which assured her livelihood from then onwards.

↗ I called up my old boss at Groupe SM to see what was going on. He said they had landed a contract to build two post-tensioned concrete bridges, and two others using prestressed girders. I'd always wanted to build bridges. "I want in" I said, and was re-hired. I knew nothing about designing bridges, so I signed up for a post-graduate course that was given at night at McGill by professor Saïd Mirza. He was a real nice student-friendly professor with whom I'd taken the Advanced Concrete Design course way back when. There were no assignments or exams;

---

25. Pronounced "Dee-ahr"
26. Transl: "They should pay us to live in Paris!"

for your final grade you had to submit a brief on bridge design. So I simply handed in the calculations and drawings of the bridge I was actually working on in the *real* world.

On a crisp, fresh evening in October, it was very quiet in the classroom. The sky outside the window was already dark. Mirza was explaining in detail how the chemical reactions in the cement paste formed the bonds that gave rise to hardened concrete. He was explaining this calmly, and in the room you could have heard a pin drop. The atmosphere was very peaceful and my mind was crystal clear. All of a sudden, I sensed the whole of the universe expand before me, rushing to an infinite horizon. I felt part of it, and all was well with the world. I had just experienced a genuine highly lucid satori.

Imagine—an honest-to-goodness, true satori during a course in *Bridge Engineering*. There was a worse way to begin the rest of my life.

26

EPILOGUES

1—*The Death Of My Brother*

When Caroline and I moved back to Montreal in 2003, we couldn't find a suitable babysitter for our two-year-old toddler Nico. In desperation we decided to give it a try with our chronic substance-abusing friends Mario and Réjane. They turned out to be great; they took care of him wonderfully, made meals, snacks and entertained him, and what's more they were very sweet and loving with him. And accomplishing this stone cold sober. They actually became his virtual godparents, joined us in the Magog house we'd inherited on weekends, and in the summer pitched a tent in the garden and enjoyed fussing over Nico.

Eventually Nico was accepted in Quebec's awesome CPE pre-kindergarten system, and Mario and Réjane went back to their old ways, which included a drunken brawl in March of 2004, during which Mario beat her and wound up in jail. The condition for his release was a restraining order saying he couldn't see Réjane for 2 weeks—plus, no drinking, and he had to stay away from bars. He knocked at our door on Hutchison. I was on crutches, my leg in a cast, and Nico was going through a phase of waking up screaming at night, so we couldn't take him in. I wanted to pay him a hotel room, but he refused and shuffled off.

≷ In the fall of 2004 Mario and I had a serious tiff and broke off our friendship of 24 years.

After a long while I decided to try reconciliation, and sent him a timid e-mail in February of 2006, to see how he was doing. There was no answer. A few days later I received a phone call from Réjane. "Mario died," she said laconically. I said: "What do you mean, *Mario died*?" She said: "He died a few days ago, from cancer of the esophagus." I started railing and cursing at her, asking why the fuck she hadn't informed me of his cancer. She said: "He told me not to tell you," and also that they would often walk by our house without knocking.

Had I learned of his cancer, I would have dropped everything and rushed to his side, moving heaven and earth to save him. He probably knew this and didn't want to be a bother to me and my family.

I went to their apartment and saw the stain of dried blood on the armchair he died on. And his empty bikers' boots. And empty studded leather jacket.

He died on that armchair because due to the discomfort of the tumor growing in his throat, he had to sleep propped up. It was impossible for him to get a good night's sleep. The tumor was stuck to an artery, so surgery was out of the question, but he didn't want to go through radiation therapy. He couldn't take the agony anymore, so he grabbed a bottle of Réjane's blood pressure pills and emptied it down his gullet. After so many attempts to kill himself, Mario had finally succeeded.

Thoroughly dejected, I organized a memorial wake at the *Chercheur de trésors*[1] bookstore on Ontario street, where he attended the poetry nights of *Le Steak Haché*[2]—the monthly poezine that regularly featured his poems. I draped his eternal leather punk's jacket over a chair, the empty sleeves now hugging his books and publications.

I became guardian of Mario's archives by default—Réjane gave me all of his writings, papers, and books. Except for the heart-rending intimate last note he left her, which I glimpsed lying on their bedroom dresser.

Come spring, I joined Réjane, her friend Paule and another, along with Mario's brother Bertrand and wife Nicole, to inhume Mario's ashes in the Campo family plot at the *Repos Saint-François d'Assise*

---

1. Transl: The Treasure Hunter
2. Transl: Ground steak

cemetery off Sherbrooke near Langelier. Eerily enough, Bertrand had the same voice as his brother.

I can assure you there's nothing sadder in the world than holding in your hands a small pine box containing the ashes of your blood brother. From then on I swore to never again have a tiff with a friend. Closure was no longer possible for me. You just have to learn how to live with big holes in your heart.

In early 2016, to commemorate the tenth year of his passing, I put together a website in his memory with the help of Zovilé, featuring chosen texts, photos, anecdotes and condolences[3].

Francoeur finally proved to me beyond a doubt his true worth as a poet, by best summing up the emotions that Mario Campo aroused, both through his writing and his life:

> *"Mario ... this dear, sensitive and so fragile a being ... he alone could testify to the loneliness of poets that was his, and to the anguish that dwelled in him and dwells in me and imprisons me in my incurable melancholy ..."*

Out of the blue one day, Mario had turned to Caroline and said: "I know that my life will have been pathetic and ridiculous."

I don't think so Mario, I don't think so.

---

3. https://mario-campo-poete.com

2—*Herbert Huncke—A Special Appreciation*

Quite simply, Huncke is the most endearing human being I've ever known. When I met him, my original plan was to mine him for tales about Kerouac. But I fell so much in love with him that I forgot about it, and out of deep respect for my wonderful friend, I never mentioned Kerouac, not even once. I wound up happy just to be in his company and gab about a million things.

I learned of Huncke's death in 1997 a few months after the fact —annoyingly enough through the internet—that laughably un-Hunckian medium of "human communication". Because Huncke was all about people, and the crucial immediacy in being brought together by life, at that very moment. Huncke communicated, all right. Cross-legged on the floor, right in front of you, baring his soul, and peering into yours, eager to see what you were made of, desperately curious to hear your life story and how it had brought you to this point in space-time. Everyone who was lucky enough to get to see or talk to him, no matter how fleeting the encounter, was indelibly affected by him, and remembered him fondly for life.

Everyone adored Huncke because he listened to you, you could tell he really cared about you, cared about all the people he came across— and that care and attention to others shines out from his stories. It's funny, I sound like one of the Apostles desperately trying to convey a sense of what Jesus meant for those he'd touched, years after his death, to anyone within earshot. Yeah, Huncke was definitely the ultimate sinner-savior—the Beat Priest listening to your confessions, absolving you de facto by afterwards regaling you with *his* sins.

Huncke was the kind who couldn't hurt a fly. Sure, he'd steal or "borrow" from you, but what the hell—that just came with the Junkie's job description. I never heard Huncke say a bad thing about anyone. He was totally incapable of sarcasm, and when I'd snicker or let fly a snide remark about anyone, he'd always offer a gently disarming qualifying reminder, without any trace of reprimand, that would instantly shame me shatteringly to the core. In this sense Huncke was the true Buddhist of the lot—he practiced by nature, whereas all the others preached. And making a career of it.

In Howard Brookner's documentary film on Burroughs, John Giorno, speaking about the tragic life and death of Burroughs' son, points out that Bill Burroughs Jr. actually lived by the principles of the Beat life as idealized by his elders, who ultimately found success in a world against which they had so much rebelled. The same can be said for Huncke. Sure, he didn't have the same literary skills and ease of verbal expression as his more illustrious compères, but his significance in the movement was just as important. In fact, I believe Huncke was the all-crucial lynch-pin, the cosmic sperm-glue that held such disparate beings as Kerouac, Ginsberg and Burroughs together. He christened them unwittingly, and more than any other ancillary figure in the Beat pantheon, Huncke arguably was pivotal in their collective decadent beatitude.

In many books people are only pawns, props, cartoons. Not in Huncke's. In *his* books, everyone he talks about is treated with the highest respect. His books are so human—*too human*—caring stories about the naïvely eccentric individuals he's known—that as soon as I start re-reading them I can only think about Huncke, whom I miss deeply—and invariably, the tears start welling up.

Kerouac's work is like fireworks, or an intense be-bop session blowing hot—exhilarating at the moment, but in the end, frankly exhausting. And Burroughs' work is like LSD—a wild, eye-opening trip, but afterwards you're glad it's over. After over forty years spent devouring and mulling over the works of the Beats, what remains for me is Huncke. Kerouac, Ginsberg and Burroughs belong in the history books, but Huncke remains in our hearts. And each year that passes doesn't diminish the pain of the hole his death left in my life.

Huncke was the Buddha of 42nd Street, the king of the truly beat—meaning the downtrodden, the dispossessed, the riff-raff abandoned by the Busy Ones rushing around attending to their oh-so important, all-consuming agendas. Those who have known real soul-crushing poverty and rejection, endless lives of bad luck, immediately recognize Huncke as their patron saint.

Huncke was the Christ of the Fuck-Ups, he was the king of all losers, the Loser King of all humanity. Because ultimately it's the losers—those who have failed in life—like my soul-buddy Campo, dead of alcohol at 54—who have a rightful claim to being truly human. It's what got them where they are.

3—*Josée Yvon And Denis Vanier*

One day Denis and Josée received a $40,000 grant from the Canada
Arts Council. They always had trouble with the Welfare authorities
because they never declared these grants. To celebrate such occasions
they liked to go to the Motel Diplomate, because when you ordered a
steak, it was delivered to your room by a topless waitress. But this time,
they had a big party with transvestites, where they circulated a syringe
full of coke. It seems that Denis, before going to bed, emptied his pockets and dumped a pile of cash and coke on the table for the guests to
help themselves. Next morning the coke, cash and trannies had disappeared. Except that a lethal dose of HIV was already circulating in
their veins.

They both went blind before slowly dying of AIDS. Josée died first,
in 1994, at age 44—and then Denis, in 2000, at the age of 51. They are
now venerated beyond belief, as two among Quebec's most cherished
tragic authors. Josée left behind an unfinished work on blindness, called
Manon[4].

---

4. Pronounced "Mah-noh"—a given name popular in Quebec before the Eighties

4—*The Last Time I Saw Kathy Acker*

Caroline and I wound up living in Toronto from 1995 to 2002. In the fall of 1996 we saw that Kathy was doing a book signing for her new novel *Pussy, King of The Pirates*. We showed up, bought a copy, and stood in line waiting to get it signed. She didn't look too healthy. She'd shrunk, lost weight. Little did we know at the time that she had cancer. When I stepped up to the table I said, "Hi, Kathy." She looked up and said, "Oh my... the past becomes the present."

That was the last time I saw her. I was shocked to learn of her death a year later, and to read about all the sadness and desperation of having to end her days in sordid, tacky Tijuana.

She died a very sad death, at the age of 50. She had cancer in her left breast. "The doctors proposed a lumpectomy followed by radiation, but she demanded a double mastectomy and declined further treatment ... to her, radiation meant evil things ... when the cancer spread into some of her lymph nodes, the doctors urged her to start chemotherapy, but she declined. She was afraid her hair would fall out, she was afraid of losing her teeth ... she consulted healers, acupuncturists, card readers, and astrologers ..."[5]

The cancer metastasized and invaded the rest of her body. She was driven to a dubious palliative care clinic in Tijuana, a few friends came down to her bedside, but no one or nothing could save her by then.

➤ You heard of the 27 Club. Now you have the 97 Club: Burroughs, Ginsberg and Acker all died in 1997. Huncke came close, beating them by a year. I'm kind of relieved they missed 9/11 and all of our 21st Century crap.

"We never know how much we learn from those who never return."
—William Burroughs

---

5. From the literary biography After Kathy Acker, by Chris Kraus

5—*David Rattray: The Poet's Poet*

David Rattray was the poet's poet. Not only for his great poetry—like *The Yoga of Anger*—but more for his brutal honesty and *unreasonableness*. In her novel *I Love Dick*, Chris Kraus quotes him as saying: "To be honest is to be almost prophetic, to upset the applecart."

And his insanity was delicious. Chris further tells us: "David Rattray was a 26-year-old American junkie when he started translating Antonin Artaud ... in 1957, living on his own in Paris, he decided to become him. At the old Bibliothèque Nationale in Paris ... that year David Rattray read every single book checked out by Antonin Artaud."

Talking about an interview she'd just done with him, Chris reports: "He was ranting ... about his hatred for everyone who'd kept him down, who were out to silence 'every bright young person who comes along with something original to say' ..."

David said this just three days before he collapsed on Avenue A with a massive and inoperable brain tumor.

6—*The Ultimatum Archives*

Thanks to the auspices of the poet Sébastien Dulude, Concordia University English Department Associate Professor and poet Jason Camlot, PhD, and post-graduate Samuel Mercier, PhD, contacted me in 2018 about collecting and digitizing my Ultimatum archives. Through their efforts and also those of my friends—the American artist tENTATIVELY, a cONVENIENCE—and Quebec pop culture archivist Martin Lamontagne—a total of 14 hours of video are presently available, although this represents only a fraction of what was filmed.

Miraculously, the stacks of boxes of audio tape from the first Ultimatum festival that I'd been lugging around throughout a dozen moves were still intact after 35 years, and the complete audio of that festival was digitized and documented, thanks to the monumental efforts of Concordia's Sadie Barker and Emma Telaro.

The video record that remains is haphazard but still captivating, and constitutes the final proof of the vitality of that era. Right now we are in the COVID one, so Concordia's plans to exhibit and make the material available to the public is in the same holding pattern we are all in.

For over 30 years I had thought the audiovisual archives of Ultimatum II lost forever. Fortuitously, it turned out that Tentatively surreptitiously asked the video crew for a copy of those Videotron mixdowns, and in 2017 he told me he had the mixdown tapes for five nights of the festival. He was kind enough to digitize them, so we have at least that. But soundman Guy Bou—who'd held the audiotapes for ransom—wound up erasing them just to spite me. His mindless destruction of culture would have been greatly appreciated by ISIS.

Overall, Cynthia Jervis did a great job, but she was gender biased to say the least, and preferred long rambling texts by women, instead of much stronger performances by male iconoclasts. Thus, left on her cutting room floor were the SCP, Gordon W, and Steve McCaffrey's superlative *Bachelor Machine*.

In addition to the performances left out by Jervis willfully, unfortunately we have nothing of three whole days of the festival. Lost forever are the videos of David Rattray's *Yoga of Anger*, Lisa Blaushild's shockingly hilarious *Love Letter To My Rapist*, John Giorno's solo performance, and more.

When I imploded after Ultimatum II, manager Joe Martek stored the towering stacks of ¾" U-matic tapes of both festivals in the offices of *The Montreal Mirror*. After the *Mirror* eventually folded, who knows what happened to those precious documents. Years later I tried to find out, but was unable to contact either Eyal Kattan or Cathy Salisbury.

Too much chaos, too much entropy.

7—Last Words

After this book I never want to hear about Canada being a boring place ever again. And I hope I've also destroyed forever the moronic knee-jerk association of Montreal with Cirque du Soleil, Smoked Meat, and Leonard Fucking Cohen.

This book proves in spades that what we had going on here in the Eighties was a world-class underground art scene rivalling any other in History. At the very least, I've managed to share with you the stories of all the amazing people it was my pleasure to know, people you would never have heard of otherwise.

On a personal level however, self-doubt always persists. Did I waste my time, waste my life, could I have done something better with it, were all the paths I chose the wrong ones?

What could I have done differently? Luckily, you can't do a retake in your life. Had I chosen any other path, I wouldn't have ended up with Caroline and the wonderful son we made together. Raising a kid properly is the hardest thing in the world, and by all accounts I at least succeeded in giving someone a happy, drama-free childhood, and helped shape a decent, thoughtful, accomplished human being. I've finally settled on my epitaph:

Alan Lord
Best Dad In The World

I made tons of drawings from the age of six onwards, then paintings and cartoons as a teenager. I should have gone into a Liberal Arts program, but my surly upbringing in a joyless working class household dictated the more pragmatic profession of Engineering. Thankfully, with time I became self-taught in what mattered most to me—art, literature, and rebellious counterculture.

On Christmas day 2019 I sent an e-mail to Angel containing a link to the Julien Temple documentary *Christmas '77 with The Sex Pistols*. Angel's response was: "Wow. Thank you very much, a great Christmas present. It justifies the choices I made in my youth."

Hearing that was a revelation. *Of course* he was right. How could I *not* be excited by The Sex Pistols? Like Alan Vega said when he saw The Ramones at CBGB's in 1974—*It's what I'd been waiting for.* And it turned out to be the vital spark that led me down the road of indispensable self-expression, of artistic exploration and discovery.

乙 My whole life has been a schizoid tug of war, a constant push and pull between conventional jobs and radical self-expression, one always offsetting the other. Even though the violently capitalist engineering milieu was oppressive, it nevertheless provided me a harbor of sanity when I needed one. I loved losing myself in the perfect, pristine universe of elegant math and physics equations, which I could then shape into tangible concrete and steel structures. When I was in my stratospheric world of pure intellect, no one or nothing could touch me. My structural solutions were often way more creative than anything you'd find in art. Unlike all insular art snobs, Picabia and Duchamp understood and respected that. Bonus: whenever I feel down, I can always go look at and even touch what I've built.

乙 Writing about the Eighties in 2022—this awful year of unrelenting COVID, unstoppable climate change, and incredibly—*War in Europe*—makes me feel like old Sol in Soylent Green, reminiscing about how great things once were. In the Eighties, we thought Reagan and Thatcher were bad. Sorry kids, but it's been downhill ever since. And who knows where the bottom is.

In truth, the real reason behind all the crazy shit I did was to meet my heroes and the people I found fascinating. I put on festivals as an excuse to meet and hear them—so yes, ultimately it was a vast selfish enterprise—*I wanted kicks.* And of course, I wanted to share my enthusiasm with as many people as possible, turning them on to the great cutting-edge writers, artists and musicians I loved—just like I'm still doing right now.

So I got a little over-enthusiastic and fucked up. *Big time.* I can laugh about it now, but it took 35 years.

乙 I was right to follow my conviction of cramming as much living as I could into my life. I got an NHL cancer at age 61, and then colon cancer at age 66. They're in remission, but the grim reaper's definitely after me. Still, a lot of people died younger, so I consider myself lucky.

Mario's death was the moment I realized I had to share all the crazy stories I had to tell about him, and also the stories of all the other amazing people I knew, plus my unlikely adventures in the music and art world. So every month I had a new chapter for the chronicle I held in *Le Steak Haché*. And these were the genesis for this present book. In the end, memories are all we have, and if they're not written down, they'll evaporate along with us.

➤ After making it to old age and surviving a few close calls, you realise that what matters isn't what you may have done or accomplished, *it's the people you were with*. Suddenly, your memories of them is the only precious commodity that's left to you. In the end, it doesn't matter what you did or didn't do, what you had or didn't have, or the path you chose or didn't choose. *Because we're all the same.* Only our ideals and delusions are different. We all have to go through life one way or another, by hook or by crook. We all have our summits and our depths, our heartbreaks and ecstasies, our soaring moments and failures.

➤ And so, after my decade-long hour of fretting and strutting upon my strange stage, what's my big takeaway, the crucial bits of advice I may have for you?

Take care of things, or things will take care of you. And for God's sake, don't *plan* your life like a spreadsheet—take the plunge head-first and *live it*.

Also, I know it may be hard for you, but try being a bit more of a punk. This doesn't require any studded leather jacket or spiky green hair—it's about *attitude*: never bullshit or swallow it either. Zero in on the brutal truth, and speak your mind at all times. It's often caused me a lot of grief, but I couldn't live with myself any other way.

And lastly, give your Asshole Radar a regular tune-up. Because they're everywhere now, and it's getting worse. Remember: their purpose is to fuck you up at the slightest chance. So identify them, and steer clear. "Hell on Earth, it exists," Gagnon once told me. And he's absolutely right. Life is *not* a dream. But thanks to others, it can sure be a nightmare. Sooner or later, some asshole will make life difficult for you. It's an inescapable constant of life on this penal colony called Earth.

⇝ For a while there in the Eighties, we truly, sincerely believed we could change the world by being highly creative—because it had changed *ours*. But the rest of the universe didn't go our way. David Sapin summed it up best:

> "The noble quest for absolute inevitable abject failure in our opposition to social norms that we wholeheartedly rejected—that was our Holy Grail."

We tried, and now our time is up. If we can survive Putin, after the COVID Era, people will go back to their mindless lives of jetting around on holiday, packing the cruise line ships, and continuing to fry the planet to the last crisp of fossil fuel. Being angry at human folly all the time is damn exhausting. Anyway, a glance at the headlines is daily proof that the idiots won. And the Punks and Post Punks lost. As Robert F. Kennedy said: "You do your best, and then fuck it." In other words ... *Culo la balena.*

I'll just stay home and cause no more trouble, keep a low profile and go on being a technological monk, just like during the COVID lockdowns. I'll be safe, six feet under, when the water levels rise.

"Old punks never die, they just go to bed earlier"
—Zilon

SELECTED TEXTS

Lucien Francoeur / Aut'chose

The Freak of Montreal

My head freezes, my skull cracks
I'm the Freak of Montreal ...
I slapped wings on my suspenders
A stereo in my brain
I got the universe in my spoon

It was during the week of three Fridays
We sniffed some patchouli
She had a Mustang Skylolo
And didn't have any pimples on her back
We went to see Pink Floyd
We ate hot doys
We made it to 7th heaven
The Good Lord asked us for an encore

I gulp mothballs and I'm gnawed by my myth
I drink rotgut and dream about Janis Joplin
I'm fucked up, I love her cause she's ugly
She's a real cunt
It's with her I wanna get my rocks off

My head freezes, my skull cracks
I'm the Freak of Montreal ...
I slapped wings on my suspenders
A stereo in my brain
I got the universe in my spoon

I'm the toppest of top dogs
I sing for mops
I sing for fags
And stealers of Corvettes
For those who eat their boogers
And those who can't get it up
I'm never on time
Too bad, cause I'm the bogeyman

I eat sardines
Cause I don't have a big paycheck
I'm a panty sniffer
And have a right to my place in the sun
I'm not asking for too much
It's not too dark tonight
And it ain't with mirrors
That we'll wind up seeing each other

My head freezes, my skull cracks
I'm the Freak of Montreal ...
I slapped wings on my suspenders
A stereo in my brain
Cranked the volume to 11

Song DNA by VEX

Let me tell you 'bout the latest kick
Based in part on research done by Watson-Crick
Take a "D", an "N", and then an "A"

DNA: You don't have to stay that way
DNA: Recombination is the way
DNA: Your future lies in the lab tray
DNA ...

There's no end to all the crazy tricks
You can pull off the double-stranded coiled helix
All you need's the kitchen sink—you're on your way

DNA: Gather all the tools you'll need
DNA: Just follow all the recipes
DNA: Jump as many steps as you please
DNA ...

(Gagnon's Wagnerian Mini-Moog Tape-Loop Solo)

Tell your friends about the latest scene
Bring them home and mend their old blew genes
One, two, three or more can play the game

DNA: We can take turns as we play!
DNA: What a way to spend the day!
DNA: Which amino acids can you name?
DNA ...

MARIO CAMPO

Translated excerpts from his novella *Le Délire* (*Delirium*)

One evening, about seven years ago, I had sex with a transvestite dressed as Jean Harlow. My friends tell me that I take risks, but what I love about risks is that they're never safe. I hate safe things. I'm not an insurance salesman or an American preacher. The chick I'm currently obsessed with is a Tunisian girl who lives on the floor below. When it's super hot, the air stifling, and her door is ajar, I feel like going downstairs buck naked and embrace her clitorisk as if it were the liquid of an oasis after crossing the desert ... like Rimbaud sucking a female camel after 20 days in Somalia.

Suzanne had never seen a guy jerk off. One night, she asked me if I wanted to masturbate in front of her. While I wanked, she asked if she could do anything. I told her to massage my balls. When I ejaculated, she began to count the jets of sperm. Looking at her eyes, you'd think she'd just discovered the law of gravity.

Is there anything more ridiculous than an egg looking at you in the morning? I come in my bath and watch the sperm particles turn into misshaped seahorses. One thousand stillborn children, and all those infertile couples. What's your problem? I masturbate again and I come on the mirror. By the way, do you like turkey, other than during Thanksgiving and Christmas?

On New Year's Eve, I came on the radiator. My father still has three years of work before his retirement. I'm vulnerable. Others are accountants. I smoke because we are ashes and will return to ashes. To die is to live a little. What gets to me is that bars close at 3 AM.

To my astonishment, my wife, who isn't lesbian for a second, starts licking little Josée everywhere, from the neck down to you know where. She works her up so much with her tongue that she gets her in a tizzy. As for me, excited by such a scene, I fuck my wife from behind and—oh boy—to my surprise, the girl starts sucking my balls. How will I react when my mother dies?

JEAN-LUC BONSPIEL

A Toronto Poem
(for Alan Lord[1])

I saw a trillion dollar bill
floating playfully on the wind
above a downtown intersection

far above the oblivious heads
of the milling crowd

and I knew that it should soon fall into a sewer
but instead it alighted
on the Spadina streetcar wire
and instantaneously incinerated

Expiry Notification

in a human pyramid
the understander
doesn't understand
he stands under

until the pope shows up
pope yes

if you don't want to talk to your partner
while having sex
don't answer the phone

pacific islanders
who were cannibals
are fond of spam

---

1. Based on an inside joke: I once told Bonspiel that every poem about Toronto
mentioned Spadina

Sample Neoist Tract

THE SERVICE

INSTITUTE OF RESEARCH AND INVESTIGATION

P.O. BOX 524
TOUR DE LA BOURSE
MONTREAL H4Z IJ8

Perhaps, inasmuch as we strive toghether towards this or that, perhaps and therefore not obligatorily, perhaps our respective progressions may be but for a moment halted, perhaps to reflect. At this time, as at any other, our deformed heads rise above whatever becomes below them, drinking in whatever happens to be available. The gaze is not unlike two dimly burning coals overgrown with ash. The isolated combats, struggles summoned up by conscious consent. Or not. Someone going off somewhere to fight, no-one else can begin to understand it, as they're doing something else anyway. Not that it isn't alright to expect a change. Just don't count on it.

First you get into trouble, then they kick the living shit right out of you. At least that's the way we always heard it worked. So we like to think about heavily armoured buildings. Often.

And when some guy says "JUMP", take his word for it, he knows what he's talking about. Don't worry.

And don't do us any favours.

J.L. BONSPIEL   KAZIMIR STRASSMAN   KIKI BONBON

(WE'RE NOT CONFUSED, NOT ANYMORE)

ALAIN-NAPOLÉON MOFFAT

Technological Monk

Convoked to the summit of reality, we shall find only horror and resignation. However, it will appear to us that this reality isn't so; it is eminently improbable, fugitive and simulated. We are passing from a sensitive reality to a technological reality. From a human reality to things media-bound. Through the prism of objectivisation, we enter into the world of simulacrum and perpetual boredom.

On the screen are obsolete souls and uncertain shapes. In the world of special effects, we declare that we are not data callers for the system. We declare war on the images that are never quite real, which are images of control and dissuasion. We refuse this exile from ourselves and others that constitutes this display.

This coldness behind us represents the majority of eyes and hands, of mouths and legs, catching up to us and bleeding dry our will and eternal anger. Electronic flavored fascination.

We'll never enter into that media-bound coma. With the energy of total youth, trained for the new challenge: spread between this world and us a distance so great, so passionate, that the image before us will exhaust itself, without the least prompting.

SILVER AMUSEMENTS (SAMPLES OF POP ART POETRY)

Colorado

Foxbat Sunoco
Winston Cools
Tex Mex Flavor
Dreamwhip Nevada

Bronco Radar
Sidewinder Magnum
Champion Marilyn
Valvoline Lube Job

Lunar Landau

That's one small step for Man
One Giant Super Sale
Going on now at your
Local Chev/Olds dealer!

Fabulash

Spring Mylar
Micro Rayon
Miniskirt Swipes

Accident Proof
Sperm Splotches
Up In a Wink!

MOHAMUD TOGANE

In Money We Trust

Bushman, you wanna be civilized?
Go get money!
It don't matter how
Get it honestly if you can
Get it dishonestly if you must
But by all means get money

Bushman, put money in thy loincloth!
In God we trust
In money we must
Money is defence:
Money makes a hedge about you
Money is the sixth sense
Without which the other five are useless!
Bushman, without money you don't make no sense,
Period

Without money you can't get
Tight pussy, loose shoes
Or a warm place to shit
Without money
Rich man's shoes better than you

Without money, you dirt, nigger dirt
Without money, you really unhappy lonesome nigger
Lonelier than Jesus in the Garden of Gethsemane
Before they crucified him
Without money, you without papa, without mama
Without descent—you born orphan

Money makes the oil of gladness shine on your face
Money makes everything possible and permissible
Blond, blue-eyed, pale-skinned Billy Graham Jee-sus
Failed to make you white as snow
But money will make coal black nigger like you
White right
Even in South Africa
Where Japs are white because they got money
Where your kind are called kaffirs and sacrificed to
Mammon because they ain't got no money

Money makes friends who make you laugh
Who laugh with you and for you
But if you poor, you separated even
From yourself and from society

Oh God! Don't make me poor
Lest I steal and take your goddamn name in vain
Brother, can you spare a dime?
Chinese, Japanese, money please
I heard a brother in Harlem holler:
"Eenie, meenie, minee, moe
Catch that motherfucker honky by the throat
If he's got money, don't let him go!"

Bushman, I ain't interested in
How long you been in America
How many degrees you got
How many black oaks you split
How many blondes you balled
How many times you got drunk and stoned
Out of your bushy head in Reggie's
I wanna know
How big is your bank account?

Bushman, if you were born in a civilized country
And were properly toilet-trained instead of
Pooping anywhere in the bush,
By now you'd have big bucks in the bank

Bushman, if you have the gift of prophecy
And understand all mysteries
And all knowledge
And if you have all faith
So you could remove mountains—
But have no money,
You ain't shit!

The Black Tin God

It is astounding what outrages
a black bully with guns can perpetrate in Africa.
He can exalt himself above God, Allah, and Juju &
force a whole nation to worship him.
He can prove his baboonery and outbaboon
white colonialists and castrate a whole nation
by plunging it into abject servility:
he can fancy himself a Napoleon and crown himself Emperor;
he can style himself a teacher, a prophet, a savior, a revolutionary
philosopher equal to Mao, Marx, and Lenin
and teach the nation ad nauseam;
he can seize the attention of the whole world
by personally beating up foreign journalists,
like Bokassa beat up Michael Goldsmith;
he can piss on Uhuru, embrace tribalism and clanism
and call them Scientific Socialism;
he can loot the land and declare himself PRESIDENT FOR LIFE:
he can appropriate any name, any land, any title, any degree, any medal—
why he can even call himself
like General Mobutu did:
"THE PEPPERY ALL-CONQUERING WARRIOR,
THE COCK WHO LEAVES NO HEN INTACT."
And rape every chick in sight.

VENT DU MONT SCHÄRR—*SELECTED LYRICS*

Surfin' Suicide

Brad met Sue on the beach at Malibu
He had great big muscles and a suntan too
She had great big titties and an iceberg ass
Now tell me what more could a little boy ask for

But they were deeply disturbed and hopelessly depressed
No matter how beautiful or well-dressed

  Surfin' Suicide—they committed
  Surfin' Suicide—they were totally committed
  Surfin' Suicide—that's how I wanna die
  Surfin' Suicide, n' my insides are hurtin' now

  Surf now, surf is down, Surfin' Suicide

Chuck met Debbie when he knew that she was ready
To go all the way to neck and touch and kiss and play
But their tale ended up tragic when they messed with voodoo magic
In the nightmare of confusion they abandoned all illusion

Deeply disturbed and hopelessly depressed
No matter how beautiful or well-dressed

  Surfin' Suicide—they committed
  Surfin' Suicide—they were totally committed
  Surfin' Suicide—that's how I wanna die
  Surfin' Suicide, n' my insides are hurtin' now

  Surf now, surf is down, Surfin' Suicide

Jump Off a Building

Uh oh, uh oh, I wanna jump off a building
Uh oh, uh oh, I wanna make a big mess on the sidewalk
Jump off a building, have a good time on the way down
Jump off a building, say goodbye to my care and my worries

Jump off a building, Jump off a building
Jump off a building, Jump off a building

Welfare Babies

Welfare Babies they grow's up dumb
They's ain't got nutrition when they's born
Welfare Babies they grow's up dumb
They's ain't got nutrition when they's born

Welfare Babies, Welfare Babies

Welfare Babies they stick you up
They stick you up in the ass
They stick you up in the ass
When youz in the penitentiary

Welfare Babies, Welfare Babies

Welfare Babies they grow's up dumb
They's ain't got nutrition when they's born
Welfare Babies they grow's up dumb
They's ain't got nutrition when they's born

Welfare Babies, Welfare Babies

I Need a Rug Cleaner

I need a rug cleaner, I need a rug cleaner

I have areas of heavy traffic
In my hallways and my rooms
I have areas of heavy traffic
In my hallways and my rooms

I need a rug cleaner, I need a rug cleaner

So I'll go to the supermarket
And get me a steam machine
Yes I'll go to the supermarket
And get me a steam machine

I need a rug cleaner, I need a rug cleaner

And on Mondays, Tuesdays and Wednesdays
I'll rent for two days and get one free

I need a rug cleaner, I need a rug cleaner

Normal

He wanted to live a normal life
And have a normal career
A normal wife and children

He wanted to live a normal life
But he had an abnormal life
And had an abnormal career
An abnormal wife and children
But he wanted to live a normal life

Gonna Kill Myself

There's only one thing dumber than to write a song and that's to sing it
There's only one thing dumber than to sleep and that's to stay awake

Gonna kill myself

There's only one thing dumber than being unemployed and that's to work
There's only one thing dumber than to have a job and that's to go to it

Gonna kill myself

Woo hoo hoo hoo

Gonna kill myself

There's only one thing dumber than to to get a cheque and that's to
    change it
There's only one thing dumber than to have a car and that's to drive it

Gonna kill myself

There's only one thing dumber than to write a song and that's to sing it
There's only one thing dumber than to sleep and that's to stay awake

Gonna kill myself

Woo hoo hoo hoo

Gonna kill myself

JOEL ROSE

Kill The Poor (excerpt)

Let me tell you how we can afford to buy a place on the Lower East Side, no matter how cheap:

We got some money from an incident that went down at the Gotham, where Annabelle worked as an exotic dancer.

"Say what, Zho?"

Ahem ... Bite my tongue. Rather, Annabelle got some money from an incident that occurred at the Gotham dime-a-dance strip joint where she worked just to pay the rent. She didn't really like it.

Stay with me here. There's a certain mentality today—moneywise. Do you agree or what? Every fat fuck on the make. Not that Annabelle didn't deserve the money Leonardo wound up paying her. Not to mention, otherwise, we'd still be living over all those blind people, hearing the squeal of brakes, those horrific screams ...

Right after I was born my old man used to sell his papers off a standpipe sticking out of a building on Seventh Avenue and Forty-seventh Street. Right outside the hottest strip joint in New York City. That's how I remember it when I was a kid. Me and my sister. My father in earmuffs, his nose red.

One night, nothing personal, Leonardo, the Gotham floor manager, who has the same basic shape and size as a mirror armoir, cut Annabelle's face with a bottle opener. He claimed he lost control. Didn't know what it was about, didn't know why he did it. High on something. Smoking crack. Cut her one hell of a slice right across the cheek, hooked her lip and tore it pretty good. When I go inside people are backed up, looking. I push some away, step in front of him. Blood running down her face, but no tears. I tell him, "Leonardo, put it down, bro," and he laughs at me, and says, "Listen, you little Jew!.."

Later he apologizes, repeats that he didn't know what came over him, this mindless violence. He smiles, pays her thirty thousand bucks to keep her mouth shut, no cops, no authorities, keep his business open, keep his liquor license. He arranges to have the cut stitched up by a customer he claims is an "A number one" Park Avenue plastic surgeon. Later, I swear, I see the guy advertising on tv, looking at me through the void, the voidoid, "A number one," saying that you too can be all you ever dreamed and more, me thinking, looking back at him, watching him at his table, drooling over the girls, the spittle running down his chin, pulling his six-dollar Beck's that much closer across the table, my folks calling me in the bedroom, six months after my sister died, saying, Jo-Jo, we been talking, you seem depressed, would you like a nose job, the guy looking at me out of the screen, his eyes saying, we can do a number on you too, sir, me thinking, man, you can kiss my skinny white ass ...

Annabelle looks at me, blank, no comprehension, and asks me what kind of doctor advertises on television. "I'm not an American. I never heard of such a thing. In France doctors don't advertise ..."

I say that's exactly the point.

Fucking Leonardo. She fingers the scar, says she'll hold a grudge till the day she dies, longer. She'll get him back, no matter when it is. This man, the size of a deep freeze, with a heart like a pint of Häagen-Dazs deep in its cavity.

(Reprinted from *Kill The Poor*, by the kind permission of Joel Rose)

LISA BLAUSHILD

The Men in My Life

On Monday nights I sleep with a murderer. He likes to shoot randomly into crowds from tall buildings. If he doesn't miss, he kills people. But he also enjoys a simple evening at my place: we eat take-out food, watch cable television, and then we go down on each other. It's okay, as long as I don't get too involved.

On Tuesday nights I go all the way with a man who is terminally ill. He hasn't much time, we make it a quickie. Afterwards, he spits up blood into a Dixie cup and tells me he doesn't want to die. I remind him that we've all got to go someday; and read out loud from books on life after death to give him false hope.

On Wednesday nights a former lover fucks me for old times' sake. He says he doesn't really like me, but he can't let go of the past.

On Thursday afternoons I take a cab to an office building and have sex with my best friend's husband. We don't take off our clothes, I just lift my skirt, while he complains to me that his wife is too possessive.

On Friday nights I try to be patient with a man who can't get it up. I shout obscene suggestions and pull roughly on his thing, but he never responds. That's alright, I tell him, it's really not important, and he watches while I prove it and do it to myself.

I spend the weekends with my boyfriend. He is still my boyfriend even though we both see other people. We make love in our favourite positions and spread cream cheese over bagels and talk about our relationship.

Gay Cancer

My lover thinks I'm a man. I play along because I don't want to lose him.

He calls me big fella, his partner, his pal, hey mister, and Mack the Knife.

For my birthday he buys me gifts from the men's department at
    Bloomingdale's.

We wear Levi's and brown leather bomber jackets. I hide my hair
    under a cap. I paste on a moustache, similar to his but darker.

We walk up and down Christopher Street, keeping in step.

He sends me gay men's greeting cards.

He gives me gay men's diseases.

We make love but inside out.

Roommates

I don't do anything until the woman who lives in the apartment above
mine arrives home.

When she slams her front door I get up and slam my front door. When
she stomps into her bathroom I stomp into my bathroom. When she
flushes her toilet I flush my toilet. When she stomps into her kitchen I
stomp into my kitchen. When she clangs pots and pans I clang pots and
pans. When she stomps into her living room I stomp into my living
room. When she plays the drums I play the drums. When she does
aerobics I do aerobics. When she moves furniture I move furniture. When
she stomps into her bedroom I stomp into my bedroom. When she laughs
I laugh. When she moans I moan. When I press my ear to the wall and
there is silence I go to sleep.

How to Pick Up Impotent Men

Go to that famous bar in the village for men who can't get it up.

Sit next to the man who looks the most depressed.

Whisper in his ear that fucking isn't everything. Tell him you like walking in the rain and holding hands just as much. Tell him your favourite part of sex is the hugging and the kissing. Tell him he probably just hasn't met the right woman. Ask him to come home with you.

Later in bed tell him what you really want is to get laid. Order him to try or get out. When it's over ask him if he started yet. Accuse him of liking boys. Tell him you'd see him again but you think he's too old to change. Have him leave without car fare in the middle of the night.

How to Photograph the Blind

Buy a pencil from a blind man and ask him if you can take his picture. If he asks what it's for, tell him you're a professional photographer and you have a feeling that being blind isn't much fun. Ask him if you can document what it's like. If he says yes, get rid of the dog and dark glasses. Move him in front of an artificial waterfall. Hand him your pocket comb and tell him to do something about his hair. And then tell him to lick his lips and smile, before you hurry quickly away.

Boyfriend

I close my eyes and imagine his phone: long, black, cordless.

He says it doesn't turn him off that mine is pink and attached to a wall in the kitchen.

I wait for him to call me. I know it's him when I say "Hello" and there's heavy breathing.

I'm in the living room, he says. Now I'm walking upstairs. Now I'm in the bedroom.

What would you like me to do to you? he whispers.

At the same time I can defrost the refrigerator, clean the oven, cut out coupons from the back of House & Garden.

You get me so hard, he says. Touch yourself.

I'm coming, he moans.

The sound of water running. A toilet flushes.

Then we each smoke a cigarette in silence.

If he falls asleep I slam the receiver several times against the dishwasher.

That was great, he says. How was it for you?

Sometimes he takes a drive in the country and calls me from his car.

He's also called me from the men's room at Area, a Quality Inn in Toledo, Ohio, and a phone booth at the corner of 45th Street and Eighth Avenue.

Why don't we ever meet your boyfriend? friends ask me.

Once I thought I saw him on the street. He looked the other way. I ducked into a shop.

Love Letter To My Rapist (excerpt)

Howdy, stranger!

Remember me? That's okay, it's not as if we were ever formally introduced (ha ha). I'm the girl you beat up, then poked without permission on my kitchen floor at 164 N. Main Street, apartment 4C. Ring a bell? Sorry the place was such a mess, but I wasn't expecting company. I'm just writing to say "Hi" and hope there are no hard feelings, okay? The bruises and welts have almost completely disappeared, the bloodstains came right out of my favourite sweater with a little club soda, and the couple places on my face where you slashed me easily vanish under concealing cream. No fuss, no muss. After all, it's not like I'm a fashion model and you've ruined my career! And since statistics prove it was bound to happen to me sooner or later, I'm grateful it happened in the privacy of my own home. That is, at least you didn't force me into sexual submission on a deserted rooftop (fear of heights), in the back seat of a moving vehicle (motion sickness), around children (we'd have had to keep our voices down), near animals (too stinky!), in a cheap motel (creaky bed, no room service), or anywhere in the great outdoors (I don't even like to picnic in the woods, much less do the nasty act there). So mucho gracious for your consideration, kind sir! After you left I wondered, why *me?* But now I think, Hell, why *not* me? I'm not such a dog! It's flattering to learn even though I'm pushing thirty I'm still considered quite a fetching piece of ass. Besides, you didn't dismember me then store my various parts in your freezer as a souvenir, or keep me chained in a damp cellar somewhere as your love slave. No, you quickly accomplished what you came to do, then you were outta here. A true professional!

(Reprinted from *Love is Strange: Stories of Postmodern Romance,* by the kind permission of editors Joel Rose and Catherine Texier)

David Rattray

The Yoga Of Anger

I didn't come in here tonight to talk about love and sex. God doesn't love a single person in this place. Who cares for the love of God anyhow. I don't. I'd rather deal with something more tangible like a pair of breasts for instance; and I don't believe God has breasts. Now my friend here has called me "the Mad Preacher." But that has nothing to do with mad-insane. What we are dealing with at this point is anger. Anger is more than the name of a filmmaker, it's universal. Anger is all over the place and rightly so. Did you know there was a yoga of anger? Right. All these swamis coming over here with a message of sweetness and light. What we haven't yet seen is the yoga of anger. They were the true mad preachers. These guys sitting up on Kailash in full lotus, screaming with rage, perfecting a glare that could zap anything at any range. Telling the sirenlike demonesses flitting in front of their eyes to fuck off, female spirits that were always making other lesser men have an involuntary ejaculation into the nearest river and it would get carried downstream where a doe would swallow it and a child with antlers would be born, or fish would get it and so, mermaids and mermen. Well since all of the above are nothing but figments of the collective uncon-scious, the yoga of anger would have nothing to do with them, it cor-rectly rejected them, chased them into the woodwork where they belong without exception. You don't need ups, downs, goofers, speed. alcohol, psychedelics, or any of that shit. Just go for the pure nerve, adrenaline. Anger. Anger is the name of the game. Fuck peace. Fuck quiet. Go for anger. Be like the headlight of an oncoming freight train. Climb down the world's throat like a locomotive. Freedom from anxiety was one of the Four Freedoms spelled out by FDR. It turned out to be a fraud. You have a constitutional right, a duty even to get angry, vent your rage, act out any fucking way you please. When I heard the entire poetry estab-lishment was gathered under one roof at John the Divine, the whole lot, Church, non Church, Academe, Naropa, together with the Dalai Lama, an assembly worthy of the Questions of Milinda, 400 pederastic

philosophers in league with Nagasena and the emerald Buddha of
Bangkok, I had the power to strike that roof like a giant laser and bring
the whole fucking building down on those people, let God recognize
his own, and I might have done just that, except for the fact Eileen
Myles and a couple of others could have been in there too, and there are
places where legitimate anger does and does not apply. I realize that for
me to merely mention I would prefer to deal with something more tangible like a pair of tits could be construed in some quarters as sexist.
Now if I were to talk about kneeling down over in the trucks and getting reamed in the rumbleseat while sucking on a dirty exhaust pipe
that would be okay because gay and the male homosexual is above criticism to anybody except angry women. Well let me tell you kids I
couldn't care less what position any one of you may take on this, I've
got my own. As a matter of fact I think about 90 percent of any given
crowd is like Mechanical Man, bionically constituted of drugs, 3-4
veins on each limb, nostrils, lungs, a mouth, and a well greased anus for
the insertion of toxic suppositories. A couple of orgasms and maybe one
good shit a day. Eardrums shattered, thinking processes totally fried,
and most of you not even half my age. How a man of seventy can find
himself attractive and talk about jerking off in front of a mirror with a
movie camera rolling, trained on him, till he "shoots," is beyond me. It
is something I'll never understand until I reach that age myself. How
would I know? I don't go around fucking sixty-year-olds. "Shoot" indeed. Every shot I ever fired was in anger. I killed a man in Mexico. Shot
the motherfucker dead. Watched him bounce in the moonlight. This
town on a plateau, volcanic fault lines, gaps bridged by rotten planks,
and the son of a bitch was out to get me so I killed him, and I have never
lost an hour of sleep over it because I was angry then, when I was
twenty-five, and I am angry now. There's a line by Bessie Smith, Nobody
knows my name, nobody knows what I done. That line applies to me.
Every shot fired in anger. I shot my life and several other people's full
of holes and never will forget John Wieners, "If a man were to die with
the needle plunged in his vein he would not have died in vain." If you
can believe in anything it's a volcanic fault. Eruptions happen when the
sulphur sleeping underground has a dream and this swells into a mountain bringing it closer to the heat of the sun causing the sulphur to

explode, "shoot" if you will. As for gaps, I think people ought to stay in their own age bracket. Want to play around outside your age? Why not just kill 'em, that would be the angry way, the correct way. If you think I have an ax to grind you're right, I do, and fuck you, I mean you, you know who I mean, you know who you are and what you are. Fuck you. Why anybody should be turned on by a person twenty years their senior is a mystery, a superstition. It doesn't fit, I distrust it, I reject it, I spit on it. Anybody hangs you up, you have a duty to get angry. Go for the jugular if it's within reach. I'll never forget this conversation between Vaccaro and Jackie Curtis bickering over who wrote this play and Vaccaro suddenly said, I'm gonna kill you Jackie, hang me up a whole fuckin summer over a fuckin play (and I wrote it) I'm gonna rip your eyes out, I'm gonna tear your tongue out of your head, go in Max's Kansas City. I'll get Mickey to really fix your ass, I'll kill you I'll kill you I'll kill you you'll never act again . . . Right fuckin on was my reaction and I like Jackie too but that was the spirit. Or when Valerie Solanas took that gun and went after Warhol's ass. This is what we need more of. Anger. That's my message. Dare to dream like a volcano dreams. Blow your stack. Kill. Smash 'em through the floor.

(Reprinted from *How I Became One of the Invisible*, a collection of Rattray's work, by the kind permission of editor Chris Kraus)

SPDP Art Test—*Sample Questions*

Which of these painters isn't of Spanish origin?
  A) Goya
  B) Velazquez
  C) Ribera
  D) El Greco
  E) Gris

Who founded the "Bauhaus"?
  A) Walter Gropius
  B) Piet Mondrian
  C) Mies Van der Rohe
  D) Joseph Beuys
  E) Josef Albers

Which name doesn't belong in the following list?
  A) Satie
  B) Shönberg
  C) Berg
  D) Webern
  E) Ludendorff

Who composed "The Art Of The Fugue"?
  A) Glenn Gould
  B) Bonnard
  C) Bach
  D) Brueghel
  E) Offenbach

Who did Baudelaire translate?
  A) Emily Bronté
  B) Herman Melville
  C) Norman Mailer
  D) Amos Poe
  E) Edgar Allan Poe

Who filmed "Lady of Shanghai"?
  A) John Huston
  B) Fritz Lang
  C) Eisenstein
  D) Orson Welles
  E) Louis Malle

Fragments For a 1000-Year Farewell *(Translated excerpt)*

Exaggerate my friends, exaggerate
Eat, drink, fuck
And ask for more
While staring-down those morons
Who make things difficult for you

Eat a rabbit
Eat life
Cause it'll disappear real fast
Whole days were made for ejaculating
And others risk enjoying themselves
In your place

Laugh at the "why's"
And identifiable possibilities
Because we've learned nothing
Even after fifty centuries
Of art and intelligence
Thanks, but it was only good for
Kitchen conversations
At boring snooty parties

Don't ever go to school anymore, my friends
Cause the future will transplant us
Into a nice clean ambulance
With our biocarcasses
Frustrated, no doubt, to have lasted so long
Till the end of days
That wind up finishing us off anyhow

Abandon your sociophilic habits
And run around in the vast green outdoors
Ah, if only I was still a punk...
Courage, my little Salman of Existence, courage!

Because Tranquility, robed with justice,
Which fairly makes us understand what's normal
And the computerese of neurons
Where Man ain't alive
Well, that's for someone else

Let us smash our own heads, severely
We who are accompanied by no one
Able to think that happiness lies
In a calm existence
Amid the cruel game of circumstances

There will always be the Alps, and good game
And terror for a friend
When the newly-jackbooted Germans
Will pummel the crowd with sympathy
While passing on banners stuffed with
Remarkably stylish symbols

I'm searching for childhood images
Secret gestures, and silence
I feel there will be a lasting peace
That will come after the black hunger

I had wonderful stupidities to demonstrate
With huge gazes often in mid-mission
But now I want joyful companions
Who'll set fire to no one
Asleep at a table brimming with
Empty bottles

But I certainly want to see bosses die
Then give them a bit of water
And to know that at their cottages
Will only remain a jealousy of ants

I want to learn how to be someone else
Because "I" is an idiot
And variety is fun
Them people, they got Logic with a big "L"
But *we* can fuck ourselves in the ass

Le Groupe Absence

LE GROUPE ABSENCE

ON TO
ON PART POUR ///ARS

OFFICIAL NEWSLETTER OF LE GROUPE ABSENCE   SPRING 1993

When I say "The Future", I mean tomorrow or the day after.

Ted Koppel, *ABC News Nightline*

Dear Member and/or Friend of *Le Groupe Absence*,

Spring has come at last, and indeed it is a rare pleasure for *Le Groupe Absence* to indulge in that classic reminder of corporate luxury, the newsletter. The perfect vehicule to assault you with such banal gems as "spring has come at last !" Since — as always — we're all working on other things and don't have that much time to lose, we will make this one a quick one.

SO, WHAT'S NEW WITH *LE GROUPE ABSENCE* ?

If you aren't late to date you will be soon. Now that would be far from telling the whole truth. So, what's new with *Le Groupe Absence* ? Nothing. Of course. Toujours rien. Come on, now. The whole truth. As a matter of fact, there's plenty of new and exciting goings on at *Le Groupe Absence*. Like how about...

NEW SLOGAN OF THE MONTH !

*Be as clear as necessary
and as vague as possible.*

FONT OF THE MONTH : HELVETICA BOLD !*

**Be as clear as necessary
and as vague as possible.**

DISPELLING FALSE RUMOURS DEPT.

Contrary to what you may have heard, *Le Groupe Absence* is not against Art and Great Artists. In fact, quite the opposite. *Le Groupe Absence* encourages absolutely anyone to express him or herself through the use of charts, graphs, sundry business graphics, clip art, trademarks, copyrights, and the free use of office supplies. Remember that one of *Le Groupe Absence*'s favorite slogans is "Let your imaginations run wild !" So grab those mice, and "let a hundred spreadsheets bloom".

GET A LOAD OF THIS : THE LOGOSPHERE

It has been recently scientifically determined that in addition to the earth's inner and outer mantles, continental shelves,

atmosphere, ionosphere and exosphere, there lies a region called the Logosphere. The Logosphere is that part of the earth's environment which is plastered with the corporate logos we have all grown to love through relentless, inexorable, repeated exposure. The only problem now for *Le Groupe Absence* is to establish the upper and lower limits of the Logosphere. So we ask all budding Logologists out there to start investigating the deepest subway tunnel or industrial shaft in which a logo is to be found, and the exact height in a tall building or free-standing structure where a logo is to be found. Sorry, the *Goodyear* and *Fuji* blimps don't count, and neither does a lone *NASA* logo on a stray astronaut's orbiting glove. The logos have to be fixed on a permanent — make that a semi-permanent — basis to count as part of the Logosphere. Now the *Tour Absence* even has a virtual reason to exist : to top off the building at 6000 feet of altitude with the highest logo in the world. And whose lucky corporate logo will be scraping the roof of the Logosphere ? Why, *Le Groupe Absence*'s logo, natch. A semi-permanent logo on a semi-permanent free-standing structure. Can't do much better than that.

LEGGO MY LOGO ! (SAVE THE LOGOS FOUNDATION)

And speaking of ludicrously outsized buildings and logos, you may have heard that the *Pan Am* logo, of the threatened Airline Species, once the proud emblem of that landmark Manhattan building of the same name which was designed by Walter Gropius is no more. We wish all serious logo lovers out there to register a formal protest with all the authorities who took part in this inexcusable Logological disaster of immense proportions. How many more species will fall prey to this veritable LOGOCAUST going on under our very noses ? Think about it.

BAUDRILLARD RUNNING OUT OF IDEAS ?

Finally, for info purposes only, please note that in his latest book, irrepressibly attention-prone French *philosophe minceur* Jean Baudrillard has nicked a few ideas from *Le Groupe Absence*.

"*L'Agence Stealthy ?*" Complete with slogans and divisions ? *Absence ? L'Illusion de la fin ?* Now... Where have we seen this before ? Come on, "Ti-Baud"... We really don't think *Mr. Random* is at work here. Why not admit you've been visiting *Monsieur Plagiat* lately ? But then again, who could blame you ? How can anyone resist *Le Groupe Absence !*

---

* For the third month in a row !

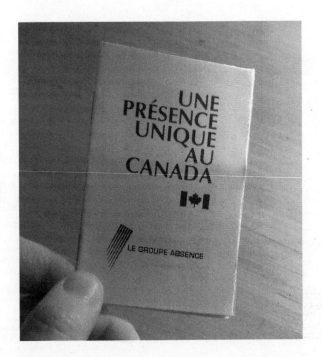

You'd think *people* would

take the little spare time they have to

think things out in a rational way, to

slow down the information

overload long enough to

make things simpler. **But no.**

The paperwork

keeps piling up. No one

knows where to put

the stacks of

COMPUTER

output. Countless boxes **of**

u s e l e s s

information get

to CLOG up what's left

of **your** ever dwindling

office space.

DOMTAROMARTADOMTA

AT

Le Groupe Absence

WE BELIEVE
IN SLOWING DOWN
THE DATA
PILE-UP

VOUS ÊTES ICI

Marriott

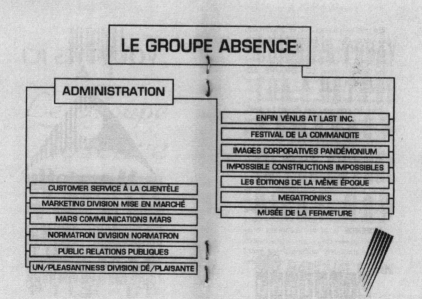

LE GROUPE ABSENCE

ADMINISTRATION

CUSTOMER SERVICE À LA CLIENTÈLE
MARKETING DIVISION MISE EN MARCHÉ
MARS COMMUNICATIONS MARS
NORMATRON DIVISION NORMATRON
PUBLIC RELATIONS PUBLIQUES
UN/PLEASANTNESS DIVISION DÉ/PLAISANTE

ENFIN VÉNUS AT LAST INC.
FESTIVAL DE LA COMMANDITE
IMAGES CORPORATIVES PANDÉMONIUM
IMPOSSIBLE CONSTRUCTIONS IMPOSSIBLES
LES ÉDITIONS DE LA MÊME ÉPOQUE
MEGATRONIKS
MUSÉE DE LA FERMETURE

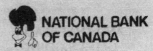

OUR BUSINESS IS KEEPING YOUR MIND OFF YOURS

LA DIRECTION ET LE PERSONNEL DU GROUPE ABSENCE VOUS SOUHAITENT UNE BONNE FIN DE SIÈCLE

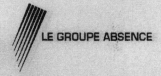

LE GROUPE ABSENCE

MAKING OUR PRESENCE FELT ACROSS CANADA

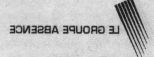

LE GROUPE ABSENCE

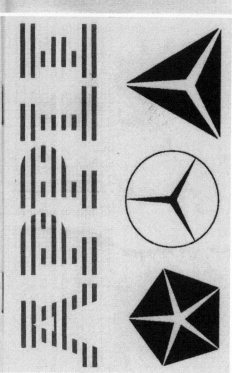

VIDEO WEB LINKS

ULTIMATUM (1985)

The John Giorno Band: https://vimeo.com/553330473

VIDEO 1—Performances in French: https://vimeo.com/553300131
CBC TV News Feature, Geneviève Letarte, Michel Lefebvre,
Steve Montambault, Janou Saint-Denis, André Tcetera ... ,
Michael Delisle

VIDEO 2—Performances in French: https://vimeo.com/553305367
Claude Beausoleil, Colette Tougas, Jean-Paul Daoust, Anonyme
Sanregret, Daniel Guimond, Josée Yvon, Denis Vanier, Mario
Campo, Pauline Harvey

VIDEO 3—Performances in French: https://vimeo.com/553321768
The Woeurks, Jean-Claude Gagnon, Alain Martin Richard,
Richard Martel, Jean-Yves Fréchette, Pierre-André Arcand,
Concept Variable, Paul Chamberland, Jack Five, Boris
Wanowitch / Boys du Sévère, Sylvère Lotringer

ULTIMATUM Record Launch (Part 1): https://vimeo.com/553712997
Anonyme Sanregret, Concept Variable

ULTIMATUM Record Launch (Part 2): https://vimeo.com/553715734
Vent du Mont Schärr (first show ever), Mario Campo

ULTIMATUM TUESDAYS (1986—1987)

Kathy Acker Reading (Part 1): https://vimeo.com/554680291

Kathy Acker Reading (Part 2): https://vimeo.com/554683748

Between C & D (from New York): https://vimeo.com/551972168
Introduction by Alan Lord, Joel Rose, Lisa Blaushild, Catherine Texier, Darius James

Un Cycle Laurentien (Bernard Gagnon): https://vimeo.com/551939471

ULTIMATUM II (1987)

DAY I—SALUT LES RICHES (French Montreal): https://vimeo.com/554710556
Festival kickoff by Alan Lord, The Pantry Partners, and emcee Jean-Luc Bonspiel, Jack Five, Poutines Productions (Myriam Cliche), Claude-Michel Prévost, Nitroglycérine with artists David Sapin, Christian Dion, reading by Jean-Luc Bonspiel, VDMS (Vent du Mont Schärr)

DAY 2—COLD CITY FICTION (Toronto): https://vimeo.com/554719049
Emcee Jean-Luc Bonspiel, Eldon Garnet, Arnie Achtman, The Nibelungenbüro (John Bentley Mays), Violence & The Sacred, Karl Jirgens, Judith Doyle, Donna Lypchuk, Susan Parker

DAY 3—BORDERLINES (Vancouver & Baltimore): https://vimeo.com/554728366
Emcee Jean-Luc Bonspiel, John Berndt, Ken Lester, Mecca Normal, Judy Radul, tENTATIVELY, a cONVENIENCE, I, Braineater

DAY 4—ANGLOMANIACS! (English Montreal): https://vimeo.com/554738018

Joy Lou G, Mohamud Togane, Ian Stephens, Darrell Ecklund, Anne Seymour, Nick Toczek, Rhythm Activism

DAY 7—AU DELÀ DE LA 'MODERNITÉ' (Quebec Poetry): https://vimeo.com/554748778

L'ATTACQ Orchestra (Alain-Arthur Painchaud, René Lussier), Josée Yvon, Irène Mayer, Hélène Monette, Nicole Brossard, L'ATTACQ Orchestra, Les Sanscoeurs, Paul Chamberland

ULTIMATUM II TRAILER (IN ENGLISH): https://vimeo.com/554696423

Ultimatum II trailer, then clips from Ultimatum 1985: Monty Cantsin, a Miguel Raymond video, Anonyme Sanregret, Concept Variable, Red Shift, Geneviève Letarte, Jack Five, The John Giorno Band, Boys du Sévère, Colette Tougas

GENERIC AS-BEENISM (tENTATIVELY, a cONVENIENCE): https://vimeo.com/552128815

ACKNOWLEDGEMENTS

I would especially like to thank Chris Kraus, who was the first to read my manuscript critically and offer priceless suggestions. More crucially though, she buoyed me with her enthusiasm for the book. The same thanks go to Michael Mirolla of Guernica, for his diligent editorship and patience.

Special thanks also go to James Grauerholz, for sharing his recollections about Burroughs, and correcting the flaws in an article I'd previously posted on a website.

I wish to thank Hilary Holladay, Joel Rose, Catherine Texier, and again Chris Kraus, for kindly allowing me to quote from their books.

Thanks must also be given to Jason Camlot, Samuel Mercier, and their staff at Concordia University, as well as Martin Lamontagne, for digitizing the audio and videotapes of my Ultimatum archives. But more importantly, I have to thank tENTATIVELY, a cONVENIENCE for sharing his precious hoard of Ultimatum II videos, that I thought were lost forever.

And of course, I have to thank my wonderful wife Caroline, who encouraged me to write this book. The poor gal had no idea.

Apart from those already mentioned, I wish to thank the following people—in order of their appearance in the book—for sharing their stories with me. Without their kind help, there would have been many holes left unfilled in my tale. They are:

David Sapin, Robert Ditchburn, Louie Rondo, Angel Calvo, Allan Fine, Rick Trembles, Pièr Major, John von Aichinger (Spike), Dave Hill,

Bernard Gagnon, Lorne Ranger, Lucien Francoeur, Marc de Mouy, Jean-François St-Georges ("JF"), Al Gunn, Istvan Kantor (Monty Cantsin Amen), Jean-Luc Bonspiel, Tristan Stéphane Renaud, Pierre Zovilé (Boris Wanowitch), François Alfred Mignault ("Fred"), Jean-Martin Mignault ("JM"), tENTATIVELY, a cONVENIENCE, Jack Five, Jerome Poynton, Alain Bergeron, Karl Jirgens, Philippe Bézy, Bernard Schütze, Guy Gendron (for his background on CP Meen), Sheila Urbanoski, Joel Rose, Catherine Texier, Lisa Blaushild, and Ava Rave.

ABOUT THE AUTHOR

Alan Lord is a bilingual writer (English, French), guitarist, songwriter, retired civil/structural engineer, and was a multidisciplinary artist and event organizer in the cutting-edge arts scene of Montreal in the 1980's. He is featured in the documentary films *MTL Punk* and *Montreal New Wave*, issued dozens of albums with several bands, and opened for The Ramones, The B-52's and Nina Hagen. His current bands include The Pagan Gurus and Les CYNIQZ. He published four books (including the book of savage satire *ATM SEX*), has poems published in two anthologies and is mentioned in several books, notably the biography of Beat legend Herbert Huncke. His Ultimatum series of avant-lit festivals featured hundreds of poets, musicians and writers, included such luminaries as William Burroughs, Kathy Acker, John Giorno, Herbert Huncke, Chris Kraus, Sylvère Lotringer and Karen Finley. His major civil works include the Montreal Biodôme (for which he received an award from mayor Pierre Bourque), as well as the signature cable-stayed St-Jacques Street bridge next to The McGill University Health Centre. After living in Paris, Toronto, and Santiago, Chile, he returned to Montreal with Caroline, his wife of 34 years and conference interpreter. They have a 20-year-old son who is enrolled in the Physics department of the Université de Montréal.

Printed in April 2022
by Gauvin Press,
Gatineau, Québec